D1414471

Folie à Deux

Dedication:
This one's for me.

Folie à deux – *Folie à deux* is a psychiatric syndrome used to describe similarly delusional ideas in two, closely associated persons. The expression comes from the French, "Madness shared by two." The belief may be shared by more than two people, *folie à trois* involves three, *folie en famille* is a family madness and *folie à plusieurs* is of many. The simple clinical name is, "Shared Psychotic Disorder," or "Induced Delusional Disorder." The syndrome was first theorized in late nineteenth century French psychiatry thanks to a high profile occurrence in 1901 known as the, "Moberly-Jourdain Incident."

On August 10th, in the gardens of Versailles two women, Charlotte Ann Moberly and Eleanor Jourdain allegedly experienced a time slip. Weeks later, comparing notes with friends revealed that their collective memory, despite the absence of collaboration, was identical. Both women spoke of seeing Marie Antoinette and other people from the same era. Despite both being of educated backgrounds and respected in their individual professions their pseudonymously published book, "An Adventure" caused ridicule and criticism ranging from psychosis to cover-up of their homosexuality.

The conclusion they collectively reached is that the grounds of Versailles were haunted and what they saw was a result of paranormal activity. Further trips to the landmark only furthered their theory due to anomalies in their investigation. After years of independent research by prominent figures in the psychological circle it was agreed that the women suffered from an episode of *folie à deux,* where one of them successfully influenced the delusion of the other. From that point the disorder has been an accepted diagnosis as an explanation of atypical behavior by two individuals.

Part One

Chapter 1

I'm your son. I'm your brother. I'm the kid that sat behind you in English class, the one who accidentally kicked the book bag under your seat. I'm your cousin, your neighbor, your paperboy, your average, nondescript teenager in suburban New Jersey. But very soon, I will be anything but typical.

I live in a typical neighborhood, in a two story, three bedroom house. I share a room with my brother who is ten years younger. My sister, born between us, is in the room next door. I want to be a rock star, a famous actor or play in the N.F.L., in that order of preference. I love alternative music and want to grow my hair out but don't think my parents would like that.

My dad is still my hero, having stopped dressing like him just recently. I also admire my grandfather, amazed at all he knows and has accomplished. I idolize Joe Paterno and my own football coach for their own fatherly qualities. I love to read and am infatuated with whatever biography I'm currently into, Douglas MacArthur, Abraham Lincoln or Anne Frank. My life is simple so I vicariously live their adversity from a safe distance.

I'm always scared, fifteen years old and figuring out high school. Freshman year went by uneventfully but not without personal tribulation. Ninth grade was the first time I changed classes, used a locker combination and met more people than ever before in my life. Nothing in my skill set has prepared me for the daunting daily task of being cool, likeable and normal, however my classmates define that. Thankfully I played football and wrestled growing up so I have a handful of guys who provide greater odds that someone will talk to me during lunch or study hall. I had my first kiss last year and the second it was over, I sprinted away from the park bench where it happened, mortified.

Now a sophomore, I'm not the bottom of the food chain, but not an upperclassman either. I'm commonplace, stuck in an unremarkable stage. I graduated from a Catholic grammar school with only 20 other poor souls. We were all taught to obey and never, ever question the infallibility of our teachers. Especially the nuns. Laic teachers might make a mistake once in a great while, but that was exclusively for my parents to decide. This won't be the first time I curse my Catholicism.

I love my parents and enjoy being the oldest even though I think my siblings benefit from the overcautious approach taken with me. I wish I could talk to my parents about emotional things yet they don't seem to understand me. But it's not a big deal. Life is mundane, I go to school, play sports, go home to play video games and then start over again. I don't have a girlfriend and think I prefer things that way to not complicate the awkwardness I already feel walking through the halls.

That's the depth of my world right before I'm smacked with more reality than any kid could imagine, right before I go from average to extraordinary. I wish I could say that I won an award, or saved a friend from drowning but my switch is darker. It's fluid, transcendent, and unnoticeable until I wake up one morning amazed at who I've become. I never have and never will know anyone who will endure and survive the existence that I will wear for the next three years.

Chapter 2

Kevin's mom died on December 11th 1991, and the end of my life will soon follow. Kevin is not a good friend but he's the best friend I have. He's pushy, girl crazy and a bully. A good looking kid and well-built but unfortunately, he knows this. I'm more his lackey than true friend. He knows the benefits of my unthreatening manner and uses it frequently when I approach girls on his behalf. This is the first relationship of many that will revolve around a power imbalance and without the help of foreshadowing, dictate much of my immediate future. But I need this type of friend with balls and swagger to help me navigate the rocky landscape.

Kevin's mom is sick, her illness as mysterious to me as adolescence. When I ask him what's wrong with her the only response he gives is, "It's some sort of infection that the doctors can't find."

He replies with sincerity but I feel his confusion, so I let him alone. I wish he would be more open because she is deteriorating at such a rapid rate and it's gut-wrenching to witness. I hate my own lonely sadness so his must be unbearable. She makes repetitive visits to the hospital, keeping current with when she is home or away almost impossible. She looks sicklier every time I see her but luckily Kevin does not notice or doesn't remark when I shy away from visiting. In November of our sophomore year she is taken to the emergency room and admitted to the Intensive Care Unit.

Days later I'm met by Frank, a friend Kevin and I share, as I walk out of the boy's bathroom, he mumbles, "Kevin's dad and sister are in the guidance office. His mom died." Death cannot touch me yet. All four of my grandparents are alive and I knew my great-grandfather well until he died just two years ago. Frank says, "I came to find you. Let's go."

I walk into the guidance counselor, Mrs. Beecher's office to see Kevin sitting in a single chair across from her, two other friends kneel beside him. Kevin has his head down, he is silent. He almost looks to be praying until a sob escapes. Boys don't cry in my world. The last time I let anyone see me cry was the day my mom dropped me off for CCD and I was so scared that all I could do was bawl. That was first grade.

I'm unable to grasp what I see. This is Kevin, who constantly informs everyone that he's a brown belt in karate. Kevin, who taught me everything I know about weightlifting. All the girls think he is cute, conceited but cute. He has a German Shepherd, befitting the machismo identity he is cultivating. Kevin, who wears his toughness like a second skin, takes advantage of his size and intimidating personality, hits me when I do something he dislikes, and when I don't do as he demands. Laughs when he gives out ball taps and titty twisters and nobody protests, save a few other kids who play tough. He gets away with this because he is Kevin.

And now he's crying. Helpless, against the backdrop of his father behind him, sunglasses hiding his own tears. Kevin's sister, Amanda is holding her dad's arm, but he offers no solace, too stunned himself. I'm not prepared for the grief of right now. My mind is flipping between two different channels. I'm absorbing every essence of the moment, the guidance counselor's futile consolation, Kevin and Amanda releasing sobs at an almost simultaneous pace, the expressionless look on Mr. Sumac's face and two other friends looking exactly as I must. I see their effort to avoid eye contact with anyone, looking to each other for support. On the other channel I see myself in Kevin's seat, the same two friends kneeling before me and my siblings standing behind. I imagine the surviving parent trying to plan out the rest of our family's life solo. Without any hesitation, when I snap out of my daymare, I kneel down next to Kevin and take his hand. This is also taboo but on the day Kevin cries I may as well hold his hand. With my index finger, I swipe his cheek as a tear collects at his eyelashes and rolls down. I say the only thing that anyone ignorantly says at such a scene, "It'll be ok." This moment is so far from ok that no one in the room knows how to articulate the gravity. I immediately regret and resent my attempt on Kevin's behalf. But the land of tears is strange. Kevin never looks up thankfully, but his sister won't stop staring at me. The look on her face begs me to take away the pain. How I wish I could but I'm barely holding my own composure. I've never felt so alone in a room full of other people.

Mrs. Beecher rescues us, "Ok, boys thank you for coming. I'd like to have a moment alone with Kevin and his family. Please ask for a pass at the front desk."

My heart finally stops racing once in the hallway and although I've been here countless times before I feel lost, as though I've never laid eyes on this part of the school. The other guys all go in the same direction while I stand still, unable to move. I stumble toward a bench, no, I see the auditorium at the other end of the common area and I think I should sit in there to have a moment alone. The perceived significance of this decision freezes me and

I stand immobile, solitary in my grief. As I process to fight the paralysis, my French teacher from freshman year, Miss D. greets me from behind, "Bonjour Jacques. Ca va?"

I'm silent. She turns serious upon seeing my expression and puts her hand on my shoulder, "Oh my goodness what's wrong? You're white as a sheet."

On the verge of tears I say, "My best friend's mother just died."

Her hand moves from my shoulder to rubbing high on my back, "Oh no. What grade is he in?"

I never notice before today that she has colored contact lenses that make her irises purple. I wonder what her real eye color is, pretty sure it isn't violet. She asks other perfunctory questions before offering, "I have a free period now and my classroom is empty. You could sit with me."

She speaks these words softly and with so much care that refusing her is impossible. She leads us through the stairway doors toward her room. I hear the beads she's wearing click together as she walks and instinctively, I move to the beat.

Her room has two entrance doors, opposite one another and she closes both. I'm reassured by the privacy and her undivided attention. I cry but am unsure why. My mind is back to channel surfing. Firstly, life is unpredictable, followed by the crippling reality that I could have easily been in that grieving chair.

In the second feed I see Kevin crying and his father helpless. I see Amanda looking at me in despair and feel the naked exposure with which all of us in the room were struggling. As I begin to cry harder I feel Miss D. sit behind me and put both of her hands on my shoulders. The physical contact only unleashes more tears. I hear an audible "Shhhhh" followed by the same mistake I made, "It'll be ok."

She also uses the more generic grown-up statement, "She's in a better place now." I'm not sure what that means to accomplish because Kevin and Amanda need her and what place could possibly be good enough to leave her children? Miss D. says sweetly, "The bell will be ending 4th period in five minutes but if you'd like, I'll find an empty classroom for you. Unfortunately, I have a class coming in next." I look at the clock wondering where the last forty-five minutes have gone because I just sat down.

After composing myself, I tell her, "I'll be fine. I can skate through the rest of the day." I control my emotions better than expected but break down when I say the words to my wrestling coach, "Kevin's mom died and I need to go home," despite his, "Take all of the time you need."

All day long I hate being in school with this burden, but as eighth period nears the thought of leaving is equally as daunting. Once I leave life progresses. I need to attend a wake and a funeral and worse yet, I need to reach out to Kevin. Right now the thought of making that call brings incomparable waves of nausea. There is a certain comfort in knowing that I'm still linked to the beginning of this day and this morning she wasn't dead. Being a part of today means that I have a link to her life and my life before all of this sadness that I don't want to surrender.

As soon as I arrive home I call my mom and tell her the sad news. I don't know how I expect her to react because my own mind is swirling. Her questions are equally as dutiful as Miss D.'s. The where and when are natural but she asks about the cause of her death, to which my response is the same. What is missing is condolence. I don't expect her to know exactly how I hurt or that I cried today. I could tell her that all day long I was thankful to have my mother, but I think it's her place to offer sympathy.

After moving the conversation to something benign like dinner, we hang up. I call my dad hoping that he might help, but he doesn't. He asks, verbatim the same questions as my mom which saddens me anew to repeat, except he adds, "Hang in there bud, it'll be ok."

My loneliness drives me to dial the only other person with whom I have a connection to this sad day. I call Kevin but Amanda answers. I should ask her how she is but that's an asinine question so after, "Hello," I hurry through, "Can I speak to Kevin please?"

He says, "Hello," barely above a whisper and I ask what I was unable to ask his sister. He responds, "Fine." I want to cut him slack because his mother died today, but all I can think is how upset I am too yet I can't find anyone to comfort me. My parents arrive home and within minutes everyone is carrying on with life. I'm silent through dinner, don't even attempt to do my homework and lie in bed long before bedtime, unable to sleep. Not until after I hear my parents go to bed does my mind begin to slow. I don't remember my last thought but the first of the new day is how early my alarm sounds.

Chapter 3

I feel different entering the building, out of place. Something has changed that I have not had nearly enough time to digest. I'm thrown back into the flow of life grossly unprepared, peppered with stares, less forgiving than yesterday. Today is different. Kevin's at home and no one mentions his name. Nobody asks how he is or if I spoke to him or any of the things over which I'm obsessing. When I walk out of my first period class Miss D. is standing at the door.

She asks sympathetically, "How are you, Jim?"

I mumble, "Ok, I guess."

She frowns, "Come to my room before you go to lunch."

I don't ask why but she was nice enough in class last year and a big help yesterday so I don't think I'm in trouble. Still I wonder what she may want.

When I enter her room a few hours later she comes around her desk, approaches me and asks again, "How are you?"

She still has purple irises. She stands close and smells good. She asks, "Didn't you sleep well? I can see it in your eyes."

Her sincerity borders on overbearing.

I feel inexplicably guilty when she wonders what I'm doing after school and I tell her, "Wrestling practice."

She suggests, "Why don't you speak to your coach to see if he would allow you to be late?" With a dismissive wave of her hand that implies no power is greater than hers she tells me, "Come to my room after school and I'll take care of whatever else." The rest of my day I'm not so upset that no one seems concerned about Kevin, someone is taking an interest in me. Now I'm being cared for too and selfishly, I want to ride the wave.

I arrive at her room after hurrying from my locker, avoiding eye contact with anyone else. I feel pampered when she tells me, "I spoke to your wrestling coach and he said its fine for you to miss practice." She closes the doors and we sit on adjacent desk tops. She is close enough that I notice her perfume again when she asks softly, "How are you?"

I tell her a little bit about what I've been thinking, expressing how unfair it is that Kevin's mom died and she will be able to see him neither graduate nor marry. Maybe because of how close I am to my grandparents I can't shake the fact that she will never meet her grandchildren. "God has a plan for all of us, Jim and this is just part of his plan for Kevin," she offers.

Her ideas match everything I was taught in grammar school, touching upon infantile comforts. She asks who I'm able to speak to at home when upset.

I lie, "My parents."

She believes me, "Well, that's good," but something in her voice rings doubtful. A moment after, she hands me a post-it note with a phone number written on it. She reads my perplexed expression and tells me, "That's my phone number. If you need to talk, just call me."

This is Miss Danza. All the boys fawn over her while the girls try to be her. I've heard all of the descriptions about wanting to bend her over the desk and do dirty things, some of which I can't even visualize. She always looks good in her short skirts or tight pants, never taking a day off from her trendy outfits and elaborate hair styles. This is the same petite and muscular Miss Danza whose phone number is in my hand. I want to escape this moment because there is so much to process and I have no idea where to begin. I also feel like I want to tell my mom and dad of her kindness, but am unsure they would understand. I don't know exactly why it would be ill-received but I foresee questions to which I have no answers.

I think I play it cool, "Thank you," but I'm really grinning from ear to ear.

She tells her own stories of loss finishing with, "Time heals all wounds." I don't understand what that means and despite not seeking clarification she explains that Kevin's family will struggle but be stronger for what they are enduring now. Although the individual parts confuse me, the whole of what she says provides comfort.

Before I leave she reminds me again, "Do not hesitate to use my phone number," emphasizing, "Do not."

During an earlier pause in our conversation I told myself, "I will not call her unless she mentions it again." I play this game because I still think it impossible that her phone number is in my pocket. She outfoxes my escape clause. It seems a bit like overkill to make a kind gesture and then repeat it so many times, but maybe her concern for students is this great.

When I arrive home dinner is on the table. I hear nothing of the conversation because all I can think about is what I am going to say to Miss D. when I call. Should I continue about my sadness or strike up a normal conversation? But what is normal with a teacher who I don't even have for class this year? In addition to being one year removed, I barely eked out a "B" average when she was my teacher so I can't talk about French. What could she know about the things that interest me which amount to not much more than sports and video games? And I really know nothing about her. I finish dinner and run upstairs to my room without saying a word to anyone.

My next dilemma is when to call. I just got home so now would seem desperate. I can't wait too long because I don't know what time she goes to bed. I don't know where she lives so maybe she isn't even home yet. It nags at me again that my parents won't be crazy about me talking to a teacher, plus if she lives far away it will show up on the phone bill. I don't recognize the exchange so the bulk of my predicament remains unresolved as I sit, deliberating on my bed.

A year ago, as I entered ninth grade my parents had an additional phone line installed for me and my sister to share. For twelve dollars a month nobody has to prematurely end their calls. This also provides the necessary privacy to call Miss D. without immediate fear of getting caught. I decide to casually ask her where she lives to gauge whether or not she is a toll call. If so, I'll speak briefly then create an excuse to end the conversation. I can always explain that as a wrong number.

At the conclusion of my circular deliberation I call her at 8:30. Long enough past dinner and not quite time that a grown woman should go to bed. She picks up on the 4th ring and her voice sounds strikingly seductive, much more than in person. All she says is, "Hello," having no idea who is on the other end, her voice deep and rich as I picture her with the receiver to her face.

I stumble, "Eh, hello, Miss Danza? It's Jimi" short pause, "Cunneely."

Very calmly, absent surprise she says just as alluringly, "Hi Jimi, I'm glad you called." I need to kill the dead air but don't know how.

"First, thank you for spending time with me today to talk and stuff," I stagger, "You don't know how much it helped."

She says, "I'm so glad I can help. I'm happy you feel comfortable talking to me especially since I'm not even your teacher this year."

There is a brief and uncomfortable pause I'm hoping she will break but painfully, leaves for me, "I hope you don't mind that I called you and all? I was just feeling sad," inflecting my voice so she will complete my thought.

I silently beg for her to say anything to stop my heart from pounding and alleviate the ringing in my ears. She eases my anguish, "No, no, I don't mind at all, I said you could call and I'm glad you did."

Silence again. I knew this was going to be difficult but neglected to foresee the difference between standing in front of her and being on the phone. Being together allows for small talk inspired by our surroundings, but over the phone there is no such minutia.

"So what's on your mind?" she asks, sparing me the agony of further reflecting on my regret. When she asks I realize, truly realize with the full gravity of my life that I didn't call her because I needed, but rather because I wanted to talk. I now have to either confess or create something upsetting enough to have reached out to her.

I hate how helpless I sound when I say, "I'm upset about Kevin's mom."

Her response is unimaginable, "I know you are, Jimi. I spoke to Kevin's dad today and mentioned how deeply affected you were by the passing of his wife." Confusion overwhelms me to a mute.

"Why were you speaking to him?" I say, succumbing to the adolescent weakness of people talking behind my back. I need to know what was said.

She sighs, "Well I knew you were upset today so I looked up their phone number. I explained how I don't have Kevin, but I have his friend. We spoke a while and after he asked me about my last name he proudly told me that he's also Italian. I offered to help anyway I could so I'm singing at the funeral mass and baking a lasagna to bring over tomorrow when we pick some hymns."

Too many thoughts and too many emotions crowd my mind, leaving me speechless. I'm confused how this all happened but also touched. She must have done this for me. I become uncomfortable immediately. I realize that I've already planned to go to Kevin's tomorrow after school which means we will be there at the same time. I feel a smile coming on that I try to hide despite being invisible to anyone.

I wonder if she made the call so she could see me too. Even if I'm overanalyzing, I feel substantial in a way for which I can't recall a parallel. Piecing everything together intensifies the smile I'm still trying to cram down. I cannot put a name to the emotions pervading the forefront of my mind because they're simultaneously comfortable yet awkward. So much lately feels a dichotomy, normal but slightly amiss.

I change the subject to save more discomfort. I tell Miss D. my experience with death and she responds about her own grandparent's and her uncle who recently died from cancer. I hang on every word as if there will be a quiz afterward. I ask questions to show I'm interested. "How old were your grandparents when they died?" "How old were you?" "Where are they buried?"

Some responses form an innocent bond, "Well just like you, Jimi my great-grandfather died when I was in eighth grade." Our conversation never achieves greater depth so I thank her and say, "It was nice to get my mind off of things for a while." Her response has an adamancy that was lacking earlier, "Call me anytime you want." The emphasis placed on, "Anytime," and a diphthong created with, "You".

I hang up the phone and look at the clock. It's eleven. While on the phone my sister came in to say goodnight as always, my brother went to bed five feet away and my parents came in to kiss us both. I was oblivious, deeply engrossed in conversation. I don't think anything I said could have revealed Miss Danza, but I can't remember. I'm awake another few hours trying desperately to remember if I told her I was going to Kevin's house tomorrow, fraught with wonder if she called his father for me. I'm embarrassed in my own head because the reality that I'm fifteen and she's a teacher makes that a ridiculous presumption. I'm sure she has better things to do than arrange to be in my presence. Regardless, I cannot shake the feeling. The last time I look, the clock reads two-thirty.

Chapter 4

Six forty-five comes early and I'm tired but anxious for school, interested to see how Miss D. treats me. Maybe she speaks to many students on the phone making our conversation inconsequential but to me its significance is undeniable. I may not even run into her today which only heightens my anticipation. I know the places and times I sometimes see her so I make sure that I'm not talking to anyone and my head is on a swivel walking through the hall.

As I sit in seventh period Geometry, I still haven't seen her. The end of the day is close, preventing me from paying attention to anything. I was hoping to talk to her in school, assuming the mood at Kevin's will be uncomfortable. I hear the door to the classroom open but don't look. The quiet buzz in the room is the perfect soundtrack of my wandering questions about last night.

At the same time I realize that someone is walking toward me I see it's Miss Danza. She walks to the edge of my desk, winks and puts her hand on my forearm. A gentle touch, which if I'm reading correctly means, "I'm thinking of the tough time you're going through and I'm here." I wanted to know if it was going to be awkward when I saw her today and as a matter of fact, it was even better than I thought. So many answers with one touch.

Once school ends, I run to Kevin's house, having decided it crucial to arrive before her. As I tire I ask myself why it's of paramount importance to arrive first. The only reason I can find as my pace slows is because she's coming into my world. I want to appear as though I have a grasp on the elements she is seeing for the first time. She seems more like a friend than a former teacher which makes it difficult to determine certain boundaries. Should I be formal or casual? How should I introduce her? Do I shake her hand or hug? These questions race through my head as I return to a panicked sprint through the woods.

When I turn the last corner I'm relieved that her car is not parked in front. Now I refocus on seeing Kevin and his family for the first time since that day. I bounce up the front stoop, ring the bell and wait an eternity to hear someone struggle with the deadbolt. A woman I do not recognize opens the door with a melancholy smile, "Hello, I'm here to see Kevin," I say.

She steps aside as she says, "Come in. He's in his bedroom."

I walk down the hall to the last door on the left where Kevin sits silently on his bed, head cast down. It seems redundant after having walked past Amanda's room to see her sitting with the same posture, joined by two girlfriends on either side. "Hey, what's up?" I say trying not to sound too upbeat but at the same time not wanting to drag him further down.

He tilts his head and raises an eyebrow in the typical, "What's up?" gesture. I sit close and put my arm around him. He simply nods.

"You hungry? There's a shitload of food. Come on," he says as I hear the doorbell ring.

By the time we reach the foyer Miss D. is already inside being greeted by a flock of adults. Kevin has always had a temper and his mother's death has done nothing to calm him. When he sees the scene unfolding he turns to me and says, "What is she doing here? Is she trying to fuck my father or something?"

He makes me so angry that I have to fight the urge to set him straight. If I were to speak I would explain that she is here out of the goodness of her heart and to be perfectly frank, I believe she came to see me. I refrain from saying anything on my mind because Kevin would beat the shit out of me on the spot. Secondly, I don't speak my thoughts because they're inappropriate to say or even think. And lastly, Kevin is simply lashing out at whoever is in front of him.

I respond, "I don't know," and the second I say it, become irate with myself for not defending her. He walks back into his room and I follow.

We become lost in a conversation that borders on comfortably normal. I'm engrossed in listing everyone who sends their sympathy when I suddenly see his father and Miss D. standing at the bedroom door.

Mr. Sumac says, "Kevin, this is Miss Danza. She's a French teacher at your school." He speaks slowly and softly with a slight Italian accent mixed with a bit of Brooklyn. The effort of enunciating his words too much to bear. Kevin is thankfully less hard hearted than earlier. He looks at them and says, "Hi," understandably unable to possess more decorum. She approaches and hugs him with the appropriate condolences spoken softly. He says nothing in response, only wipes away tears.

I'm thankful she makes no eye contact with me because I'm smacked with something unforeseen since our budding friendship. When she entered the room I was in mid-sentence, "Then she said, so I said." The gossipy nuances of adolescence. When the two adults entered I had no time to switch egos. I got caught in the transition between a high school kid and the façade I've been carrying in my individual contact with Miss D.

This is my first awareness of a pretense. I've been acting how I see fit in any given situation but did not know my interactions with her are consistently different from the usual me. She doesn't seem to disapprove but I feel like I'm something less than what she may have thought prior to this humiliating moment. I'm embarrassed for being a teenager.

Chapter 5

Mrs. Sumac's wake is the same night as the Holiday dance, a semi-formal event so my suit serves both affairs. My dad drops me off at the funeral parlor knowing Frank's mom is taking me to the dance afterward. I sit next to Frank after paying my respect at the casket, relieved he's already there. Kevin's family is in the front row of arranged chairs. As people approach them I watch the embraces and mutual tears with unspeakable sadness. As Frank, his mom and I sit silently, Derek and his dad join us, followed by Jacob with his mom, Rick, next to his dad and when Mike and his father take their place near us I'm struck. I'm here alone.

I explain a variety of excuses to myself, speculating all the adults were family friends, sat on the same committees, or grew up together but none of my theories rest as a conclusion. It's impossible that all of these parents could have known Mrs. Sumac because they are from different towns and different ages with different interests and commitments. I try to remember that I'm here for Kevin, his family and the tragedy they are enduring but it's becoming impenetrable to dismiss my loneliness.

While working this out, Miss D. enters the parlor. I'm happy to see her, instantly relaxed. She signs the registry and waits on line. She must be going to the dance afterwards too, except her dress is not quite as dual functioning as my suit. She doesn't see me and I'm not sure I want her to, I feel especially vulnerable. I asked my dad if they were coming with me, he answered simply, "No."

I see her kneel down at the casket and know I'm not the only person watching. She makes the sign of the cross as she stands, walks to Kevin's father and embraces him, then Amanda, and finally Kevin. Before walking out the door, she approaches to say, "How are you?"

I shrug. The gravity of the evening too much to articulate, compounded by new confusion. "Are you going to the dance?" she asks.

"I am."

She smiles, "Maybe I'll see you there and if not you always know how to reach me." I'm tempted to tell her what I'm really upset about but cannot, still creating vicarious apologies for my parents.

Monday after the dance is the funeral. Although my parents seem reluctant for me to miss a day of school they agree since I've arranged my own transportation. Mass is at my parish, providing a small amount of comfort but I'm still unable to concentrate on anything except Kevin's family sitting in the front pew. I think I feel Miss D. looking at me but it's hard to tell because she's on the other side of the church. There is audible weeping as she sings the hymn, "And He Will Raise You Up on Eagles Wings" and most specifically during the recessional hymn, "On the Last Day." I know she isn't here for me but just having her present adds comfort, like I'm in a safe place where my childhood is meeting my future.

After mass, we go directly to the cemetery where Mrs. Sumac is being interred. When the priest says his final blessing and Kevin and his family return to their limousine everyone is left standing at the grave, lost. The first person I lock eyes with is Frank, ironically the person who broke this news to me. I feel the panic of knowing the day is coming to an end and the uncertainty of the next phase. He looks at me and with tears welling in his eyes, embraces me in a hug that shakes both of us with his sobbing.

Once home, at one o'clock in the afternoon, I take off my suit, lie down and sleep as though I have not in weeks. I know my late night conversations are contributing to my fatigue. I sleep for hours until my sister comes home from school, followed by my parents and my brother shortly after dark. My mom makes dinner, we eat, take our showers and not one word is mentioned about my day. Nothing about the funeral, Kevin, or his family is spoken.

As I lay down in bed I decide to address my feelings with my parents. It still hurts to recall the image of myself sitting alone at the wake. I've been trying, in vain, to articulate something all day. When only their bedroom television illuminates the hall I stand in my doorway deciding how to present my thoughts. I rehearse several openers before I decide on the most concise; crippling fear drives my internal resistance. I walk into their room, stop at the foot of their bed and they both look directly at me.

Nobody speaks a word during an uncomfortable silence that I must break, "I just wanted to tell you that I felt lucky today. I realized that life is fragile and can end anytime. I'm glad I have both of my parents." It's staccato, disjointed and lacks the preamble that might have made it succinct, but it's the best I can do. The moment freezes for me and I become hypersensitive to every reaction. My mom puts her head back on the pillow as though collecting her thoughts.

My father, still sitting up, legs crossed says, "Well," and pauses as though he has no idea what should follow, "It's good you realized that. Some people take a lot of things for granted and miss them when they're gone." He seems to squirm, looking in vain for something else. Mom closes her eyes either satisfied or desperate to escape.

That is apparently the only response. A pat on the back for coming to a realization through the tragic death of my best friend's mother is my reward. There is no hug, no invitation to discuss and no reciprocation. I walk back to my room and lay in bed. I pick up my phone and call Miss D. apologizing profusely for calling so late but she stops me mid-sentence, "Jimi, I told you to call me whenever you needed," this time emphasizing, "Whenever." I never tell her what happened in my parent's room, unable to think about my feelings. I want to bury them and hope they go away without ever having to actually face the truth.

Chapter 6

Each time I dial her number becomes easier and the conversations shift to more normal topics. When we discover that my second period study hall coincides with her free period she tells me, "Stop by first thing in the morning and I'll give you a pass. You can come to my room in case you wanted to do homework or just talk."

I seize the opportunity to spend more time with her. We discuss less death and more of our lives. How long she has worked at the school and the arc of her career. She sporadically asks me about Kevin and his family but the topic ends quickly regardless of my answer. Our nightly conversations resemble the small talk that two friends would share but I have difficulty viewing this as typical friendship.

She enjoys talking about how well we communicate and reiterates constantly, "I never have to dumb anything down when I'm talking to you." She compliments my broad vocabulary and how speaking to me isn't even like talking to a fifteen year old, "I feel as though I'm talking to someone in their twenties if not my own age," she elaborates. I'm tempted to ask her age but avoid being impolite.

On the tail of a similar conversation she asks, "What are your feelings on getting together sometime to talk?" The idea confuses me because we talk so often. She clarifies, "Well, I mean being able to talk outside of school."

I ask innocently, "Where do you mean?" still confused.

She stammers. She is very good with words, knowing exactly what to say at the right time so I feel bad for putting her on the spot. "Well, I just thought that it might be nice if sometime we could, uh, maybe get together and like, have a cup of coffee, or maybe a bite to eat?"

She's right. Our conversations are always cut short and there never seems to be a lack of things to discuss, our uncomfortable silences having vanished long ago. There are a wealth of topics that we have yet to complete and even more that have never been broached. I wonder what made her want to become a French teacher and what summer vacations are like for an adult. I want to know what kinds of cars she has driven in the past because the one she has now is cool. Where did she grow up and what is Paris like? How hard it is to be fluent in French, why isn't she married and so many other things that need time.

For some reason our conversations always revolve around me. Not just my past but also my life now. How I'm so different from other boys my age and how I'm able to get along with them despite my unique personality. These topics, of course are nice to hear but make me uncomfortable once belabored.

I respond naturally, "Sounds good, let me just ask my parents."

She ends our conversation to grade tests. Not too long after we hang up, as I'm sitting on my bed, my dad comes to my room. As he places clean laundry next to me, I run the idea by him, "Dad, do you remember my French teacher from last year?"

He doesn't. "Miss Danza," I remind him, "Dark hair, very pretty."

"Ok," he says because he knows no description will help.

"Well she came to Mrs. Sumac's funeral and has been a big help getting through things recently," I pause to wait for verification. I wonder if he feels any remorse when I tell him I've sought help from another adult. "Anyway, she asked me if I'd like to get together with her outside of school so I told her I'd ask you first," I continue.

He has the same initial question, "What do you mean outside of school?"

"Well like a cup of coffee or a bite to eat," I repeat her words because it's all I can say.

He thinks again, as though struggling to find an answer, "Let me talk to your mother and I'll let you know." His typical answer whenever I make plans.

I relay his answer when I speak to Miss D. to say goodnight, "I'll let you know as soon as he gets back to me but he doesn't seem to have a problem."

It isn't until two nights later that my dad comes into my room, ironically while speaking to Miss D. I put my hand over the mouthpiece in case I'm about to be scolded. Instead he says, "I spoke to your mother and we're not sure it's a good idea for you to go out with a teacher. I understand that there's nothing going on but I'm afraid how it would look."

He leaves no room for debate but I don't have a counterpoint anyway. I hadn't accounted for the appearance of impropriety and he raises a good point. I put the phone back to my ear, apologize and allow her to finish what she was saying.

When she pauses I say nonchalantly, "Hey, my dad just got back to me about dinner or whatever. He didn't think it was a good idea." I don't think to speak gently and don't think it's an upsetting answer. It's an invitation and for circumstances beyond my control I have to decline, similar to countless others on the grounds, "My parents said, 'No.'" Annoying but not terrible.

I'm mistaken.

I wait for her to say something but nothing comes. Her silence becomes unsettling, open-ended. I finally hear what I think sounds like crying but cannot imagine what would cause such a reaction. Before I can ask I hear an audible and unmistakable sniffle.

"Um, are you crying?" I ask, afraid she'll laugh at my question. When she says, "No," I know she's lying.

I fall silent, bewildered. I've never been good at consoling anyone in tears. Despite the fact that we have crossed some lines into becoming a friendship she is still my teacher. "Why are you crying?" I ask. Her silence lasting so long.

During the pause I retrace our conversation to recall if there was something I said that could have upset her. I'm scared I did something wrong. If it weren't for definite sobs I would think our call got disconnected. After letting out a deep staccato sigh she says, "What you just told me made a reality of something I've been afraid of."

She doesn't say anything else so I ask, "What's that?"

"Jimi, there's so much I'm afraid of when it comes to you," she responds immediately.

Youthful ignorance prevents me from understanding innuendo. I'm nothing more than a student going through a rough time and she reached out to help. What about me could possibly cause this visceral reaction? I feel the sensation of spiraling when she says, "I've been feeling some crazy feelings toward you, Jimi. I've been fighting telling you because I was hoping to do so in a different setting. I really didn't want to do tell you over the phone but I guess I have to."

Her repetitive use of my name draws me in and continuously bridges the chasm that my parent's prohibition created. She tells me, "What I'm most afraid of is that I'll never be able to act on the deep emotions I feel every time we talk." Her cryptic speech is maddening and makes me feel like everything is happening at Fast-Forward speed.

"What are those emotions?" I naively ask, surprised by my quick draw response.

Silence again.

Another long sigh, "Oh Jimi, the feeling I'm afraid that I'll never be able to act on is that I'm falling in love with you."

Now it's my silence ringing in my ears. Is this really happening? I need a second. This comes out of nowhere. "What the fuck?" rambles through my head. My heart pounds, I feel it in my feet. My ears burn. This is Miss Danza. Every boy in the school talks about how hot she is. The two boys I sit next to in History class tell me all the time about how badly they want to, "Lay her on her desk and fuck her." The Miss Danza that causes boys to crane their necks and almost fall out of their seats when she bends over to pick something up in her tight pants. The same teacher who is crying to me.

I ask her, trying to start small, "What can I do to make you feel better?"

She answers immediately almost snapping, "Please stop calling me Miss Danza or Miss D. Call me Carla."

I think I can do that, though it will probably feel weird.

"What else?"

"Do you love me too?" she asks too quickly. She dictates the cadence of the conversation and I can't keep pace.

"Yes."

She's crying on the phone and it's my adolescent answers causing these tears. I definitely feel something I can't describe. I know I look forward to seeing her. I like talking to her at night. When she walks by me and says, "Excuse me," placing her hand on my shoulder I feel chills. I guess that's love. So my response seems the truth. She doesn't ask me to elaborate and doesn't ask me how I know, she just takes my one word answer and runs.

I hear her cry again and although I'm afraid of the answer, I ask, "Why are you crying now?" This time sounds like a low grade wail out of sheer agony. I feel bad for having said, "Yes."

She says through sobs, "In some ways I wish that you didn't say that you loved me." Her calculated pause allows my mind to wander feverishly. "Now that I've told you that I love you and you have told me too, I'm tortured by having to wait until you're eighteen to kiss you."

Through a tornado of thoughts it occurs to me that I did not tell her I love her. I didn't say the words, "I love you." She asked and I said, "Yes." I see a distinct difference. Also, when did we arrive at the topic of kissing?

"Well, I guess we have to wait but eighteen isn't too far," I say.

Wrong answer. What I thought was a valid response, elicits a full-fledged sobbing fit.

"Ok, wait, wait, why did you just get more upset?" I ask.

"Because that is a long time and I don't want to wait because I'm in love with you now," she snaps before I'm done with the question.

"Ok, well Carla, whether or not we wait until I am eighteen is up to you because you're the one who can get in trouble."

I am so confused I'm panting. I speak before thinking, trying to protect myself.

She immediately attacks issues at the heart of a budding romance skipping right over legality and morality. The topics she broaches are ones a high school couple needs to discuss. She keeps sniffling and snorting, wrestling to gain control of herself.

"So let me ask you something," she starts, "What sorts of rumors have you heard about me and be honest because I'm sure I've heard them already. I just want to be truthful with you."

I pause, it feels like a trap. After a moment, deciding I have nothing to lose I admit, "For as long as I have been at the school I have heard two names." She summarily denies any involvement with either of them, telling me stories of innocuous and trivial contact with both boys but nothing that even provides opportunity for indecency.

It sounds convincing as she details her believably benign interaction but does not seem surprised by the names either. It's almost as if she has heard these rumors too but before I can read too much into her responses she comes back with another question preceded by the same long and drawn out sigh. "So my next question," she begins with an almost sarcastic tone, "My next question has to be something that you have heard about one time or another."

I stay quiet, afraid to speak.

Another sigh heightens my panic, "How old do you think I am?"

I didn't bring up the age issue in previous conversations trying to avoid being rude. However, I think it equally impolite to prompt a guess. Do I come up with a number and knock a few years off to be careful? I don't have the time or mental energy to play these games so I create an answer that seems in the right range. "Thirty-five?" I guess. My mom is thirty-six so I think I'm safe as well as close.

Quivering accompanies her exhale. "Well James," she says, "I am the ripe old age of," and pauses. The pause seems unnatural as though the dead air is being filled with creativity instead of honesty; the same game I just played. "Forty-two," and silence.

I'm fifteen. I have no concept of old. To me the seniors in the cafeteria are old. I have no frame for forty-two years old. Thirty-five was a harmless guess because that makes her younger than my mother. But now I just confessed my love, as per Carla's recollection, to someone older than my mother.

We talk until somewhere after three a.m. because I'm afraid to leave this conversation. I know that by ending it I'm solidifying what was said. I don't know if I want to take anything back or if I even can. I know our words are not digested yet, not applied. They are all fresh and perhaps can be slowed down or processed differently. But if we hang up they are committed to memory as having been spoken in the confines of this conversation on this night.

My reluctance means she's the one who says, "Well I'm up at five thirty and that's only a few hours away so I guess I should get some sleep."

I agree, still ignorant to what any of this means. She ends the conversation with a heartfelt and romantic, "I love you," and now I have no choice but to say what I avoided earlier. I speak before I can think, before I can attach meaning to my words and before I am anywhere near developed enough to grasp the consequences.

"I love you too. Goodnight."

I lay awake for hours replaying the crucial parts of the conversation. I try to remember how we went from talking to crying to consoling to solidifying the foundations of a romantic relationship and I simply cannot. All I can remember is what was said but the words are now absent the bonus of context. What

I said was so quickly synthesized and enacted into the fabric of what we just created but how did those words leave my mouth? I never even knew that sort of conversation was in my head.

I think I have a girlfriend. I think I just found a forty-two year old girlfriend who was my French teacher and probably will be again next year. How do I look at my mom in the morning? How do I look at Miss Danza or Carla or whoever she just became? How do I look at my friends as we sit and have a bagel before first period? Do I tell them? Do I tell anyone?

I think this conversation has to remain a secret but she didn't say one way or another. I think she can get in trouble but only because of my dad's words earlier. As I was conveying those rumors I know they were spread with a sense how cool it would be if they were true. I envied the boys in the stories for having her attention and now I'm not sure that I want the uncertainty with which it comes. I was much more comfortable admiring her from afar because that was safe, like a crush on a movie star. Never did I imagine I would be the recipient of her affection.

I think I fall asleep but I'm not sure. All I know is that when my alarm sounds I have to start a new day in a new life that snuck up on me from somewhere beyond my wildest dreams.

Chapter 7

I'm apprehensive to see her, not knowing what her demeanor will be. Will she have regrets? Was she simply overcome with emotion? Was she drunk? So many scenarios emerge that I consider the possibility that I imagined the whole exchange. I walk into her room second period expecting to discover I fashioned the conversation out of a subliminal fantasy. Instead, I'm greeted with a giant smile. She says, brimming with excitement, "Bonjour, Ça va?" which I know means, "Good morning, how are you?"

I respond, "Bien, et tu?" which is wrong but she does not correct.

She answers, "Très bien."

Obviously, my memory matches reality.

I don't know if it's appropriate to continue the conversation, ignore it or embrace it. I just had history class with other kids who were talking about kid stuff, some even talking about problems with boyfriends and girlfriends but I'm sure they were manageable ones. I decide to be myself and imagine what I would have said yesterday, before last night. But all I can think about is what makes sense now in the context of those irreversible words, nothing meaningful reaching my mind.

She moves rapidly into topics that she has clearly given more thought than I am afforded. She suggests plans that involve

Christmas Caroling in her hometown, twenty minutes outside of New York City. Leaving me with only the same disastrous response, "I'd love to go but I have to check with my parents." I'm nervous because if my parents don't go for this invitation either what does that mean when I have to break the news? I'm already trying to concoct how I can make sure this time is more readily accepted.

The next item she mentions has caused me a great deal of anxiety since recent developments. This subject predates last night as well as the passing of Kevin's mom. It goes back to a place before there was even a hint of anything more than just a teacher-student relationship. Sometime in the fall, Miss D. spoke to all French classes about a trip she was planning to France. I knew she took students abroad every few years because I had seen pictures. She was fond of showing slides of those trips to illustrate aspects of art and architecture in her lessons.

This time was to be different though. She explained that although past trips were educational they were too much like field trips, not immersion into another culture. This year she was planning a true exchange. The students who were selected would be staying with French families and although there would be daily excursions most of the time would be spent alone in a French household. I thought it sounded amazing so I went home that same day and asked my parents.

They were open to the idea, saying they would consider the trip but I had to provide more information. It was expensive but my parents recognized this as a once in a lifetime opportunity. So much so that my grandfather offered to defray the cost if I were accepted to participate.

The context of this trip is much different now. She gushes how excited she is to show me the places that she holds so dear and what a wonderful thing this will be to experience together. The whole concept, which had excited me, now takes on a new meaning I'm unable to define. I don't know if she senses my apprehension but drops that topic quickly despite the fact that it seems to be the most significant on her checklist.

Every night we stay on the phone until early morning. We become better acquainted, talking about our lives, "What do you see in your future, Jimi?" she asks.

My contribution is nebulous, "I really don't know. I kinda just want to play football and wrestle. Maybe I'll be a professional football player one day."

"What if that doesn't happen?" she presses.

"Maybe work with my dad at his business," I appease because I simply don't have a direction.

She says with no segue, "I watch you talk sometimes and I watch your lips. They look very soft and I want to kiss them." Panic rises in my chest. I squirm on my bed. "I really don't want to wait until you are eighteen years old to be able to feel your lips," she continues yet I hope desperately that she stops.

Thankfully the conversation concludes, "Ya, me too," punctuated with my nervous giggle.

Chapter 8

Our routine forms quickly. She works in her classroom while I'm at wrestling practice and afterward, I go to her room for the few minutes before I catch the bus. I find myself very excited when practice lets out early and I can spend more time with her. The last day of school before Christmas break practice ends at four o'clock, I shower and rush to her room capitalizing on the most time we ever spend alone.

We make small talk while she packs boxes of classroom decorations. She breaks the lull of a comfortable silence by broaching, for the first time face to face, the subject of kissing. She's playfully coy, alleviating some of the uncomfortable pressure but I still find it hard to breathe when she asks, "So I never asked you if you even want to kiss me?" seductively biting her lower lip.

Despite the taboo, I promised myself after last time's awkward ending to be more confident. I courageously say, "Of course I want to kiss you, who wouldn't? But I guess it's not that easy because you're a teacher." Her expression darkens when I add the last clarification. I assume she doesn't like to be reminded.

She rebounds quickly, "Well I don't think it's that difficult. I know I'm a teacher and I still want to kiss you."

I shrug, validating her counterpoint. Wallowing in the distress only momentarily before she says, "I guess we'll know when the time is right, don't you think?"

We continue cleaning and talking about nothing serious until 6:00 approaches when I say, "I need to be heading to the bus."

"I'll walk out with you if you wait just a minute," she replies. I watch her put on a long black overcoat and grab a shopping bag with each hand. Most of the lights on the second floor hallway are off and all of the stairways are dark too. Neither of us speaks as she locks her door and we make our way to the staircase. My mind wanders to Christmas vacation, looking forward to sleeping late and playing video games.

I open the heavy orange fire door and let her go first. The scent of imitation pine cleaner is overpowering as we reach the large landing that separates two sets of ten steps. Halfway down the second flight of stairs, still silent, she stops but I take one more step in rhythm. The first floor hallway is illuminated so as I turn, her face is slightly obscured but there is no doubt that she is looking at me. She drops the shopping bag from her left hand and pulls me by my coat toward her. One step below, I'm slightly shorter. Without a word she gently touches her lips to mine in a manner I can only describe as chaste.

We stay still with our mouths touching. Her lips part, guiding mine with them. I feel her tongue touch both lips as she slides into my mouth. This is not my first kiss but it may as well be. I'm useless. I'm neither worried about someone entering in the stairway nor about what my mom would think nor about the fact that I'm kissing a teacher. I close my eyes to block everything except the sensation at my mouth. Her hand is still clasped on my coat, her grip tightens at regular intervals. Her tongue meets mine deep inside my mouth. Shock leaves me immobile. As she tilts her head to one side I push my tongue forward not to drive hers out but to create a shared kiss, rather than an assail on my innocence. I don't know how long we last but as she pulls away I'm satiated yet want more.

She picks up the dropped shopping bag and says with a smirk, "Wow, that was nice. I don't want you to miss your bus."

I step aside unable to move anywhere else and watch her walk down the last four steps. She reaches the bottom of the stairs before I'm able to move and when I finally take a step my right leg buckles underneath me.

We walk down the hall together in silence. When we reach the crowd of students waiting to take the same bus as me she says, "Ok Jimi, goodnight and have a nice Christmas. I'll see you after the break."

Something in the tone feels cold and hurts me. She says goodbye as if I were any one of those other kids, as if we didn't just kiss. I think I understand this to be a show but I'm suspicious. Was I not a good kisser? Did I do something wrong? Does she regret having kissed? I'm distraught.

My bigger problem though is facing my parents. I don't know how to speak to them with the same tongue that was in her mouth. I think I've done a good job of keeping things close to my chest but I don't know about this. I'm looking at the other kids around me to gauge their reaction. No one is looking like they suspect anything but I'm not certain that my face isn't screaming my astonishment.

Aren't most life altering events visible on one's face? I can't imagine this isn't written all over mine. If the speed with which my mind is racing is indicative of the rest of my body then it must be obvious. What if my parents notice? Confusion prevents any clear thought. I spend the bus ride home systematically analyzing each boy riding with me to figure out what makes me stand apart. What makes me desirable? Despite my best effort to denigrate myself and improve their adolescent traits I come up with nothing. I surrender and escape by thinking about anything but my new twist on reality.

I come home, put my books in my room and come down for dinner. I don't eat a thing which is not abnormal during wrestling season but has nothing to do with making weight and everything to do with the weight on my mind. I hear the usual speech from my parents about being healthy, complete with the threat that if I don't eat well they'll pull me from the team. I say nothing, just nod in agreement. Apparently there is no suspicion, so as my life depressurizes the kiss seeps into consciousness

I try to occupy myself until a reasonable time to call Carla, but it doesn't work. I am baffled how she could say goodbye as if we had not shared the same experience. Maybe that was just a kiss for her but it was a big deal for me, impossible to just leave on the stairs. I finally succumb and call. As soon as I say, "Hello," I hear, "Wow, that was the most amazing kiss of my life, let alone our first." I can't agree because I haven't allowed myself to process. I am, however, immediately washed over with relief. I was hurt by how we parted, absent any emotion but my fear disappears when her voice soothes me.

Once over that confusion I begin to fathom that we even kissed. Relief leads to reality. I don't have a notion of what romance is but I'm fairly certain standing in a high school stairwell that reeks of a mystery cleaning product basking in the fluorescent glow of hallway lights is not true love's first kiss. I replay my memory now and the feeling is dirty. I tasted coffee and I hate coffee. Something tried, unsuccessfully to hide coffee breath, like a fruit flavored "Certs".

"What did you think of our kiss?" she says.

I'm silent for those few seconds while she waits for my reciprocation of how great it was. "Oh," I say to buy myself time.

"You're absolutely right, it was pretty amazing," I lie.

My life since I called her the first time feels like being lost on a highway. Instead of exiting to recalculate, I keep driving. I pass exit after exit having absolutely no idea why I have yet to stop. It's as though every chance where I could speak up and express the thoughts in my head about coffee breath, age and love I ignore. And with each missed exit the car picks up speed, heading toward an unknown destination.

She talks incessantly, asking an endless stream of questions. It seems our kiss was a stimulant. She asks, "Have you asked your parents about Christmas Caroling?"

She asks, "Have your parents said anything about the exchange trip to France because I have so many ideas."

She tells me, "I am a little bit nervous about Christmas break because I don't want to go that long without seeing you." Carefully peppered among the real questions is bait. I have no responses, unable to think that quickly. She concludes, "So, I've been thinking a lot about what our next step should be since we've kissed," the thought left hanging endlessly between us. I no longer want to be me. And in the true spirit of the season, she wraps everything up in a nice package by saying, "I know what I'm going to get you for Christmas by the way."

This comes in rapid fire succession with neither solicitation nor opportunity to respond. My inventory is as follows and I try to express it in the prioritized order with which it was delivered: I've asked my father about Christmas Caroling. He will get back to me. France has not come up again, but I have a feeling I'll be able to go. I forget the rest of what she says because my heart races like I'm struggling on a final exam. She gladly and boisterously repeats in the same order, with the same verbiage, her questions. I'm only able to ask with ignorant innocence, "How would it be possible for us to get together during break if there's no school?"

She responds quickly, clearly after preliminary planning, "Well I know that there is the holiday wrestling tournament on the 28th of December."

Her silence again leaves the issue looming over my head to clarify. All I can say is, "Um, yeah I know. I'm wrestling in it."

"I know but since the tournament is all day whenever you are done, we could see one another," she responds again without pause. "Plus your parents wouldn't be expecting you until later in the evening so we'd have a lot of time together." She doesn't ask me if I have plans that day, or if, very specifically, I had plans on possibly winning the tournament which would then keep me at school until the finals.

"Well okay, I guess that could work, since I'm not expected home until later."

She continues, "I mean I would love for you to do well but the consolation prize if you happen to lose in the first round is that we could spend all day together."

Her words hurt. I feel pressure to lose, a painfully foreign feeling. Immediately my mind is clouded by the guilt of imagining her waiting for me so that we can spend time together because she, "misses," me.

A compromise occurs to me. If I do well at the tournament I can still see her between matches. The thought excites me because that would provide a place to get away from the commotion in the gymnasium. When I mention the possibility she sighs, a familiar exhalation.

"Well, I thought that we could go to my apartment for the day. It's only about fifteen minutes from school," she says unassumingly.

I don't know where her apartment is, what it looks like, who lives nearby or much else about her outside of school but when she proposes this idea my palms become sweaty. A low grade ringing develops in my ears. I try to imagine her apartment and how it's decorated. What does she do there in the evenings? I visualize her sitting on a couch I've never seen in an apartment located in a town I've never been through talking on the phone, telling me she loves me. I see her crying over my age and trying to cope with the obstacle of my parents' skepticism.

My daydream is broken by, "I can give you your Christmas present that day too unless that'd make you uncomfortable."

I answer quickly, "No, that's fine."

The whole idea makes me very uncomfortable although I don't know why. I simply take the path of least resistance.

I think I can interpret her invitation but it's hazy around the edges and I'm scared to imagine too much. I know what it meant when my last girlfriend told me to come over because her mom was working late. We kissed and made out and I even went up her shirt but we were both uncomfortable and regretful for being in that situation. The difference was that our remorse was softened by shared inexperience.

Carla and I stay on the phone until three o'clock in the morning and just as late the next four nights. We talk about ideas that two people in our circumstances should not. She asks, "Are you a virgin?" quite abruptly. I don't want to lie but want to give the answer that will most please her. However, I don't know what that is. I think I should be because if I'm not then that means that I have been living pretty fast for my age.

"I am," I say almost too quick to be intelligible.

Her response is cold in its simplicity, "I thought you were. Well, that's a good thing." I'm neither sure what led her to believe that I've never had sex nor why that's appealing. I only know a few people in my grade that have had sex and they're trashy. I shudder to think what their parents must think if they have been so lax as to let their high school sophomore have sex.

I'm severely ill-prepared for what comes next. She says, very naturally, with a bounce in her voice as if she is concurring with a preference of ice cream flavors, "Oh, me too."

"You too what?" I ask, unable to make the connection.

"I'm a virgin too."

I sense that she doesn't like the implication of my reply, "How can that be?" I don't mean to be offensive but am taken off guard. I was sure that she had boyfriends and lovers before especially considering how attractive she is.

"What do you mean how could I be a virgin?" she snaps. I feel bad for having a natural reaction.

I tell her immediately, "I'm sorry. I didn't mean anything by it. I just figured by the time I am your age I would have had sex."

With a tone that makes me instantly regretful for not keeping a tighter harness on my thoughts she says, "Well maybe I haven't had sex because I haven't found the right person and that's why I'm talking about it with you."

I remain silent because if I didn't have the right response the first time, I'm definitely not going to now. I remain motionless so she only hears silence on the phone, hoping her anger will soften.

She explains, "I've had boyfriends and most, have tried to convince me to have sex but I wanted to wait until I was married. I was even engaged once but before we were married, I found out that my fiancé, John, wanted to have an open marriage and I ended it immediately."

I ask nervously, "What's an open marriage?"

She describes, with what seems like misdirected anger, "An open relationship is where the people involved can sleep with whoever they want, whenever they want. And because of that, I called it off immediately."

Now I'm dying to know what makes me different. I can't ask because she is already upset and that may only exacerbate her. Although a logical question, I know I would convey a distinct hint of disbelief.

She drops the topic saying with renewed candor, "Let's not worry because we'll know when the time is right." I remember that platitude from the discussion about kissing and I had no say when that time was right.

We end our call early in the morning and once again she says, "I love you, Jimi." I know the only response is, "I love you too," so I comply. I speak from the same place that I recite everything else, void of emotion. The same voice I use to pledge allegiance every morning.

As usual, after I hang up I play back the conversation and figure out what was decided. I think I'm going to lose my first match of the wrestling tournament. I think we're going to have sex but not on that day. I have to ask my parents again regarding Christmas Caroling and I need to pin them down about the exchange trip. I think that covers the bigger issues but I know there are smaller matters requiring more attention than I can spare.

A chaotic noise resonates in my head. I feel it from the time that I wake up until I close my eyes early in the morning to sleep. Matters arise that I have to remember whether it's something that Carla has asked, my responsibilities at home, a request from a friend, or what should be most important, school.

Kevin is still having great difficulty and I want to be strong for him but simply cannot. I'm overwhelmed and feel panicky most of the time, like I'm drowning in something viscous I can't scrape off. I have this feeling most predominantly after speaking with Carla because she is counting on me to come through on so many issues. Some of them are tangible and require an answer, and some are too nebulous to mold into any comprehensible form. As I finally fall asleep I feel like I'm coming down with a cold. I'm worn down and there's a tickle in my throat. I'm undoubtedly exhausted and with the obscure things that have been coming out of my mouth I have no doubt that my throat has suffered some ill effects.

Chapter 9

I walk through my life as if in a dense fog. Certain things catch my attention and I can focus for a moment. Schoolwork suffers tremendously in just a few weeks. I have no energy for wrestling practice and find it difficult to participate in phys-ed class. The people I call friends treat me a little bit differently I think, but that might just be my own refracted self-perception. I feel tainted. I think people know what is behind my eyes even though I'm not sure myself. I'm jumpy and frightened by everyday things, often feeling like someone is going to grab me on the shoulder and say, "Mr. Cunneely, please come with us."

I know I'm doing something wrong but don't know what and don't know if it's even my fault. It seems like I'm watching my story unfold from a great seat in the mezzanine. All the places I hope for the protagonist to act differently go awry. The good vibes I send never have the effect for which I hope. Now all I can do is watch as the surrounding action leads him further down the spiral.

In the days leading up to Christmas I feel gradually worse but at any decent time when I ask to go to sleep Carla says, "Oh, ok, just one more thing."

That one thing, inevitably turns into some conversation about how mature I am and how she can't believe I'm fifteen. She marvels at how she never has to dumb anything down for me. That becomes how I'm so different from anyone else my age and consequently, our tremendous bond. It concludes with a list of the reasons she loves me like she does. I already feel feverish and achy but it's the gravity of these conversations that makes me dizzy.

Christmas Eve I cannot sit up without feeling like I'm going to faint. I regret every night that I stayed up late on the phone talking about things that seem unimportant now. I wish I had eaten healthier and not been so concerned with my weight. I've come down with nasty, flu-like symptoms that leave me without energy to even answer the constantly ringing phone. I hear the incessant noise but have no energy to pick up. When I finally give in, thinking that it could be an emergency, it's Carla. She doesn't even say, "Hello." Instead, leading with, "What's wrong? Why haven't you answered?"

There is concern in her voice but she sounds scolding, like when my mom doesn't hear from me in what she considers too long. I try to talk but cough instead. After composing myself I explain my symptoms and she softens her tone, "Oh, I'm so sorry you're sick. I wish I could take care of you."

Her sincerity sounds believable and comforts me slightly. I drift in and out of sleep as she tells me what I should eat and how often I should go stand in the shower to unclog my sinuses. "Uh-huh," is all I mumble.

"Ok, sweetheart, feel better and I'll call you tomorrow ok?" I don't realize that I miss the cradle when I drop the phone until I hear the obnoxious beeping from being off the hook.

Christmas morning I try to open presents but can barely stand. I make the effort so my mom can take pictures. As soon as I open the last stick of lip balm from my stocking my dad tells me, "Go upstairs and lay down," without a word, I do. I lay in bed all day feeling the full brunt of not having gotten more than three consecutive hours of sleep for the last two weeks. I drift all day, in and out of consciousness teetering on the edge of what was my childhood and whatever lies on the other side of the precipice. The big present I opened this morning was a stereo system with my first compact disc player. My parents also bought me the Led Zeppelin boxed set I've begged for since its release last year. I put all four CD's in the machine with what feels like the last bit of energy I will ever have and press, "Play," and, "Shuffle," and the CD player does exactly what my head is doing. It randomizes the songs like my mind is trundling through the memories of the last few weeks. As I focus on the events that have taken place over the last month it feels like a year. The panic is indescribable that so much emotional and mental energy has been crammed into such a short stretch of my life.

I finally drift despite the aching that prevents me from finding a comfortable position. I hear the music in the background and the only way that I know how long I've slept is that I hear "Tangerine" play for the second time, "Living reflection from a dream." That means all four CD's have played through once. It's the background music to the same fever-dream that I remember having every illness since pre-school, nightmarish but consoling in its familiarity.

A few moments of clarity reveal the sounds of the new toys that my brother and sister are playing with downstairs. I hear my mom using the new KitchenAid mixer my dad bought her and I think I smell fresh baked cookies that christen it. I hear the faint din of dinner conversation and the sound of forks and knives clanging against plates, and I know that I have missed the whole day. I have sacrificed my entire Christmas for the sake of staying up late to talk about many things that all add up to nothing.

Folie à Deux

What I don't hear for a change, is my phone. I turned it off before I went to bed last night and I haven't thought about Carla since. In a rare moment of lucidity, it occurs to me that, not only have I avoided speaking to her but she hasn't crossed my mind in hours. I wouldn't characterize my days as thinking about Carla so much as being consumed by her presence, making today a welcome respite. I'm left alone in complete darkness, in near silence except for the barely audible boxed set playing underneath. I will remember this day as the first time in my life that I want to be alone but am terrified of the loneliness simultaneously.

As I start to feel better the next day, I long to be sick again. There was a certain protection in being ill, a built-in excuse for avoiding my phone, a reason not to face my parents with my giant secret looming. Both apices of my triangular life were content to know I was convalescing on my own time but neither knew that I was starting to spiral further downward. I'm scared to ask my parents about Christmas Caroling because I know what my father has already said, plus I asked him to go out to dinner with Carla at a time when even I thought it was innocent. Will they become suspicious that I'm asking for another out of school meeting? Will they ask me questions about her involvement in my life? They know I'll be at wrestling practice every day during Christmas break and I'll be gone all day at the tournament on the December 28th but I'm still scared to be caught.

I lose my first match of the tournament at 8:30 in the morning, my head down and hands shaking. I tell myself I lost because I'm recovering from a nasty flu and try to convince myself that since I'm an underclassman, it's also inexperience. It helps to think that I haven't been sleeping, I still can't breathe well and I missed two days of practice. I clutch for anything to soothe the disappointment I feel for putting my wishes so far behind hers.

Part One

I decided to give this half-hearted effort because I had something else on my mind. As I walk off the mat and see the disappointment on my coach's face, over his shoulder I see Carla in the bleachers clapping. It could be the applause of a supporter lauding my effort or it could be the overspill of arousal for watching me star in six minutes of soft-core porn. Most likely, it's that I can be showered and with her in minutes. The instant that I'm in the locker room alone I realize with full force the finality of indecision that controls my life.

I didn't lose purposely but I also didn't try to win. My ambiguity to neither displease her nor act on my behalf has left me at the mercy of unknown factors. I may have won had I tried, but I'll never know. My fate was decided for me and the feeling is terrible.

Chapter 10

I take a long shower and a longer, lonely walk to her classroom where she is anxiously waiting. The first thing I think when I walk into her classroom is that she looks pretty. A long black sweater worn over leggings that have vertical black and white stripes and she smells good. She sees the dejection on my face and hugs me, "You did well. That was close."

Bullshit. I did horribly and should have won.

She can barely hide her excitement that I'm free to leave, "Are you ready? I'll cook you a delicious breakfast to cheer you up." I don't know how I feel about today. I'm excited but nervous. Want to stay but want to go with her, ambiguity again dictating my life.

We walk to her car as though engaging in the most normal, mutually enjoyable activity. She talks non-stop the entire ride, "I'm so excited to give you your present. Do you like cranberry juice or orange because I have both? How do you like your eggs? Do you prefer wheat toast or white? I'm so sorry you were sick for Christmas." Her forced conversation interspersed with, "Cheer up, I know you're sad you lost but there's always next year," which makes me feel even worse.

The ride is fifteen minutes and I'm only fifteen years old so by the time we arrive I feel better thanks to disassociation more than coping skills. I enter her apartment to see the table is already set for breakfast with nice china. The pans are on the stove and the coffee pot set up so all she has to do is press start. When I see the little box on the table wrapped in contemporary paper I release the last vestiges of my bitterness. Even though I still want to be a kid, I push through and present my best version of what I think a grown-up is.

She says, "I'll do the eggs and you can be in charge of juice and toast but first can I give you your gift? I'm so excited to see if you like it." She walks to the table and holds out the small, carefully wrapped box with a tiny silver bow offset on the lid.

Before I take it from her I explain, "Listen, I couldn't get a ride to pick something up for you and I feel bad."

She tilts her head and gives a wounded puppy dog expression, "Oh, Jimi, that's so sweet of you. I didn't get you this so that you would buy me a gift. I bought it because I want you to have it."

She sounds genuine but I think I should still have a present and am obsessing that I don't. She pulls me by the hand to the loveseat, I pull the bow and begin to unwrap what looks like a jewelry box. I move slowly, trying to avoid participation in whatever ritual this is. I feel the tether on me tighten as I realize it's probably a talisman that marks me as her property or a piece of jewelry that I will not wear, causing hurt feelings. Before laborious turns into ridiculous I open the box to find a single diamond stud earring.

As I'm creating a response she asks through a barely audible panting, "Do you like it? Will you wear it?"

"I like it a lot" I answer truthfully, as the light reflects from the facets of the jewel.

My first thought is what I will tell my parents when they notice I'm wearing a real diamond. She cleans that up quickly, "Just tell them it's fake. It's an imitation that was a gift from a friend."

I remove the silver ball earring I put in after my match. She is sitting on my right side so after I feel the earring back slide over the lock I turn my head so she can see.

She puts her hand on my chin and says, "Wow, I like it. It looks very nice." Sitting this close, with her hand on my chin, I start to tremble. It could be from exertion, but I don't think so. She leans in and her grip tightens on my chin as she pulls me gently to her lips.

This kiss is different than our first. I'm slightly driven back by the force of her mouth, hungry for me. Her left hand remains cupped on my chin, her right on the armrest, pinning me into the corner. Her tongue is deep in my throat and before long the hand holding my chin moves to my chest.

I feel the beginning of an erection I want to hide. I can't imagine she would put her hand there. Not now, not today but she did talk of our next step and we have all day. Anxiety battles arousal for the forefront of my mind. It seems instantaneous that as her left hand is on my chest her right is on the back of my head moving down to the nape of my neck. It moves down the collar of my shirt and when it returns to the center of my head she plunges her tongue more deeply inside. She prevents me from pulling back. My penis is as rigid from excitement as my back is from tension. My hands remain clutching the partially wrapped jewelry box providing purchase on something safe.

She moves her hands around my upper body as if frisking me. When her hands reach the bottom of my wrists she tosses the paper on the floor. My hands lock on my lap partially because I don't know an appropriate place for them and I'm still embarrassed by my body's response. When I realize that her hands are now so well acquainted with my entire upper body, front and back I think it offensive that we are both touching me. After another few moments of deliberation I put my right arm around her and my other on her thigh. I keep my right hand immobile on her back and my left rubs her thigh from knee to just short of what might suggest an interest in more than kissing. In reality, I have no idea where any boundary line is anymore. I can't say how long we kiss because the velocity of my thoughts makes time hard to track. Maybe ten minutes? It could be an hour.

When my stomach growls audibly she slows the kiss at an unnoticeable pace, "I guess you're hungry and I did promise you breakfast didn't I?" She giggles as though embarrassed but only because my physical hunger was louder than her sexual.

I open my eyes when the kiss slows to see a satisfied smile on her face. She opens hers slowly and draws near to join our lips once more, this time ending with the sound of a smooch. "You are a very good kisser, I must say," she whispers and stands up before I can respond. With no further debriefing she walks into the kitchen and begins breakfast. "You got the drinks and toast, right Hon?" she calls to me.

I have not yet moved and am not ready to join her. I'm conscious not to give the appearance of something wrong so I rise and walk into the kitchen trying to deemphasize my bulging crotch.

Her tiny apartment is the ground floor of a converted bungalow. I walked from the dining room to the living room in three steps. It seems as though the bed barely fits in the bedroom but I avoided looking to not seem curious. I pour the juice and drop the bread in their slots attempting to be present but really, I feel catatonic. More engulfing than what has happened is what still could the rest of this day. Every time one of the channels in my mind becomes too heavy I switch to the other. I think about what my mom is doing. I imagine playing a video game with my sister, or taking a walk with my brother. Eventually those thoughts join in the overwhelming static clouding my ability to function also.

"Oh shit, I burned the toast," I say when it pops. "Oh shit," I just cursed in front of her I say in my head and I burned the toast. She assures me that she likes her toast exactly that way. I continue to apologize which convinces her I don't believe her contrived forgiveness.

She responds, "If you were to call my mom right now and ask her how her daughter likes toast she would say, 'Black.'"

I think, "If I were to call my mother and ask her to guess where I am I bet she couldn't." But I say nothing.

The only way I'm going to survive this day is to detach from the enormity around me. I'm able to discuss school, my holiday and her holiday as though my presence in her apartment at ten-thirty on a Wednesday morning is quite normal. All the while thoughts of my parents at work, my younger siblings at daycare and my teammates supporting one another creep in, reminding me of my other life.

We eat breakfast, eggs sunny side up, toast, and crumb buns with one orange juice and one cranberry over normal conversation. When we are long finished eating and seem to have run out of topics, she asks, "So would you like to sit someplace more comfortable?" Had I not already disconnected from the dysfunction such a question would have made all newly found comfort disappear. But the carved off piece of me is able to say, "Sure, that sounds like a good idea."

"Leave the dirty dishes. I'll take care of them later," she says as she demurely places her napkin on the chair.

She walks in front of me, stops abruptly at the loveseat and turns. She delicately takes the diamond earring between her thumb and forefinger and says, "That looks so nice on you. I love you." She pauses and shifts her attention between my ear lobe and my eyes, "I don't know, Jimi Cunneely, you are one handsome man."

I giggle because I'm not a man and I don't think of myself in the terms with which she perpetually describes me. It feels as though she is trying to convince herself of these attributes, not me.

She leans in and kisses me, this time with her whole body. I feel her thighs and breasts press against me, slightly taller than her, she tilts her head upward. Instantly when I feel the warmth in my pants I pull my hips back only to feel her palm crushed flat on the small of my back. As her hand pulls me her hips push and the pressure causes a sensation of pleasure intertwined with pain I've never felt before. She lets go of my lips for a second to produce a barely audible moan that arouses me even more. She rises on her toes as if searching a better vantage point, pushes her whole body into me but I have long forgotten where I am. I fail to recall that there is a loveseat behind me, so while this has been calculated by her it causes intense panic until I fall back safely.

Before I can process that I did not hit the ground she is straddling me and in one motion, grinding. Her moans are louder now and her hips moving not so much faster but harder. It causes quite a stir as my body and mind try to decode the gratification of the throbbing. What feels good in my body makes me feel bad in my head. I'm not supposed to see her like this. I enjoyed it when it was a fantasy I heard out of the mouth of someone else but this is too real. My nerves or my anxiety or my body's inability to direct any part of me except my dick is keeping my hands on the cushion beside me. She forcefully places them on her back. I play the same game as I did earlier with her thigh. I feel vulgar as the words that scream through my head are all the slang terms used in the locker room. I'm too overcome to keep any composure regarding the language I use to describe the narrative of what is happening.

She rises for a second to pull her sweater out from underneath which I know means she wants my hand on her bare skin. I discover her flesh, warm and soft. Her back tight and muscular. I start by touching her tenderly, but then to keep with the pace I move my hands faster, grabbing muscle with a slight massage. She pulls her mouth from mine and latches onto my left ear saying in a throaty voice that startles me, "Your hands are strong. That feels so good."

Without thought and almost as involuntarily as the beating of my heart, my hips rise in rhythm to meet hers sending a shock wave up my body I feel in the back of my neck. Her first couple moans I mistake for heavy breathing but my thrust leads to unmistakable clamor born from unbridled bliss.

My hand dares touch her oblique. She buckles, as if tickled. Time again has no value and can't be quantified. She says to me after what seems like hours of grinding, "We should stop." But she doesn't. I think she wants me to ask why. She leaves her statement dangling but I've had little, if anything to do with the planning of this entire day so I'm not about to exert any now. It seems like another thirty minutes of the same when she jumps off and says, "Ok, ok, I have to stop this now."

I'm no longer concealed by her body so I instinctively fold my hands in my lap as if she doesn't already know I'm hard. My mind, still being elsewhere doesn't react as she wants so she asks, with frustration, "Do you know why we have to stop?"

"I don't," afraid my response invites her to climb back on, which I may want.

"Because if I don't stop, I'm afraid I'm going to overstep my boundaries," she offers through the slowing of her breath. I'm reminded of her saying how upset she is that she'll never be able to act on her feelings. I cannot guess what she is implying but I know there is definitely a right response to this statement. I don't know what it is so I remain silent, muted by confusion.

Right now I'm tired. I wrestled and lost a match I should have won. I'm drained of the mental energy I've been forced to wield for survival and mostly because I've had to hide my ambivalence to exist. Too tired to reply, "Yeah, you're right", is the best I can do.

I look at the clock to find we have spent more than three hours on the loveseat. My penis feels beat up from rubbing up against the inside of my underwear and her pants for so long. My back aches. The same atrophy that formed in my back, settled in my mind from detachment. After I waken my muscles and re-pose myself for the first few seconds I feel a rush of indescribable guilt for being a part of what just happened.

I remind her that she needs to drive me to school so I can catch my ride home but when I think of my mom, I no longer want to leave. I'm not faced with having to account for my where-abouts. There is a certain security involved in being here because this is still happening. Questions have not yet been asked. Lies have not yet created tension for however long they will hang in the air between me and my interrogator. For some inexplicable reason, I relish the avoidance of having to deal with this but I tell her anyway, "We probably should get going."

Because she is sitting next to me she only has to tilt her head to rest it on my shoulder protesting, "I don't want you to leave yet. I'm having such a nice day with you." Her playful objection weighs on me like another trap. It's always with bait that is too simple to ignore but too complex to evade either. It wasn't a nice day for me. From the first waking dilemma of the tournament and everything since, I unfastened me from me.

"I did too," I say quietly, as if speaking too loudly would confirm it doubly. I'm upset enough that it leaves my lips in the first place.

"Ok, let's get you back to school," she finally says with overt reluctance.

Chapter 11

"So I want to ask you something," is the common phrase helpful in preparing me to expect absolutely any ensuing question. The topics that have been broached with only that preamble run the gamut. It's used on the phone, late one night with my brother already asleep in the bed next to me. "I've been thinking about something very serious and important to me," she says.

I try to concentrate but my fear of what may come is crippling. "We said we loved each other on December 20th," her pause allows me to reflect on that random fact momentarily. "So what do you think of making love for the first time on our one month anniversary?" She asks as though we're planning a picnic or some event that will have more emotional value if the calendar reflects one number instead of another.

I thought I was ready for anything but I'm not. Like a standardized test, the questions become increasingly difficult as time rolls on. Unfortunately, I can't skip the ones I don't know and continue. The choices are too multiple to eliminate. My odds never improve.

She soft peddles once faced with my silence, "I hope I didn't overstep my boundaries by asking you that, it's just been on my mind so much since the day at my apartment."

"Oh no," I falsely assure her. My answer is the absolute truth because boundaries have been so blurred that I couldn't even begin to define what I should accept as normal. She is a teacher and I have gone multiple places with her that I never should. Clearly, the margins are on a sliding scale. They have been covered over with so much debris, kicked up in the last month that unearthing them is a hope I've long abandoned.

"That sounds fine."

Fine is the best adjective I can imagine, fully aware that my input is a formality. Before she can question my word choice, I remind her that I'm a virgin. Not to endear myself but to pre-forgive my shortcomings.

"Oh Jimi, I know and I think it's beautiful that we'll be sharing that wonderful gift with each other," spoken more like coercion than comfort.

From somewhere that has abandoned refinement, to eliminate the stresses of my life I say, "Listen, Carla, I don't want to come across as though I think you lied, but how have you never had sex before? It just seems odd because I can tell you thirty people in our school that have lost their virginity before they've even turned eighteen."

I speak quickly before she can interrupt but am certain she receives all of the disbelief that I intended. She responds with stories of insecurity about her weight and the size of her breasts. She describes how she dislikes being looked at by men because being objectified is disgusting, the irony completely lost on me.

I think it best to avoid any follow up questions because I can sense by the few sarcastic barbs that she is upset by my accusation. Some of the men in her stories are teachers that I know, others are nameless and faceless, but endearing only because we've shared a kiss and maybe a dry hump with the same woman. She speaks of defending her chastity as though it were the last virtue she would ever possess, not giving it to just anyone. Her explanations work on so many levels because they not only make me blameworthy for doubting her but the backhand to this conversation solidifies me. She subliminally reminds me that I hold a special place in her life, that I, alone, am worthy to bestow her virginity after a lifetime of undeserving suitors.

I feel terrible so I apologize and backpedal, "I can't imagine that among all the men who would clearly want to be with a woman as special as you, not one of them was good enough." It appeases her because it prompts the familiar conversation about our destiny to have met here and now. She launches into, "How thankful I am that I waited for you, Jimi." My attempt to reenter her good graces has worked, yet I don't understand how I feel ugly inside for being the simultaneous source of her happiness as well as displeasure.

I have no success extracting some truth on this topic but opening it has diverted the flow of pressure, albeit momentarily. We set a date based on our one-month anniversary which I didn't even know begged a celebration. She redirects, "Is there a day this week that you can skip wrestling practice and come to my apartment? I'm so lonely by myself. It cheered me up to have you here for a whole day." Her nasally voice sounds so much like begging I actually pity her.

"Um," I run through the schedule in my mind knowing that I have a match on Wednesday immediately regretful when I realize mollifying her makes me an accomplice. "Well, the days we have matches we can leave right after school and don't have to be back until six. I have a match this Wednesday," I offer.

She asks in the playful voice to which I am now accustomed, "Well, do you have any plans after school on Wednesday? Oh say, between two-thirty and six?" How do I say no when she is being coy, knowing I just provided my own alibi?

"That works for me," unsuccessfully replicating her boisterous tone.

She is nothing short of giddy on Wednesday from the first time I see her. It seems she wears a new sense of anticipation for the world to see although impossible for anyone but me to know. It amazes me how comfortable she is walking to her car with a student after school.

Each classmate we pass on our exit makes me increasingly jealous that I can't stay and be a kid alongside them. This is a phenomenon that will occur time and again for years. Other kids will see me with her, see the attention she dotes on me and I'll catch an envious glance or a curious stare. They don't think I perceive it and they'll never know that I crave her ignorance to their existence. I wish desperately that I was also a face in the crowd to Carla, coveting their insignificant place in her life.

It's cold and dreary, a typical January day; conversely the conversation on the way to her apartment is light and inconsequential. I notice things I didn't on our first trip, certain houses that overlook the lake and different landscaping. Because I know where I'm going the trip seems shorter but that's only due to the absence of curiosity. I know we're not going to have sex because we have already set a date so I'm anxious to find out what we explore. Instinctively, I sit on the loveseat in the same spot where we spent the majority of our last day. She walks past saying nothing as she enters the bathroom.

After being lost in my thoughts for a few peaceful moments she walks out and pulls me to the middle of the loveseat so that she can straddle me again. She locks her fingers together and puts her arms around my head, resting her forearms on my shoulders. She smirks as if to remind me of the secret that exists between us. The dirty feeling I have lived with since the day in the stairwell has been the only souvenir I need to ensure my reticence. Her expression persists long enough for me to think it's not about the secret. I raise my chin quickly to her and ask, "What?" mirroring her expression.

"I'm happy to have you back here," she sighs as though snuggling into a warm cozy blanket. I don't know what to say so I let escape a nervous chuckle that makes me more uncomfortable. She slowly touches her lips to mine making the faintest sounds of kissing. The smacking of my lips is an instant behind hers as I try to participate in spirit if not in person.

Our kiss is noticeably short before she stands up and leads me to the bedroom. Once inside, she lays me down on her bed and climbs over top to lie beside me. I look around, trying to take inventory of the room without seeming like I'm in a museum. I am awestruck that I'm in a grown woman's bedroom, not to mention, a teacher. I see a dresser and two night tables. Nothing visible decorates the walls except a rack hanging next to the dresser, necklaces hanging from protruding knobs.

I feel the warmth between her legs purposely grind for a second against my semi-erection and my involuntary reply is to raise my hips. She stays only long enough to tantalize a reaction from me that I'm afraid to surrender. She moans slightly but completes the action of lying beside me, propping her head on her hand and renews the kiss where we left off in the other room.

She plays with my hair and tugs gently on my ear lobe. Her fingernails glide along the side of my head, down behind my ear and all five uniformly caress my cheek in circles. When I react to avoid the tickling her whole body moves along with mine to keep her tongue in my mouth. After my skin has lost sensitivity and she feels as though I'm no longer receptive her mouth moves someplace different. Her lips are softer on my cheek than on my own and I like it. Tingling travels down my body as she moves to the space where my jaw meets my neck.

Without control, I release a soft whimper that sounds like a puppy having a dream. Since she already inhabits my ear she only whispers, "Am I overstepping my boundaries?" This question will become synonymous with implicating me in blurring the margins that verify I am a student and she a teacher.

I wonder if this is pillow talk.

Not until years later will I realize asking that question is nothing more than an injection of paralytic venom. How can I say, "No," to Carla Danza? All of my senses and experiences in high school thus far have inculcated me to know this is an opportunity at which any other boy would eagerly leap.

How do I say, "No," when the bulge in my pants must be visible from the other room? It's letting her know exactly my level of enjoyment. How can I say, "No," when I have agreed to come to her apartment and her bedroom and told her I love her? And at every one of those junctures my failure to say, "No," is, undoubtedly, "Yes."

It's just that perception of consent that plants the seed of disgrace I will carry for the rest of my life. That's what will make it almost impossible to lay the blame exclusively at her feet when I feel implicated not as an accomplice, rather a co-conspirator.

I hear the question but cannot answer, too focused on what she is doing to my neck and now where my neck meets my shoulder. The shift from one place to another provides an instant to remember that she asked me something so I try to think with the intent of answering. I don't know where the boundaries are anymore. Two months ago this would have been absurdly over any line. But where is that frontier now? I've told her I love her. She has cried to me. We have discussed plans to make love and visit

Paris. The line seems to be buried beneath layers of raw emotion. The best I can do is a groan meant to convey, "No," completely spellbound like never before.

"Just tell me if I am", she assures me, "And I'll stop." She knows that I will never ask her to stop. The euphoria on my face and in my faint whimpers scream that I love what she is doing. She knows that this is purely carnal pleasure and she is okay that it overrides the mindfuck. She is across the front and onto the other side of my neck in one motion.

All this while my hands are at my sides, I think. I'm pretty sure she's massaging my arms while her lips gently caress my skin. As she finishes kissing my entire head and neck she works her way back to my lips and once again gently places her tongue in my mouth. As she does, she assumes her position next to me, holding herself on her elbow.

There are no windows in her bedroom and it's cloudy outside, so as four o'clock arrives it becomes very dark adding to the tantric feeling. She lifts up my shirt and rubs my stomach causing me to spasm. She reminds me again that I can stop her at any time by repeating her question. I am so lost in the visual image of her lips all over my neck that involuntarily, I say, "No."

"No," verifies that my body works much like other fifteen year old boys', efficiently and with one guiding principle into which she is fully plugged. She interprets participation, joining her in this moment. Are there even boundaries anymore? We have cooperatively normalized all of this. The preordained value system in which we both exist in the outside world is unaffected by what is taking place here. She continues to run her hands all over my chest using a combination of her nails to scratch and her fingertips to stroke my tender young flesh. As she works her way up my body she raises my shirt at the same time.

"Would you be more comfortable if we took this off?" awakens me momentarily.

I don't speak but lift my shoulders so that she can slide the shirt from underneath me. Once off, I lie back down and she continues to touch me while simultaneously kissing my torso. She starts at the center of my trunk just below my pecs in the very middle where they meet.

I like this a lot. Her hands have moved to my sides and are still stroking but her lips and tongue are creating a wild work of art around my body. I jump violently. The trembling begins to work its way down my legs. I quiver as though trying to kick out a cramp. It's neither a moan nor a sigh that leaves her mouth as she nears my hard left nipple. One, unmistakable laugh fills the silent room.

Is she laughing because I have done something wrong? Is she laughing at my body because I'm underdeveloped or because I don't have hair on my chest? Because I'm shuddering as if I have some sort of disorder? These are all the thoughts that go through my head as I hear her one inconsequential giggle.

She asks, "Are you ok?"

"Fine," I tell her, "Are you?" She says that she's great which doesn't account for what she found humorous and doesn't assuage my insecurity. But it's not something that I have to deal with at present.

Making her way up my neck she asks one more time, "Have I overstepped my boundaries?"

I find it almost comical and the satire wasted that she is looking not for my approval but my leadership. She wants me to tell her how much I like it or she may even be prompting me to use specific requests. I don't understand why she keeps asking because she knows what she has in mind. I'm sure she presumes

Part One

I knew what was in store or I was at least in the same ballpark regarding today's agenda.

She lays half of her body on mine and kisses my neck again with more teeth involved than before. As her hand touches my stomach she asks the question one last time, making it abundantly clear why we had to pass through so many checkpoints on our way to this destination. She finally unveils her ultimate goal. Realization washes over me when she says, "How about now? Am I overstepping my boundaries now?" This is at the exact instant that her hand drops below the waistline of my pants and strokes the length of my fully engorged, throbbing penis. This sensation causes my hips to first rock back and then thrust with the full strength of my pelvis, abs and diaphragm toward the ceiling. The voyeuristic show is accompanied by the soundtrack of me letting out a full-fledged groan that starts somewhere in my throat and only increases in rasp as it projects.

The sound is drawn out and I feel embarrassed when I hear it becoming conscious that I have just lost what little self-control I may have had. She is stroking as she runs her tongue down the center of my body slowly and laboriously trying desperately, it seems to keep in contact with my writhing. I think she speeds up licking the axis of my whole body for fear that I might orgasm.

As her mouth reaches my jeans she kisses the semi-circle of my stomach from hip bone to hip bone very slowly. When she arrives back to my navel she starts to unbutton the top button of my pants and then unfastens, with remarkable dexterity, every one that makes up the button fly. When she pulls my pants down my heart pounds, painfully. My lips involuntarily move to the sentence, "I can't fucking believe this." I don't think she hears, but I try to stop myself anyway.

She has my pants down just below my ass and is now working on my underwear stretching the waistband all the way out to clear the arc of my penis, now excruciating with excitement. She places each hand beside a hip so that I can feel her wrists barely touching me as she begins to kiss my newly exposed body. She encompasses my thighs and where they meet my pelvis. The area of my stomach that surrounds it is also treated to diversionary teasing. But she is very careful not to make any contact whatsoever with her target. All that has touched me so far are the wisps of hair that fall out of place causing tantalizing panic. Once she has given consideration to every, recently undressed area she starts at the tip and works her way down the length of me kissing gently.

Upon reaching the base she begins to work her way back up, arriving at the tip of me again, she takes me voraciously into her mouth. Hungry to taste, hungry to envelop and hungry to please me. My hands are locked over my head, redundantly notifying her of my surrender. They were previously in the way and I felt uncomfortable anywhere near what was going on down there so I removed them, allowing her to work. I feel about to come but know from television that it's undesirable to ejaculate quickly. I'm trying desperately to keep control over the explosion that I feel building below my stomach. My hands grip tightly on the solid wood of the headboard and it feels as though I might rip it from behind the bed.

Her right hand grabs what is exposed of my left ass cheek before she works that hand up my body and onto my hip bone. From my hip she pushes hair back behind her ear and then grabs me full force as though she is seizing a handle to keep from falling. Within five strikes I pop. She pauses a second, maybe out of surprise or how quickly it happened, but once I ejaculate I hear something amazing.

I hear her moan as she swallows me. She takes all of me, as though I am nectar she was craving. The sound of the swallow is accompanied by the sound of satisfaction one might hear from someone drinking water after having gone days without. She sounds thrilled and aroused simultaneously at having had me in her mouth and now having ingested me too. Once done she begins to move her head up and down gently.

She slows down at unnoticeable increments until I feel the warmth of her mouth replaced by the cold of the air on my wet skin. Her mouth moves back up my body faster than it moved down, stopping at my hard, right nipple to dance in one single circle and up to my face. She nestles her head in the place that drove me most crazy when kissed before. After just a few seconds rest, as I feel myself drifting off into some other state of unconsciousness she whispers in my ear, "That was beautiful."

I can't agree. I can't disagree. I can't tell what it was or how it was or absolutely anything about what happened. Although my body is relaxed and feels like I was just the sole center of the universe my mind is starting to unravel what put us here. Almost immediately, as my body begins to loosen my mind begins to wind tighter around the intangible explanation. They were working at opposite ends of the same turnbuckle earlier, tightening against one another to cause nothing but tension. My mind was disassociating from the moment to allow my body to participate. But now my thoughts are reclaiming their hold on reality and the process of how we got from any point in our past to right now is muddled.

As I rejoin myself I remember I still have to wrestle tonight. Reality takes a firmer grip when I replay the captain of the football team telling us not to jerk off after Wednesday in preparation for Saturday's game. Wednesday was the last acceptable time to jerk off because ejaculation releases testosterone, decreasing ferocity. This thought creeps up on me as I slowly open my eyes. But I did just get a blowjob from my teacher, which has to have some counterbalancing effect on the karma of depriving my body of hormones. What could possibly make me more of a man?

I win my match providing something positive to discuss with my parents. It doesn't take my mind off the afternoon but at least helps put some distance from the surreal so I can feign normalcy at momentary intervals. My phone is already ringing as I walk up the stairs after saying, "Goodnight," to my family. I know it is her wanting to debrief. I'm sure she is going to tell me how beautiful she thinks it was and if I know her at all she is going to ask at least once more if she overstepped her boundaries.

Claustrophobia envelops me. I don't know what I should think about anything. The confusion of the orgasm is unbalanced against how dirty I feel. The knowledge that she is going to lay so many unanswerable questions on my lap which all need correct answers frightens me. It was a powerful experience that I would like to somehow sort out on my own. Her suggestions and thoughts cloud the issue so much that it overlaps my own, creating uncertainty about what belongs to me and what I've been forced to adopt.

The conversation proceeds exactly as I expected and I agree with everything. She asks, "Do you think you will be comfortable enough to make love on our one month anniversary?" I have no idea how to answer because my comfort, although falsely prioritized was far from paramount today so why would it matter in the future?

She asks, "When is your next match? Was that your first time having oral sex? How great did it feel? When can you come to my apartment again?" I give answers using words that have no root in the truth. I simply rise to play on the same level of excitement and love that she projects onto my half of our relationship.

We say, "Goodnight," and, "I love you," without her even asking me if I won my match.

Regardless of my reluctance, she continues to insist I join her on match days. Two, sometimes three times a week I'm locked in foreplay leading up to our date for intercourse and she is voracious in her desire. Her interest in the things that may be important to me wanes significantly as she force feeds what she thinks I should adopt as hobbies. I am overwhelmed by how much she tries to make me be like her. The sparse moments when we are not enthralled in some sexual act are filled with suggestions of what she can teach me to, "Love as much as I do." Her offers to teach me guitar, ride horses, speak French, sing professionally lean much closer to directives. I'm not given a choice when she puts the guitar in my lap or places the open French workbook in front of me.

Even the things I never knew I knew come from her. Assuming when she pulls me into her bedroom will end with her ingesting my semen turns out to be incorrect a week before our planned love-making. After a longer than normal time with our mouths locked, she takes my hand and places it up her skirt. When I rest my hand on her pubic bone from subconscious refusal she makes her frustration known by arching her hips hard into the air. She kisses me harder and locks her small hand around my wrist. I do nothing except follow the lead her tongue is taking amongst our mouths. In order to make me to think that her arousal is at a climax she puts both of her hands on my shoulders and pushes me down her body.

My resistance is born from emotions I never knew existed. I don't know what I am supposed to do anywhere lower than her breasts. She continues to push but I lock my hips so that I cannot sink any further down this spiral. When she realizes that she has no further power to force me, she removes her hands from my shoulders and pulls her baby blue skirt up around her waist and her panty hose down in what seems like one motion despite their contradicting directions.

I'm left to wonder what she was hoping to accomplish if only to tempt instead of oblige. I neither want to know her this way nor see this part of her. I thought this would be an awesome experience when I joined conversations at the lunch table but it comes with much more pressure than I could imagine. I'll trade places now if my friends want, gladly relinquishing my good fortune. She can have the earring back and they can have the blowjobs and the late night conversations. I want out now.

In my frozen state of self-pity her one final push puts my face directly over top of her. When I freeze again her right hand palms the back of my head and pushes me lips to lips with exactly what she wanted. This is so wrong. I don't want to know this intimate part of her life. She is a teacher, an adult in my life that I have been raised to obey and respect. If she told me to stop talking, take out my homework, or sent me to the office I would have to obey or face the consequences. How is this different? If she is instructing me to pleasure her in her bedroom after school what else am I to do? I hate the taste and I hate the smell which is not something that I would characterize as bad but unwholesome.

Once she settles into a rhythm I find it nearly impossible to keep up. Her hips move wildly in every orientation imaginable.

My jaw hurts so badly that I want to stop but I'm afraid what she might say if I disappoint her. Just as I am about to quit from cramping that has turned into pain, she collapses back into the bed and lets out a loud moan. I stay exactly where I am when she let her body fall from my mouth, my eyes closed so that I do not have to see anything else. She throws her right hand at my shoulder and grabs my shirt to pull me up. She alternates exhaling between her nose and mouth as she tries desperately to catch her breath and when she finally does she says through her panting, "Wow, Jimi. Where did you ever learn that?"

Chapter 12

I feel her gaze overtake me more frequently. She used to take careful steps to not be caught staring. I would see her look, catch herself and look away. Now, when I go to her room during study hall, even when we're not talking I feel her eyes on me. Neither watching nor supervising, simply observing from close proximity. She doesn't unnerve yet validates me, separates me from everyone else. Carla not only authenticates me but certifies the compliments with which I'm showered. I've never seen her looking at anyone else the way she does me and I've never had attention like this.

She keeps her distance from some single teachers or the flirtatious custodian so I know she doesn't look at them this way. Her watch makes me feel like she is enamored with the idea of me more than who I am which is fine because my essence is all that sustains my survival. I don't know me yet because I'm too young but am trying to figure me out at an accelerated pace. Being me is becoming increasingly difficult because the need to be her boyfriend has supplanted all else.

I'm superseded by the need to engage in long conversations about where our life is going. I take a back seat to the dilemma of how to tell my parents when I turn eighteen. I'm crucial to her when she needs consolation, driven to tears by the difficulty of our relationship. There are so many demands that I could not have imagined, trying to juggle them is stressful and understandably, I lose me from time to time.

There are three times throughout the day that we walk together from one class to the next. Sometimes I miss her because someone needs to speak with her or I leave class a moment late. In those instances I feel her gaze from behind. I hear her greeting people as they pass and if she's near she must be looking at me. I sense the warmth of her eyes softly fixed on me and I wonder what she's thinking. Is she staring at my ass? Is she thinking of my face buried in her crotch or her mouth wrapped around me? I try not to laugh too loud or talk about anything immature because I don't want to seem like a high school kid.

She's always in my French class and always says, "Hello," to my classmates stealing more glances than I can count. I'm shocked the day she walks into wrestling practice to talk to my coach, staying uncomfortably long. In the time I've wrestled no teacher has ever come in to talk to anyone so the moment she spends in the auxiliary gym amazes the entire team. I hope that nobody picks up on the real reason she's here but I know her motive and it's enough to make me squirm.

Not coincidentally, in the locker room after practice, the underbelly of my life is fully exposed. Another student named James, a senior, looks at me with a wide grin and says, "How about Miss Danza coming into practice today?" Maybe because he's a senior, or because I'm embarrassed or it could even be because I'm trying to protect me and Carla, I nervously shift from looking at him to looking at the floor which only gives his suspicion credence.

"So tell me, Cunneely, does she sing to you with her guitar?"

I ignore his question because I'm not equipped to respond any other way. "I can see it now," he strums his air guitar and starts singing a song she used to teach my class last year. "But then it turns into a love song at some point because you two are love birds right?" he adds sarcastically.

The reaction of everyone in the locker room can only mean they echo his opinion. "No," I say elongating the word just to prevent him from filling the silence with anything else offensive. I feel stares soliciting my response to either validate or disprove him. Intermingled are jealous scowls that scream it couldn't be true, too unbelievable she would choose me. I even notice a few surprised glances of those who are not yet acquainted with what I just found out, is a widely accepted rumor.

All of this I see in my periphery as I'm left staring at James, strumming and singing nonsense which is exactly what smacks me in the face. I have no guess what to say or how to dismiss him. I dress as fast as I can and leave the locker room. I think the room is silent or I just can't hear anything over the nervous ringing in my ears. The outer edges of my vision become slightly obscured. I think I might pass out which I try to force because it seems like a welcome escape, but that will be an undeniable admission of guilt.

This excruciating exchange verifies with concrete reality that her grip is tightening. It seems like there are multiples of her with how deftly she moves about the building, anticipating where I will be. She has now pervaded into the parts of my life that were once safe. The boy's locker room is someplace I never thought I would be faced with answering for her actions. I don't understand how one person could be so omnipresent, in my home life, my academic life, my extra-curricular life, my nascent sex life and always with a smile and, "I love you," to make it appear pure. The expression, used so capriciously, seems to mask something she knows should not lie beneath.

Chapter 13

I wake up an hour before my alarm to the phone ringing. "Happy Anniversary, are you ready for our big day?"

I'm not. "I sure am," I say.

"I cannot wait. I don't know how I'm going to make it through today knowing we're going to make love for the first time."

I've never heard her sound so young in her thoughts. I lay still, not knowing what to say, relieved that she does all the talking. "I picked up the box of condoms at the Pathmark. A twelve pack," which means nothing to me.

She couldn't decide between lambskins or latex and I can offer no retroactive guidance but the idea of lambskin sounds funny. She chose latex. She bought candles and made a cassette tape to play. She concludes, "This could possibly be the longest day of my life waiting to make love to you, Jimi Cunneely."

I get out of bed after we hang up, unavoidably excited. Knowing what is coming does not enthuse me but the shared anticipation of her plans has an effect. I'm fine throughout the day except for the nagging fear that I will do something to disappoint her. Not living up to the preconceived notion that she has about losing our virginity frightens me.

Only a few days ago she asked me if I knew that there's blood when a girl has sex for the first time. Having no firsthand knowledge I rely on lunchroom gossip. She explains, "Since I've been riding horses from childhood you're off the hook," because, "Chances are, there won't be blood. The hymen can sometimes be broken by the constant pressure to that area of a girl while riding." What a relief because I'm certain it would be scary to see blood during sex.

The ride to her apartment is quieter than usual. A special mix tape plays to celebrate the occasion. Air Supply – Making Love Out of Nothing at All. Mr. Big – I'm the One. Rod Stewart – Broken Arrow. Peter Gabriel – In Your Eyes. Heart – We Did it All for Love. I know all of the songs because she has played them in her room during study hall but I'm not listening to lyrics. I'm futilely concentrating on meeting my expectations, as if focus will augment performance.

My anxiety has peaked. All day, trying to comprehend my life, the idea that incessantly takes shape is that I'm losing my virginity with a woman older than my mom. That thought lingers on the morning bus ride and all through first period. When I see Carla second period, it's the prevailing phrase I hear. I don't say a word at lunch, feeling above the teenage banter yet simultaneously excluded. I console myself by looking at each one of the six guys circled around the table and imagining what they're doing after school today. When I arrive back to me in the silent game I ask the same question, "What is this kid doing today after school? Oh yeah, he's having sex with a woman older than his mother."

When I sit in her car and smell her perfume, these are the exact words that echo in my brain, "Older than my mother."

Once lying in her bed, our routine remains the same. Even though there is familiarity in the agenda, I know that it's going to end differently causing unlimited panic. It hangs like a pall over the usual activities that have today become foreplay. She senses my hesitation, stopping to say, "Hey, you're okay right?"

It's not really a question because I'm sure she doesn't want an answer. She wants an affirmation that what we are doing is agreeable, which I provide. Before we can second guess my answer her tongue is back in my mouth. She works her way down my body, confusion clouds my mind, I thought we were going to make love but if I come, I'm won't be able. She only spends a few moments kissing and caressing but doesn't take me in her mouth.

She rises and lies beside, pulling me on top of her while grinding her hips. I can feel the coarseness of her pubic hair against my bare sensitive skin and it hurts. My reaction is to push back so that I feel the pressure of our bodies instead. Without warning she drops her hips back down to the bed and says, "Oh my God, I can't wait any longer," and with that, reaches to her night table and opens the foil wrapper of a condom. After removing it from the package she forcefully places it in my hand.

The room is dark and I have never seen a condom so I hold it in my hand waiting to see what she does. "Put it on and make love to me," she says in a voice too loud for the darkness.

I'm so scared. I don't know how to fulfill either of her requests but don't want to upset her either. "Um, Carla, I'm not sure how to put one of these on," I say. I'm sure she'll be angry because I've broken the mood.

She sits up, starts to sheath me, and then says, "Roll it all the way down now." She sounds annoyed but it could be the heat of the moment. I figure out the rest despite my inexperience. I'm not as hard as prior to the delay but she is still willing to try. I'm cold because the blanket has slid off, my whole body stiff from insecurity except the part that needs be.

She knows what has happened yet still seems patient. She pulls me close and kisses me hard on the mouth. My body betrays the panic reflex in my brain and I engorge immediately. She checks at regular intervals and when I'm ready removes her hand and allows me fumble the rest of the way.

I poke and thrust not knowing what I'm striving for and with every failed attempt, hurt myself. Even if there were light in the room I wouldn't do any better. She wraps her hands around my hips and gently whispers, "Shhh, relax and let me."

She takes her right hand, splits my hip from hers and I feel her thumb grab the top of me and two fingers the bottom. She moves me in circular motions while probing what I can only describe as soft, warm and even through the condom which I have never worn before, slimy.

I don't like the feeling. She's pulling me into her, dragging me away from my family, my innocence. She is drawing me to become one with her and with the intensity on her face, seemingly to be like her. Once inside, it seems a natural instinct to thrust until my pelvis presses against hers. I hear her sigh followed by a closed mouth moan. From the putrid green light of the clock radio I can see her eyes open just a slit but I can only see the whites so I assume they have rolled back.

I freeze.

I can only act according to her audible and physical reactions. She thrusts her hips quickly and then they recede. By default I withdraw, also soliciting the same blissful expression. Before I have time to figure out this choreography we are locked in a sensual yet slightly violent rhythm.

I feel about to come but really don't want to disappoint her. I put my mind elsewhere to quell my arousal. I list movies in my head, some I've seen and some forbidden because they have sex in them. When I reach Clint Eastwood's Dirty Harry movies I realize I haven't been concentrating for, well, I don't know how long. I feel guilty. Not for her, for me. I'm losing my virginity. I will never have another chance at this and I'm thinking about movies and my parents. My mind makes me feel gross, superseded only by unshakeable guilt. She's doing fine but I wish I was more involved.

She doesn't seem nervous but I'm overcome by my own apprehension. One day, I overheard a girl at lunch talk about losing her virginity. "It only hurts the first time," she said, "Definitely uncomfortable. I was afraid to do it again because of how weird it felt." I remember those words vividly because if it hurt that bad, I wondered why girls had sex at all.

Thankfully, Carla doesn't show any signs of pain. My mind travels fast, as if everything else is slow motion, allowing me to process and synthesize. It seems as though before I can even wonder about her pain, I remember the horses. Maybe the horseback riding takes away the pain too.

My mind is fluttering and I'm beginning to feel worse. Once I regain my focus I look down and see her looking at me. She asks, "Everything's ok, right?"

"Ya", I say, embarrassed, wondering if she knows what I was just thinking. Does she know I wasn't here for a while?

"How do you feel?" She says, her eyes locked on mine.

"Ok. I mean good. I feel good," I stumble because I don't know the answer. My body feels good, but my mind is clutching, trying to gain sanctuary anyway I can. I hear the words again, a final loss of composure. I look down and repeat, "Older than my mother."

"Are you sure?" she verifies. "I'm going to come. Can you?" she asks.

Without answering, as if some involuntary product of my evolution takes over I begin to fuck faster and harder. I don't know how I make the decision but she reacts with ecstasy. Her eyes roll back again and she arches her hips while forcing the back of her head into the pillow. Her breathe increases and each exhale is accompanied by the slightest whimper. I feel everything below my waist constrict and the throbbing begins to cause waves of pleasure in the same pulse as I thrust. Within seconds I hear myself grunting. When she hears me she lets out a scream. My entire lower half stiffens down to the curling of my toes and I release with an explosion.

That's it. I am hers and I know she knows it when I see her look up at me. Her gaze is satisfied, coquettish.

"That was beautiful," she recaps as usual. I hope the words convince her because I cannot share the sentiment.

Chapter 14

We fall into a routine seamlessly. Every scheduled wrestling match for the remainder of the season she simply assumes we go to her apartment. There are some weeks that she coerces me to skip practice if I only have one match. I hate giving in but the sex and her begging is irresistible. As winter progresses, she wonders aloud what we will do when wrestling season ends. I have no answer so I never reply to her rhetorical questions.

She knows where I will be throughout the school day, when I arrive home, how long I should take to shower and for how long I eat dinner. She expects my call by eight o'clock and assumes we will be on the phone for a minimum of two hours. Any deviation from this ritual causes great strife, leading to hurt feelings and sometimes tears. Many disagreements are rooted in the naiveté of a teenage boy. I learn quickly that any free time during my day is best spent in her classroom. We assimilate and evolve with little friction.

"I could use a hug this morning," she says one day as she closes her classroom doors.

"Sure," I say, finding no reason to refuse. She closes the second door and stands in the corner of the room, invisible from either of the narrow windows. The following day, as I enter she leaves her desk to repeat this and I stand, instinctively in the identical spot as yesterday. We start the day with a hug and an, "I love you, have a good day." And with rote simplicity the ritual is entered as customary.

She invites me to eat with her when she brings her mother's meatball sandwiches. Afterward, she stands up and with the same cadence as the morning lockdown, closes the doors and stands in the corner. She looks to me without saying a word, extending an invitation that we both know I cannot decline. What begins as a hug turns to a kiss. The kiss, into fondling until the bell rings. It seems she is waiting for me to advance the action but fear and the limitations of our surroundings keep me safe.

This impediment is hurdled with silent exactitude the following day. After we eat and she shutters us in, instead of walking to the corner, she turns off the lights and takes me by the hand to the back of her room. Once in the corner she takes her keys out of her blazer pocket and opens the door to the storage closet. The closet is musty and smells of dust, no larger than a typical bathroom, ten feet long by five feet wide with shelves in each corner. Every shelf full of boxes, old projects, supplies and posters. The usable floor space consists of room for two of us to stand and turn comfortably. She turns on the lights to show me where we are and then turns them off, leaving the door slightly ajar.

As I'm waiting for direction she pushes me against the wall and kisses me, informing me instantly our reason for hiding. She stops, grabs my earlobe between her teeth and whispers, "I thought this might make us both more comfortable." That is the first day that she drops to her knees and brings me to orgasm in school.

Every new foray into a sexual frontier comes with memorable lessons. It's in the back closet that I learn that my penis is larger than her face. I have never measured myself, although I hear other boys talk about size and hear comparisons. She is a grown woman and I'm shocked that I'm larger than the height of her face. She stares at me like I am a freak leaving me to wonder if she has never seen one up-close before. The look on her face reflects amazement, she is enamored. Why else would she gawk at me instead of fulfilling the only goal of our cloistering?

Chapter 15

Carla's methods of broaching a subject are confusing, wrought with questions that I can neither foresee nor for which I can prepare. Times when I think I'm following the flow of the conversation and can contribute something meaningful are often turned by an unexpected twist. An innocent explanation of how teaching contracts work, including sick and personal days turns drastically when she tells me that she has accrued over twenty five personal days.

"So, if I were to use a personal day, would you be willing to play hooky with me? We could have a lot of fun," she asks, using what feels unmistakably like a bait and switch.

Pseudo-sick days are not tolerated by my parents. Carla's suggestion to miss school for the sole purpose of having sex gives me a horrible feeling in my stomach. I have never skipped school and cannot even think of the consequences of getting caught. I feel myself begin to sweat, "Well, I missed a day for the funeral and I know the school sends a letter home after the third absence so if I have another absence what will I tell my parents?" It seems like a lucid response but anymore, I have no confidence I can sway the course of any plan.

"If a letter goes home, I'll catch it in the office before it gets sent," she says without pause, shooting a hole through my only escape.

"Sure, that sounds good," I reply.

My hesitation doesn't impede her plans even slightly, "We can make breakfast, rent a movie, have pizza for lunch and I'll make homemade pasta for dinner." She is giddy.

I leave my house the day of our tryst as always, telling my mom, "Goodbye. Have a good day. I'll see you after practice." I walk reluctantly past my bus stop to our rendezvous. I stand on the corner shivering from a combination of cold and nerves.

Crazy thoughts occur that I've never before contemplated. What if my mom leaves early today and sees me standing aimlessly in our neighborhood? Leading me to worry that my dad may come home, having forgotten something. What if my neighbor drives by or another student heading to the bus stop sees me? I panic each time I look at my watch knowing I have certainly missed the bus and Carla is late.

As I'm about to sit on the curb from the overwhelming stress I see her black sports car make the turn onto my block and I feel better. My relief shattered when I see her wearing sunglasses and a baseball cap. Her necessary disguise leaves me with an involuntary disgust so potent that I'm tempted to walk right back to my house. As she drives closer she is grinning from ear to ear, ecstatic to see me.

My emotions are scattered and despite my best efforts to harness them, I'm on the verge of tears when I shut the door behind me. She seems not to notice or deliberately ignores my demeanor, "Good morning sweetheart."

Her apartment seems a completely different place, having never seen it so early in the morning. She doesn't have the table set for breakfast but she does have coffee made and a box of doughnuts sits on her counter. She left, "Our tape" playing on a continuous loop before she left, welcoming us with Nancy Wilson singing, "We Did it All for Love".

We have sex upon arrival. I still suffer from performance anxiety as we begin our scripted foreplay, unsure if I'm doing things correctly or if her pleasure is appeasement. She keeps a running count of how many times we've made love and updates me frequently. We started with a twelve pack of condoms so it's a matter of subtraction but I wonder if she is keeping a tally somewhere for when we move past our first box. After nine times I still feel like I'm trying to figure out what sex is supposed to be. I have yet to figure out why other kids enjoy it so much. It feels good but all of the stress leading up is counter-productive.

A wave of depression overcomes me when I realize that I do not have to be accounted for until six o'clock tonight and it's only eight-thirty in the morning. I'm trapped with no one to save me, no one knows where I am.

"Isn't this wonderful? We have all day together and it's just begun," she coos.

"Uh-huh," I mumble as I put my head back on the pillow hoping to find haven in a nap at some point.

We have sex four more times and by the third, I'm in pain. I'm embarrassed but keep quiet because she has never had sex with another man so there is no way for her to explain what would cause my physical reaction. We watch TV but can't agree on what to watch so I pick up a magazine sitting on her coffee table. It's a woman's magazine from three years ago, impossible to hold my interest long enough to pass any real time. She senses my boredom and asks, "So what would you like to do?"

"Go home," I think.

"I don't know. What can we do?" I say.

She lists, "We can go for a walk, take a drive, put on a video, look at some French books, or make love again." None sound appealing.

"Any of them sound good," I say. It's only one o'clock but I'm restless. The amount of fear occupying my mind is beginning to cause great fear. This sensation of being totally confined someplace I came willingly is foreign. I use all my restraint not to pace the floor.

I take a nap and she sleeps with me. Amazingly Carla is completely oblivious to how uncomfortable I am or is still shamelessly ignoring the signs. She comes on to me and I do not protest. I welcome her because sex represents time that I won't look at the clock. When we're done she reaches under the bed, pulls out a workbook and we lay in bed naked as she tutors me in French grammar. I'm again, happy just to pass time.

She brings me back to school as the buses are pulling out of the parking lot. I jump out of her car and run to catch mine. Like every other day that I skip practice to be with Carla someone asks me why I'm on the bus. This time I hear, "Hey, I thought you weren't in school today."

I come back with the only response that cannot be disproven, "No, I was there, you must have just missed me."

Carla owns me, my essence stolen. She is the sole proprietor of my time, my thoughts and my whereabouts. She owns my truths and my lies and everything between. It is entirely possible that I have been present in my normal life yet invisible to whoever is questioning my attendance. I don't feel like I'm lying as I affirm my place in school today because my mind was in school for a great deal of the day. Each glance at the clock was followed by a reminder of where I should be instead of where I really was.

Once home, after I throw my book bag in my room, I vomit a week's worth of fear and anxiety. All of my thoughts leading up to this day were filled with unnamed dread. The day itself was worse than I could have imagined. I find it impossible to look at my mother but stare at my father, hoping he will notice that there is something wrong. Despite the fact that my mother is and always has been more in tune with the emotional well-being of everyone in my family, I think that my father should notice something with his son. Nothing is said and my life rumbles on with oblivion.

Chapter 16

I jerk off. I jerk off a lot. Twice a night during the week. Six, sometimes seven times on the weekend. It's more than just masturbating, it's an escape. It's a catharsis like vomiting or sneezing, arranging different parts of my head. There are only two constants as my life evolves, masturbation and sex. I try to grasp the patterns but just when it seems like I do, I'm lost again.

Sex in her apartment has two different itineraries depending on where we arrive. The loveseat leads to her kneeling on the floor, stomach on the cushion so that I can take her from behind. She moves her hips in every direction, writhing in pleasure. When the light is just right I can see her squeezing the crocheted afghan so hard that her knuckles turn white, moaning cautiously not be heard by her neighbors upstairs.

The bedroom is where the, "Beautiful love making," happens. This is where we lie on the bed kissing and caressing one another. My role as the follower is to never act without her approval or in some cases, insistence. When she is ready she takes my head and pushes me down between her legs until I force her to orgasm.

After, she pulls my face to hers, reaches to the night table and opens a condom. She places it in my hand to protect me from her or vice-versa. She comes multiple times, looks at me seductively then says, "Now it's your turn." I orgasm quickly, releasing my pent up desperation to please her.

When she thinks I should be ready, she touches me in ways that force my body to betray me. The monumental struggle always ends with the same winner. Carla and the carnal always triumph over Jim and his intellect. Another condom comes out of the package of twelve and is placed in my hand. I hate the smell. I don't know if it's latex or lubrication, but it's rotten.

When the odor hits my senses, it feels putrid and I feel polluted. She rides me the second time in such a violent way, absent any emotion that I fear she's going to hurt me. I'm a merely a spectator until she is finished and falls beside me. At some point every single time as she rakes her nails down my center in reflection she says, "That was beautiful." It becomes a necessary punctuation rather than a verbalized emotion. The whole event feels transactional.

Once, we don't even leave the doorway. In what I assume are known as the throes of passion she swipes all of the papers off of her dining room table, sprawls herself out, and pulls me on top of her. She takes her legs, wraps each ankle around my hips, and puts me inside. She moans as I feel her warmth. As soon as I am completely in she takes her legs and puts them on my shoulders. I instinctively place my hands on her thighs anatomically above her knees but spatially below and for the most part remain still as she grinds against me.

She spreads her arms to grab each outer edge of the perfectly circular table. This is the most visual of all the times we have sex and turns me on incredibly. I cannot help but orgasm without checking for permission. She doesn't even take the time to make me put a condom on so as I feel ready I pull out, so overcome by the waves of pleasure that I crumble to the floor. She immediately jumps down and envelops me with her entire body.

Instead of, "That was beautiful," she whispers, "I guess you enjoyed that huh?"

I don't. I enjoy none of it. Most of the time, I can dissociate from the whole affair, and be ready when she wants. I have assimilated quickly and normalized this routine. Every time my body tricks me, contrary to my reflections late at night, I hate myself. I have learned to separate the individual parts of me just like the detachable components of my mind. I grow further removed from the relationship that every male has with his penis, more controlled by it than able to govern my actions. I loathe my virility and the feeling must be mutual. My body must hate me too, otherwise why would I display such disloyalty to myself?

Given my choice I prefer the bedroom. The lights are off and there are no windows so I can close my eyes and be somewhere else. No matter where we go my body is fully functional. Stroke me and I will orgasm. At fifteen a male's body may never work with better austerity. What she mistakes as my enjoyment is the simple precision of puberty. I can escape that truth no more than I can escape Carla.

My personal routine, after a day with Carla, is static and the only way that I have found to cope. I walk into my room, put my books down, gather clothes and walk downstairs to the bathroom. I start the water a click hotter than comfortable and put a mix tape in the player that serves as the abhorrent soundtrack. A tape made specifically for this purpose, comprised mostly of The Cure. *Disintegration* is the best album I've ever heard probably because I'm disintegrating me from me a little each day. I don't know how to integrate anything into a life over which I have no control.

As soon as I rinse the shampoo out of my hair, I take the bar of soap and lather both of my hands followed by my flaccid penis. When I work up an erection, I begin. I imagine the only eroticized picture that I own with enough clarity to orgasm. She doesn't deserve this honor but I bring Carla to mind. I think of what it feels like to have her on her knees in front of me, to be inside of her. Warm and tight and constricting. I ignore the ugliness, I block that out. I can have sex with her in my head without the worries of anyone finding out and without thinking of the stain on my soul.

It's not easy to come. I've just had two orgasms this afternoon and am desensitized to my sexuality but I need this. I need to scrub off the filth. The problem, the really big problem is that the obscenity isn't on my skin. Its inside and no amount of scouring will cleanse that elusive grime. Soap is not a natural lubricant so my hand doesn't glide smoothly and I have to continuously re-lather. It begins to hurt but I don't stop even though I feel my flesh start to chafe.

My dad knocks on the door, "Come on Jim. It's been twenty minutes." Now I might be able to come. Here comes the familiar exhilaration of having to perform. It's just like being back in the closet with only five minutes left in the period. If I don't assure her that she made me feel good in those five minutes she will be upset. The pressure builds in my chest and at the base of my dick. The pleasure rises up past my insecurities, past the burnt skin rubbed raw and will cleanse me when I blow all of the afternoon's sins onto the bath tub floor. I watch it wash down the drain.

Unfortunately, no relief arrives. After I catch my breath and stand up straight the hot water reminds me how I hurt myself but I prefer this pain. I shut the water quickly even though there is still soap running down the inside of my thigh. I wipe it off with a towel and sit on the edge of the tub, disillusioned by my futile pursuit for purity.

The scornful looks when I walk out of the bathroom are familiar. They're the same ones I perceive on the faces of the students who watch me exit her room. Sometimes my parents joke, telling me they are going to take the lock off of the door. Or ask from a place of surrender, "What the heck takes you so long?"

I always say the same thing, "I was just standing under the water letting it run on me." A lame answer but I don't have the energy to care and what else can I say?

My dad reminds me, "You know, I pay for the water and don't like it wasted."

I so badly wish I could tell him that I'm paying for something every day with a currency neither of us can afford. Neither a shower nor a purge of any kind will reimburse what is taken from my intangible account.

After eating dinner, doing homework and trudging through some bullshit, one-sided conversation with Carla, I go to bed. My brother is in the room too, but usually asleep. If he's awake, I tell him, "My penis is itchy and I have to scratch it." Again, a ridiculous story, but all of my creativity is spent covering my tracks on a daily basis. He neither laughs nor questions me. He accepts my explanation and leaves me do what I need. I hate lying to him and sometimes try to wait until he goes to sleep because I don't want this blemish of mine to taint him. But I need to rub this out so I can sleep. I jerk off yet again knowing that he is, thankfully too young to understand.

I'm hurt. Sore from hunting for obscure peace. I can no longer put my finger on the source of the ache but I need to even the score of the day. Carla claimed two orgasms and I've only marked one. I still think of her. I picture her genuflected, feverish with her mouth. It turns me on to think that she is willing to bow

113

down for my pleasure. I like to picture what should be embarrassment for obeisance to a teenager.

This second time lacks the pressure of someone knocking on the door. It is completely absent of the rush to beat the bell. It's more reminiscent of the second time Carla takes me. I use my own body like she does. My flesh is raw and there is no mistaking the fine line where pleasure becomes pain. This is inexorably painful. It taps into somewhere in my brain where pain actually becomes pleasure; the self-flagellation of the penitent. As soon as the moment of ecstasy ends, the orgasm turns to ache. The throbbing in my right hand reminds me of this soiled necessity and each night I engage in this ritualized bludgeoning, I lose a little more of myself.

I reach down under my bed and grab the only T-shirt I've ever used to clean up the mess. I hide it under my bed to protect us both from ever being questioned. I love it, I hate it and I need it. I'm so exhausted and drained of life that I place it over the puddle on my stomach, hiding the last remnants of the day. I drift off with it draped over me, feeling dirty, hoping that tomorrow my T-shirt will have cleaned more than just spilled innocence.

Chapter 17

Despite my constant readiness for any topic to be broached, I'm immediately lost when she asks, "Are you familiar with the term 'forensics'"? The best that I can do is, "In grammar school I had competed in something called forensics but it was where another student and I acted out, "Who's on First" by Abbot and Costello."

"Oh that's it exactly and you've done it before?" she bursts. "Oh that's so great, well there is a Foreign Language Forensics competition in the spring and I want you to compete."

I'm not a good French student so I can't guess her angle. I know this is not an invitation rather a notification, immediately transparent when she reveals that rehearsal starts right after winter sports finish. This is the new pretext that allows me to stay after school without harassment from my parents. I accept, when she offers to explain the procedure to my mom, although I'm regularly her accomplice I refuse to be as deceitful as this necessitates.

"That's not even the big thing I have to tell you, Jimi," calling me Jimi to show just how excited she is. "Well," she starts absent any segue and audibly short of breath. She knows by now that she has complete control over me so her apprehension makes me tense too, "I was thinking that since this trip to France is an exchange where students will stay with host families, I will need a host family to stay with. So maybe you and I could be placed together. We could do the excursion trips with everyone but we would have time to ourselves to do the things we want."

She speaks faster, "I was thinking that I could just say you're my nephew, and that way, nobody would ask questions. I know you've never been to France, but it would be a great opportunity for us to spend time together. I could even introduce you to the family that I stayed with in high school because they don't live far from Fontainebleau."

Again, notification. It's framed as a suggestion but my input is invented somewhere in the shadowy context.

"That sounds good," I offer but she receives absent the cynicism.

"Great, I was hoping you would think so, because I was so excited to tell you," she concludes. Our trip is in April so I have time before facing the reality of this plan. My only immediate option is to ignore it, hoping her reality never comes to fruition. Maybe she'll forget. Hopefully the program doesn't allow students to stay with chaperones. My parents might tell me they can't afford the trip. Maybe the school will burn down and all extra-curricular activities will be cancelled. I hope for a variety of possibilities to impede her, from natural disaster to civil war.

So quickly I learn the benefit of keeping my feelings to myself. It saddens me but I cease to need what I'll never have. In face to face conversations where she forces me to react I simply nod in agreement. I can only provide a physical reaction because she strips me of speech. When I have offered counterpoints her circular arguments back me further into a corner. I leave conversations unsure why I've changed my mind but thinking she was correct from the beginning.

I watch other kids come to school and try on new personalities. Adolescence is when we're able to see who we want to be. One day, a class clown trying to be funny, the next a smart kid. Attitude and wardrobe always match. That is the existential splendor of being young. I watch jocks audition for the school play and I see members of the marching band try out for baseball but I have no such jockeying for position in my own life. My personality remains stagnant. I'm Carla's boyfriend, expected to be a man always and in all ways. I must physically perform while being able to tend to the emotional needs of a professional woman.

Worse yet, it's my fault because I made the first move. I made the phone call. I allowed her to kiss me in the staircase. I told her I loved her the night she was crying and most permanently, I never stopped her from crossing the boundaries when she afforded me so many opportunities to halt her.

Carla cannot hide her excitement the evening I reluctantly confess, "My parents said I can definitely go to France," even though I no longer want to go. Not after how she has now twisted something that was thrilling. This has also been ripped from me like so much recently but I can't back out now.

"Oh my God, Jimi, I was a little nervous, but I just knew it was going to happen, I just knew it," she squeals.

My parents attend a meeting the following week to discuss dates, prices, and procedures in preparation. They come home as excited as Carla seems but for different reasons. I can tell that my mother is nervous but also reassured that the chaperone is someone, "As sweet and thorough as Miss Danza."

The feeling gleaned from the meeting is, "Miss D. knows exactly what she's doing and since she will never be more than a phone call away, no problem will be left unaddressed."

The beginning of this affair seemed a whirlwind with the death of Kevin's mom, my Christmas flu, Wrestling season, and the loss of my virginity. Replaced now by continued demands of sexual maturity, preparing to travel abroad, and memorizing my piece for the forensics competition. The stresses never recede, only change into other elusive anxieties equally as haunting. Anticipating the end of one despicable phase of my life only frightens me about what may supplant it.

Getting out of bed each morning is an effort. Everything is set against a backdrop of Carla, my circadian clock set firmly to her. I've always been an A student. The first class that I ever earn less than B — tenth grade Biology. Not coincidentally, the second marking period, beginning in November is a challenge evidenced by my failing grade. This is unthinkable for me and my parents. They look for the cause and theorize wrestling. They threaten pulling me from the team, devastating not simply for losing my roster spot but because the blame for my failure is incorrectly placed.

I struggle whether to tell Carla because I'm terribly embarrassed. Remembering I am not exclusively responsible however, convinces me to share. I know that she has access to my grades and may already know but I tell her anyway, coldly, "I failed Biology this marking period." I want her to know that I may be forced to go home right after school as a punishment. I say it and shut my mouth hoping to torture her with silence like she does me.

When she outwaits me I continue, "So my parents said that I'll have to quit wrestling if I don't get my grade up. They might not let me go to France either." I throw in the France part to scare her.

She asks, "What happened? How did you fail?" with the exact sense of urgency I attempted to create.

I can't tell her that I don't sleep for days on end only to sleep away my weekends. I never tell her how my parents question the causes for such an abnormal schedule. I hope she makes the leap that my life is overwhelming, normal functioning impossible. I can't find the words to tell her that I feel contrasted against everyone else my age. It's slight, like ivory on white, maybe imperceptible but I know it's there and I feel contaminated. It's the reason I can't let anyone close to me because the thought of being discovered makes me shudder therefore, socially hermetic.

I lay it on thick hoping that she arrives at the obvious conclusion but instead asks, "What projects and tests do you have approaching?"

She volunteers to write my term paper for me, ignorant to the principles involved. I argue that she has missed the point but she refuses to back down. More importantly, do I need to explain why plagiarism is unethical? When I resign she takes immediate control, lacking any introspection. She writes my term paper on wild horses of the western United States. We earn an "A". Her portion is authoring, mine is going to class every day to pass the work off as my own without vomiting.

I pass Biology for the third marking period as well as finish the wrestling season with my once a week absence. With no break, I begin practicing for Forensics. The schedule includes an alibi three days a week but actually rehearsing only one. A typical week includes spending the other two days in Carla's apartment, exploring our sexual relationship. We try new positions and different rooms. We take a shower together. I master pillow talk. I receive further detailed instruction in several areas and although it disturbs me, we sixty-nine, often.

Our first day of truancy went so smoothly that Carla decides to take another. The thought of being in her apartment all day again is dreadful. I remind her of the school's policy a second time, fearful the gloating in my voice is detectable.

"Oh don't worry about that honey," she says with an unmistakable tone of triumph.

"How can I not worry Carla? What will I tell them when they see that letter?" I snap back.

I rarely use her name in conversation, refusing her the satisfaction of that personal connection. "Well," she says after clearing her throat in an attempt to be coy, "I happen to have connections at the school and can make sure that the letter never gets to your parents." Her surgical precision as prominent as the claustrophobia that tightens in my throat.

We skip school again, a carbon copy of our first day. I prepared for my anxiously awaited nap by staying up as late as possible last night. The afternoon drags on painfully slow until she pulls a French workbook from her bag out of frustration and says, "Ok, fine, let's just work on French."

She doesn't see my disgusted look as she thumbs through the pages, "Ok, here. This is stuff you won't see until college," somehow overlooking the assortment of experiences I'm too young to witness.

"Well, I guess we should be leaving now," I say after dinner, as softly as possible because she has become reluctant to drive me back lately.

"I hate being alone. It's so nice when you're here. When I come back it's lonely and makes me sad," she says in a monotone. Her hesitation to make our way to the car becomes alarming as I look at the dusty clock hanging over her kitchen sink. I know that the clock is four minutes fast compared to the clock in her car and that clock is a minute faster than the one in my kitchen.

Part One

"Um, Carla, it really is getting late and if I miss the bus, I'll need to have a very good reason." She sinks down further in the couch bowing her head.

"Just stay with me a little longer and I'll take you home. I'll drive you right to the bus stop and they'll never know. That way we can spend twenty more minutes together before we have to leave," she begs.

I'm at the end of my underdeveloped capacity. I feel a drop of sweat run down the center of my back half from fear and half from the premise of spending another twenty minutes trapped.

Chapter 18

My life is a perpetual power struggle. She drops to her knees and submits to me yet, I allow her that clout. I don't feel the authority at the moment she bows in front of me because it seems as though she's in control. I try to recapture what she is stealing with each nod of her head by employing the only defense I know which is to put my mind elsewhere. I think of my history homework. I have chores when I get home. Cleaning my room. Walking the dog. My dresser drawers have clothes that no longer fit. This closet is no bigger than the bathroom in my parent's house. I see old projects and posters from students who she has had in the past. Not like she has me.

I feel it building first right behind my balls. Tightness from underneath and between my legs. The words that pop into my head so vulgar, but so is my whole life. I have to pick a topic for my English paper on Shakespeare. She knows when I'm close. She tells me that right before I come she hears a little gurgling sound in my stomach. I wonder how much warning she has. My hip flexors tighten. I have a note in my pocket from Kevin to give to some girl. I want to watch a movie tonight on HBO. Her hand is involved now, stroking at the same pace.

I fight, wanting physical control. My grandfather is coming to my parents' house this weekend. I bought a new video game I'm anxious to play. She puts her left hand on my ass not to restrain but better keep our rhythm synced. The pressure increases to that fragile line between pleasure and pain. Have I gurgled yet? Instinctively, and what seems like involuntarily I put my hand down her shirt, into her bra and grab a breast with a hard nipple. Jason borrowed the driver's-ed handout to copy my answers, I need that back. I heard the first single from the new Cure album, *Wish* and I love it. It's ironic because of all the things that I wish were different.

Who has the power now? She's on her knees but in control of my body. What if I stopped her? I've given her this power. I have to memorize my lines for the Forensics competition. I think I hear the gurgle but maybe not, it could be something else. Do I hear someone knock on the door? She's moving so fast I can barely distinguish up or down. I heard "Smells Like Teen Spirit" on the bus this morning. It is no less dangerous with the lights out. My mouth is so dry and this closet is dank and dingy and, pop.

My mind is clear.

This is a rare moment when my head is absolutely empty. I cannot think of geometry or health class, Kevin or The Cure. I am lost in what is called "le petit mort" in French. The little death. The one moment in a person's life when the mind can be wiped clean. The seconds just before an orgasm are akin to having the clear mind of dying. Nothing has value to my wits because I have no wits about me and I have no power. I allowed her to take it. And take it she did, played with it in her mouth and as I begin to regain my conscious mind the first thing that comes into focus is the sound of her swallowing that power. She slows. I pull back my hips, sensitive to her touch, almost doubling over but she does not want to let me out. It feels like she is trying to suck me dry for fear of not knowing the next time she will have me in her mouth.

She rises and delicately pulls my pants up. As I lean back against the wall, legs trembling, she kisses me on the lips and puts her tongue in my mouth. I don't want to touch her semen coated tongue even though it is my own secretion. As I pull away she becomes insistent that I kiss her, following my face with hers. Why does she want my mouth so badly? Is she trying to regain the supremacy she just relinquished? This war for the ability to dictate the pace of our life is quickly snowballing out of control.

She knows how to work my young body masterfully. Master to a slave, not master as a craftsman. She wraps her arm around me and in one vertical barrel roll switches our positions so that now her back is against the wall. She takes my hand and puts it up her skirt, underneath her panty hose and allows me to figure out the rest. I fumble to find where she has guided me, she is slippery. So slick that my hand becomes wet and I actually cannot do what she wants. Even this clumsy choreography excites her. She bucks against my hand at the same time she takes my lower lip between her teeth.

Inside of her feels like nothing I have ever felt. In my mind more indicative of slimy than wet. It's not the first time I have done this but the trick of detaching my mind from my body worked so well I use it in reverse. As I feel the flesh that she uses to hold sway over me I might describe it as lumpy if I were writing a lab report. Bio lab is tomorrow. I think we're dissecting earth worms. I wonder what the inside of the worm feels like. She stops kissing, wraps the crook of her elbow around my neck and draws me closer, draws me as she would like me to appear. A man, her man pleasuring her. I feel her breath in my ear. It's hot and smells of coffee. She wraps both of her arms around me now and holds on as though she would otherwise fall.

Who is in charge now? I'm almost completely immobile except for the cadenced flexing of my wrist. This is enough to put her in a place of swooning from sensual gratification. I'm stuck on this idea of clout. I don't have it in her mouth and I don't have it inside of her. Her hips move violently now in no discernible pattern or rhythm.

She bites my ear lobe harder and I mouth the word, "Ouch," which she doesn't hear. She tugs, I hear the diamond stud click against her teeth. Without any warning and without gurgling she stops and presses the length of her whole body against mine and groans uncomfortably loud in my ear. I keep my hand perfectly still. Her lips mouth the words, "Oh my God," with, "God" slightly aspirated and silent by the "D". I think its sweat on my hand but it's probably a mixture of us. I don't realize how high she has somehow elevated herself until her body collapses, once again two inches shorter than me.

"Wow, that was good," she says, echoing in the pitch black of the tiny space.

As soon as I'm out of her clothing she pulls her skirt back down. I stand, uncomfortably waiting for some clue as to what should happen now. She slowly opens the door, peeking outside. I know it's all clear when she swings it fully open. I take a moment to adjust myself and desperately want to inspect my clothing and hair to make sure that I don't have any signs of what just happened.

I worry about someone pointing out my unzipped pants. I have visions of being asked, "What's that?" while pointing to a spot of viscous semen, having somehow escaped her mouth. I scrutinize my appearance because I don't know how I would explain any discrepancy. Once out of the closet, she shifts to the banal, "Will you be stopping by after school?"

I say, "Yes," but it's another involuntary reaction.

"Well, I better get something to eat. The period's almost over," I say self-consciously. Our midday romp is over and it ends as unremarkably as it began.

I often wonder what it's like to stand in front of a room full of students and speak as though everything is completely normal. I wonder what it's like to teach French when you have the semen of a fifteen year old boy still in your mouth. She acts as though everything is fine, as though every student in the room is completely engaged, but all the while I focus on the fact that she just swallowed me. I wonder how many sperm are still swimming on the inside of her cheeks. If a drop of spittle happens to fly out of her mouth is she spilling my seed? I remember that being a sin from my catholic school days. Is she the definition of a sociopath?

I don't see her chewing gum nor does she eat a Tic-Tac. Does she rinse her mouth in the water fountain? Does she feel as though she speaks French better having me coat her tongue? Every day she blows me in the back closet before greeting her students, "Bonjour classe," with candor and cheer as though the words dance from the elation of fellatio. I think of these things and the imaginary power my thoughts invent makes me perversely happy. I don't know if she thinks on this level and if she did, she would never tell me.

Chapter 19

My phone rings from the time that I walk in the door until long after I'm supposed to be asleep and my parents begin to notice. The haste with which I bound up the stairs to answer it becomes the source of a joke, "Jimi, the 'Bat Phone' is ringing." I find it funny at first, until I realize she calls me easily ten times an evening and innumerable times during the weekend.

It's her voice so often on the other end of the phone that I'm surprised when it's anyone else, slightly taken off guard to take Kevin's call one Saturday afternoon. I can tell immediately that he is pissed off about something. I'm well acquainted with his moods but had recently forgiven him in light of what he's managing. The voice that greets me is brooding, biting with sarcasm, his typical response to anger.

I'm certain he isn't angry with me, so I ask confidently, "What's wrong?"

He speaks but doesn't answer directly, "You know it would've been me if I had taken French last year, right?"

"What do you mean?" my confusion genuine.

He repeats, "If I met her first it'd be me and not you."

"Kevin, I have no idea what you are talking about," I say after a long pause, realizing that his anger is, for some reason with me.

"Carla told me, Jim. She told me everything," he spits. My pulse pounds in my throat, my need to sit overwhelms me, and his betrayed silence roars on the other end. I hear my own breathing approach panting. I guard my secret so close that this news fills me with unimaginable fear. The one person I've ever even considered telling, albeit fleetingly was Kevin. However, she disarms me once again, making me feel distant from even my closest friend. I think for a second that he might be trying to shake my tree to see what falls out. I consider lying, my forte.

"What did she tell you?" I say barely above a whisper. Now that the secret is out to even just one person the whole world is so much closer to knowing. I'm embarrassed and proud at the same time. During his silence I remember he called her Carla and not Miss D., authenticating she has gotten to him first.

Kevin prides himself on being the best looking, best built kid in school. If not for the conceited attitude that belies it all, many more girls would be willing to date him. This is quite a blow to his fragile ego, Carla knowing Kevin is on the market but choosing me. But I'm ashamed too. Disgrace still my paramount emotion for falling into this situation. I cannot put my finger on why my reaction is guilt but that is unmistakably how I feel. He recounts every detail of our relationship, his words directly regurgitated from her. I wait for, "It was beautiful," though the phrase never comes. He can't bring himself to accept that he is not exploring this physical relationship with an older woman. What he doesn't know from my silence is that he can have it. I would exchange his hushed admiration for my kidnapped childhood this very instant.

While still processing he fires, "You know you could have told me Jim. I'm supposed to be your best fucking friend."

This is already so confusing that I take no pause, coming right back with misdirected anger, "She told me not to say anything to anyone. So I was only doing what she asked," putting the emphasis of the whole sentence on the word, "Anyone." He says nothing, I imagine because she told him the same.

He returns to the only undisputable point he can argue, "Yeah, well you do know that if I'd taken French, it'd be me."

"I know Kevin," is all I can say, and all I wish.

That's not where we are though. It's me whether I want it or not. However, somewhere inside carrying my secret seems lighter, its weight distributed more evenly instead of cantilevered. I hang up, knowing he's angry but hoping he can be a source of solace when Carla becomes overbearing.

The infinitesimal relief dissipates when her plan becomes transparent. It wasn't to make me feel comfortable and it wasn't to assuage her own guilt. She secured an ally. Only one week later, while existing as a kid, my mother yells, "Jimi, phone for you."

I walk into the kitchen and say, "Who is it?" When she tells me, "Kevin," it makes sense since the ringer in my room is off. I leave the living room where I was playing cards with my sister, pick up the phone and say, "Hey, what's up?"

Without, "Hello," he scolds, "Jim, go pick up your fucking phone. Carla is trying to call you. She called me to find out where you were. I can't have her calling my house looking for you. My father is going to get pissed."

I feel ill.

My mother is sitting at the table, three feet away. I hear him clearly. Can anyone else? The insecurity makes my skin burn where my collar lies on my neck. I cannot answer without incriminating myself, "Ok, I will." I remain on the line in silence, hoping he won't' hang up long enough for me to think of what to tell my mom.

Once my lie is prepared, "Ok dude, thanks for calling. I'll talk to you later." I try to leave the room without her asking but fail.

"I have his English book from the other day. Some project we were working on and he was reminding me to bring it to school on Monday. I guess I didn't hear my, phone, I mean I guess I didn't hear the Bat Phone," I respond with a nervous chuckle. I hope to deflect any misgivings by poking fun at myself.

I walk up to my room and as soon as I move the black, oblong button from OFF to LOW it rings. It's Carla's, "I'm sorry to bother you but I just miss you so much and I had to talk to you. I know you said you were with your family but I thought I would call to say hello and that I love you," speaking so quickly I can hardly understand. I'm tethered to this phone and this room and this woman who should have no sway over me in the hovel of my parent's house.

"Why did you call Kevin looking for me?" I ask, ignoring her outburst.

"Well, honey, I couldn't get a hold of you so I called him to see if he heard from you. I didn't ask him to call you."

There is no escaping her.

Chapter 20

It's a Friday in March and I'm sitting in my business class. As far as my parents know I'm taking a bus to watch a Forensics competition in preparation for our own. Miss Danza is the chaperone so my parents have no reservations. The real trip I will be taking is to Carla's apartment, late into the evening. It's seventh period now and I'm starting to dismay that the day is coming to an end. At the height of my self-pity the intercom system buzzes, "Please send James Cunneely to the office," mispronouncing my name. I can't imagine why I would be paged to the office but am happy to take a walk.

Before I'm through the doorway to the main office the receptionist points to the phone and says sternly, "You have a call. Pick it up on line two." In the three seconds that it takes me to walk to the phone, pick up the receiver and hit the button labeled, "2" my heart pounds.

I pick up and barely whisper, "Hello?"

I hear my dad say, "Yeah, it's me."

He says it as if it's my turn to respond but I don't have the experience to guess why my dad would be calling me at school. I say nothing as my mind wanders for explanations. Has someone died? Has something bad happened to someone in my family? What kind of trouble am I in?

The next thing I hear feels like the thud of a nightmare, "A letter came to the house today from school. You've been absent three days this year? Neither your mother nor I remember that."

He is silent, waiting for a response but I'm in so far over my head, truly speechless.

"Where were you on the days that the school says you were absent?"

All I can offer is silence, I have no control over any part of my life. Nothing that comes to mind seems even slightly plausible. It seems as though any response, even if he knows it to be a lie would be better than nothing. Nothing is all I have.

In a voice that I don't ever recall having heard before he says, "I want you on the bus home right after school and we will talk about this tonight. I don't care what your plans were. Be on that bus."

I feel like I can vomit but it's coming from someplace deeper than nausea. I want to go to sleep, overcome with fatigue as if I've been awake for days. I stand still trying to think, only snapped out of my attempt at concentration by the terse receptionist, "Ok, go back to class."

I cannot though. My feet feel nailed to the floor. Any movement, in any direction is a misstep. I'm absolutely lost in the confines of my own minute life. I leave only to stop the nasty woman from staring at me.

I don't return to class, I walk directly to Carla's room. I'm on autopilot not knowing where I'm going until I've arrived. I know she's teaching her French III class but don't care. There is only one period left for me to figure out what I am supposed to do. She opens the door and upon reading my face, asks, "What's wrong, Jimi?"

I tell her coldly, "My mom got the letter. She knows I missed school." I would convey triumph in being correct if I didn't feel my life is over. A rare glimpse of panic overcomes her face, but its fleeting as she springs into action, "What class are you in?"

She steps back, looks at the clock over the doorway and says, "Ok, there are five minutes left in this period, go get your books and come right here. I'll give you a late pass to eighth period."

When Carla told me on Tuesday, "I couldn't snatch the letter because the stack was on the reception desk but there were too many people around," I was furious.

She cuts me off before I can express my ire, "But don't worry hon, I will take you to your house during lunch to grab it from your mailbox." She says this to provide comfort but instead, shocks me. Although I should no longer be surprised by her incredulity. The thought of pulling in front of my house, stealing mail that will be addressed to, "The parents/guardians of James Cunneely," drives me to the absolute edge of distress. It's clear that she sees nothing as an impediment to possessing me.

The last three days we have left school during lunch and driven to my house. We stopped across the street, I leaned out the window, and sifted through the mail to intercept any letter from school. Wednesday and Thursday, no letter. Today, when I open the mailbox to find it empty the look on my face must mirror the panic on hers. She is perpetually astute at knowing exactly what the next move should be to outsmart the would-be saboteurs of our love, this moment of alarm is rare.

"I'll come back during my free period," she says to console us.

"And if not, we'll have to come back after school before we go to my place," she adds which we both know comes with the implied risk of running into my mother coming home after work.

Obviously my mother came home early today, thwarting her last ditch plan.

During the walk back to class, one phrase echoes in my head, "I'm so fucked." I'm going to be grounded forever. Missing school is not acceptable in my house. I don't even know how much trouble I am in because I've never tested these waters. I pick up my books and upon arriving back to Carla's room, Kevin is there and already knows. His cavalier attitude does not help, "Oh just tell your parents you skipped school with me," and only scares me more that he is not taking this seriously. I stare at Carla to see what she is planning because I have no idea how to survive the next several hours. I consider not even going home. I don't know where I would go, certainly not with her, but the thought of running away is becoming increasingly conceivable.

Carla closes both doors and stands in between Kevin and me. She starts, "Ok, here's what I think. You should say that one of the days you were marked absent you were in the building but skipped classes. Some boy wanted to fight you and to avoid him you hid different places in the building. Say you were in the library or the bathroom or wherever."

I'm buying it until Kevin chuckles, "It's a good idea but just sounds gay. Why wouldn't he just fight the kid?" He is right. I'm choosing between being in trouble with my parents and looking like a chicken, completely emasculating myself.

I can hear the minutes tick off of the clock, knowing I must face this alone, embracing every facet of the lie being dictated. When I remind her that there are two absences and her story only works for one she says with almost comical delivery, "Ya, I haven't figured that out yet," intensifying my terror.

She looks at Kevin and says, "Ok, go to class now." He rolls his eyes and says with a horribly rude tone, "I need a pass." As soon as the door closes behind him I jump into her arms. I bury my face in the space between her neck and shoulder smelling her perfume and shampoo as I tremble uncontrollably. I am so afraid. Although she is trying to help, I'm nagged by the reality that it was her idea to skip school and have sex all day.

She tells me, "Go to class, get on the bus, go home and I'll call you when I've had more time to think."

I'm not sure that the phone will still be in my room by the time I'm home. My mom may have already ripped it out of the wall. For all I know, all of my belongings may be on the front lawn after how bizarre my behavior has been recently.

I can't help but feel like Carla is abandoning me. How can she tell me to go to class as if I can concentrate on anything? How can she ask me to trust her to come up with something believable? I leave after she hands me a pass with the date, time, my name, and the word, "Sorry," punctuated by a smiley face underneath.

I get on my bus, sit in the same seat as always and stare out the window. My mind is stuck on repeat, "This is so unfair," involuntarily cascades in my head. I have no problem taking my lumps for poor decisions, but I didn't choose to skip school. I couldn't plug all of this into the typical risk vs. reward calculator to see if I was willing to take the chance. I was an accomplice, why am I facing this alone?

"It's so unfair, so fucking unfair," keeps reverberating louder as time moves forward because these should not be only my consequences. I put my headphones on and turn the volume up until the music is distorted. I play the same tape that I use in the shower. I carry that tape with me everywhere I go as if the lyrics protect me. I own the songs that soothe me. They feel as though written for me exclusively. It amazes me how someone else could put down in words exactly the way that I feel so perfectly, making me feel slightly less alone. Someone understands.

I'm the third bus stop like every other day. Today, as I walk the two blocks toward my house all I wish is that I could have the life of any of the other kids who walk with me. They aren't worrying about how to cover up a day long sexual tryst. I'm sure not analyzing how their lies will be perceived. They're not petrified about what type of reaction they will receive when they walk in their door. I smile and nod along with the latest gossip, pretending like I care. All I can really think about is what awaits.

When I walk through the back door my mom walks into the bathroom. This is not a coincidence. It's her nonverbal cue to leave her alone. She is so disgusted that she doesn't want to look at me. I walk to where she was sitting and see the letter. I pick it up, needing to see exactly how it reads.

It's cold and formal yet mentions nothing of what really took place. As I read I play the video in my mind of what these days represent. I wish the words could convey the same to my parents. If I can put it on the page then I never have to speak the lurid truth. I know my mom will not come out of the bathroom until I leave so I walk upstairs to await Carla's call.

Surprisingly, my phone is still next to my bed. Just like late at night I put the ringer on low and bury the phone under all my pillows. I fear that if my mom hears the ringing she will remove it immediately. I sit on my bed to avoid collapsing. While waiting, still washed over with fatigue I fall asleep. It's not restful but provides a much needed escape. I fight the nap because I know what it's going to feel like when I wake.

There is going to be a second's worth of blissful ignorance where I will have forgotten the chaos. But then will come the rush, the feeling of transforming from a fifteen year-old to the man Carla wants him to be. Followed by the sickness.

I awake to the phone but not mine, my parents'. I tiptoe to the top of the stairs. I want to know if it's my dad but I can tell by the decorum in mom's voice that it isn't. After the greetings and pleasantries, she's silent for what feels like a long time. I hear a perplexed, "Oh?"

Then, "Well, that's interesting and makes me feel much better." I still have no idea who it is but the ambiguity of her responses piques my curiosity. I lose interest in the conversation due to her prolonged silences but dare not move for fear of being heard.

My mind wanders back to the fear of my father's arrival until she says, "Well, thank you, Miss Danza."

I think I might faint. I kick myself for not paying closer attention. What did I miss?

She hangs up and I hear her slippers shuffle across the floor, she opens the fridge and I take the opportunity to return to my room. Within minutes my phone rings. I pick up and softly say, "Hello."

Absent a greeting Carla's first words are, "I talked to your mom."

"Ok," I reply thinking we don't need to play this charade.

She continues, "I told her I was walking through the office today and heard the principal on the phone. I heard him say your name which prompted me to listen more carefully. When I heard how Jimi missed those days of school, I remembered one day I saw him in the library several times and asked him if everything was ok. He told me that he was avoiding a fight over some girl. I didn't think anything of it at the time other than it was a noble reaction but now knowing the story it makes sense. Also, he named the other date that Jimi was absent and I knew that I saw him that day too because I handed out paperwork for the forensics competition. Perhaps, when I pulled him out of class to give him the handouts his homeroom teacher marked him absent. But I'm certain that he was in school both days."

Carla tells my mother that I am to go to Dr. Bencevengo's office on Monday morning where he will give me a slip to take to each one of my teachers. If my attendance can be verified by what they have individually recorded then I will be given credit for the day. I will still receive an absence for avoiding the fight but will not suffer disciplinary action. Looks like neither of us will.

I feel skeptical relief, "Did she seem to buy it?"

"Yes, I'm sure she did," Carla replies with levity, "Your mother seemed very thankful that I was able to put her mind at ease."

The disgusting irony makes me irate. I understand lying. I have lied to my parents over the years, even prior to Carla to avoid trouble although never good at it. I'm now being groomed as a better, more seasoned liar. Underneath my mom's anger, she was genuinely worried about me. Carla assuaged her fear but I was far from safe. Those two days, like every other day that my mother ever watched me walk out the door, she put her faith in the knowledge that I was being turned over to someone who would care for me, In Loco Parentis.

Carla feigned control over everything. She alleviated any parent's worst nightmare not only hiding it in plain sight but also implicating me. This is the first time I really feel hatred. My Catholic upbringing makes hate a dirty word, reserved for evil. Like so much else I'm afraid to admit the truth to myself, Catholicism is great for making any normal emotion seem wrong. But my loathing is the only emotion that seems to make sense. In this instance, perhaps subconsciously the bystander evil I am witnessing makes my hatred permissible.

I hang up, tempted to go downstairs. I want to see if Carla's call worked, maybe my mom has softened but I shouldn't know this call even took place. My father comes home and I hear both he and my mother walk past my room into theirs. I don't dare step out to listen although I'm shaking with fear.

After fifteen minutes of anxiety my dad walks into my room, "Where were you those two days?" He uses no introduction, his voice dire.

He forewarns, "I already know the truth so your only chance to lessen the severity of this is to be honest."

I regurgitate what I have been rehearsing for the last two hours, "So Dad, there was this kid who wanted to fight me because he saw me talking to his girlfriend. To avoid him I hid in the library all day."

I play complete ignorance about the other, "Dad, I swear I was in school the other day. I cannot imagine why I would be marked absent."

I save my explanation about the third day to try to tug on his heart strings, "And the third day," which was actually the first chronologically, "Was the day I missed school to attend Mrs. Sumac's funeral." I keep every explanation short to seem neither nervous nor rambling.

He asks rapidly, "Who is the kid who wanted to fight you?" I hesitate, having forgotten to invent that detail.

Before I can think of a name or an excuse to withhold it, he interrupts, "I understand if you'd rather not say, as long as it's resolved I don't need to know."

"It's over, Dad. I promise." I hope to God as I say those words that that it could be the truth.

His tone softens as he tells me that my story matches the school's. I know what he means by, "The school." Before he speaks again I wonder what would happen if he really knew. I cannot focus on that, my survival is chief.

He asks again, almost begs, "Can you please be honest with us? If you're having problems with anyone you should tell us. That way it can be resolved without this headache." He walks out of my room and I wish so badly I could tell him who's causing me problems.

It's a long and cold weekend. The worst is over but my mother speaks not a word and my father is distant. I feel the chasm grow wider between us, grasping that I have taken tremendous steps away from them and another giant one toward Carla. Another shared secret has created a stronger bond. This is a big one that fooled a variety of people. The further we journey from the shock of the letter it seems, amazingly, as though we are going to make this work.

Monday morning, I knock on Dr. Bencevengo's door and he beckons me to enter. He does not know me so I introduce myself and he offers a seat. He walks around his desk and sits next to me, lecturing on the importance of attendance, "I understand the fear that you felt and the avoidance of embarrassment at a potential fight," he consoles.

"I am going to refrain from asking you the other boy's name as long as you can assure me that the issue is resolved and there will be no further interference with your attendance."

I tell him with as much conviction as I can convey, "I promise, it's over."

He continues, "You must also realize that if the problem does persist I will investigate on my own and bring the boy in to conclude it." With that, he hands me a slip of paper that has the numbers one through eight written on it and two columns of lines. One column represents absent and the other present. If I bring it back at the end of the day and my teachers have me recorded as being in class then I will receive credit, if not, disciplinary action.

Part One

My first period homeroom teacher initials the absent column with no discussion and I go to my seat. I avoid thinking about what will happen the rest of the day if other teachers follow suit only because I am fairly convinced that Carla has contingencies. Second period is study hall, where for the last few months I have gone to her room but today she's in a meeting.

Third period is Geometry and when I hand Mr. Paul the slip he asks, "What's this?"

I explain the problem, he looks at me with a nonchalant smirk and asks, "So what do you want me to sign? That you were here, or absent?"

His question stuns me. I know the correct answer and I know the only answer I can give so I follow the plan, "Here," and he signs accordingly.

When I enter Carla's' room for lunch she asks immediately, "How's it going?" I am too numb to answer, caught in the current of this story. I have absorbed this cover-up into my existence, each time someone asks me why I'm holding this slip of paper I say with nimble clarity the yarn that Carla spun. I detach from that whole day naked in her bed, my face buried between her legs while she writhed and bucked underneath. Those visions are buried somewhere in the limbo of my alternative reality. But the new images seem equally as damaging. They chip away more of my psyche because I'm trying to convince myself, other classmates and my teachers of the delusion.

I look at other boys in my classes and instead of wondering what their normal existence is like, I imagine if it could be them who were threatening me, wondering if they would be a formidable opponent. The story I've now adopted, I cultivate to keep interesting, altering inconsequential details with each audience to avoid monotony. The tales I tell about the origin of my quest for signatures border on gossip but since I'm already the topic why not participate in the enjoyment?

Carla takes the slip and says without hesitation, "Well I'll sign for study hall. You're with me at lunch. I know you were in French eighth period, so those are all yeses." My verification slip went from one absent and one present to one absent and four marks for present. With her check marks, a day of my life is erased. My entire existence went from evil to good as though it's a shopping list she's checking off.

As I leave her room in a daze, headed for the cafeteria I pass Dr. Bencevengo. He is speaking with another teacher but raises his hand to stop me, "How are you making out?"

I show him and he quickly tallies both columns, crumbles the slip of paper and says, "I'm sorry for the confusion, James. You were obviously here. I'll take care of it in the attendance office."

He couldn't have seen that three of the four signatures were by the same person. The same teacher hovering over this whole discrepancy. It seems suspicious to me but who am I in comparison? This is Carla Danza. An original member of the vanguard. Head of the foreign language department. Her picture adorns the trophy case memorializing all the Teachers of the Year. The driving force behind a study abroad trip every three years. She organizes the holiday concert where all the language classes sing in their respective languages, has participated in faculty talents shows and lends her hand in all types of philanthropic work that bring nothing but accolades to the school. It's underwhelming to say that she is Lenape Valley Regional because she is larger than the school. Even if he had noticed that her signature was peppered all over that piece of paper would it have caused him to question? Can this episode of my life be any more byzantine?

Chapter 21

Despite my new reluctance our trip still approaches and every conversation revolves around how much I am going to love France, listing details of all we're going to see. I want to share her excitement but simply cannot. I'm unable to grasp what I should feel, waiting to be told my emotions as well as their root. Classmates tell me, "You are so lucky."

"I guess," I reply after a shrug.

Other times I speak how I truly feel, "Not really," and either response is received with equal confusion at my ambivalence.

Carla's plan is orchestrated infallibly well. Jean-Michel, the director of the exchange program is led to believe Carla is my aunt. She tells him I'm afraid to stay alone so it would be best if I lived with her. We're staying in a town called Fontainebleau, forty-five minutes outside of Paris. Jean-Michel knows the administration of our sister school so he arranges for Carla to stay with one of the principal's friends, Luce. Luce has one son, Jean-Registe, who is about to begin his mandatory military service so I assume, older than me.

Our home-stay trip is eleven days, encompassing Easter vacation, we will miss one day before break and return the Saturday before school resumes. This is the longest I've ever been away from home. My parents are excited but I can tell my mother is anxious also. She comes to school to see us leave, providing incredible comfort. I see her wipe away tears as our goodbye hug ends, this is the first broken heart I've ever felt.

Neither of us knows that we're saying goodbye for longer than just eleven days. It will be quite longer and a much further distance traveled until the person that gives her this hug will be able to return to either of us.

Seating assignments on the plane are randomized except for mine. I'm right next to Carla and several rows away from any other student. Anxious chatter lasts until we reach cruising altitude when the movie comes on and the lights are turned down. When the mood becomes sedate she tells me all she is planning. It sounds fine but I have nothing with which to compare. There are some things I want to see but only tourist attractions so I placate her. The planning tapers and she asks about my recent confirmation ceremony. I tell her about the classes and why I choose my godmother as my sponsor.

Only a moment of silence precedes, "Do you know the only sacraments that can be performed by a laic person according to church law?"

I don't.

"Well, in the event that a baby is born sick, and it doesn't seem like a priest will arrive in time, anyone can perform a baptism so they don't die with original sin," she explains. That makes sense but I don't invest much thought.

She continues, "There is another sacrament that doesn't need a priest," her pause dramatic.

"Two people can carry out a wedding ceremony," she reveals. That seems odd because there isn't the same urgency as a dying child. I say nothing but instinctively put up my usual guard when strange segues lead to unknown topics.

She explains that two people are needed with a desire to commit to one another. "That and a ring are all you need to betroth yourself in matrimony," she purrs. With the full weight of my stupidity I know I've walked right into her trap.

"I love you Jimi, and I have never felt this way about anyone. You are the first person I have ever made love to and I want to spend the rest of my life with you. Will you marry me?"

With the real pressure continuing to build in my head I feel the figurative type reach a level of new pain. Being left speechless is a type of disarmament with which I am becoming sadly familiar. I'm reminded of the feeling in my stomach at Christmas when she bought an unrequited present for me.

"Carla, I don't have a ring," is amazingly the first concern I blurt out, the first manageable idea to reach my mind. I have no concept of forever. She is older than my mother and only another fifteen year-old kid knows about her presence in my life. How would she tell her parents? What would she tell her employer? How would I tell my parents? These questions are all hurried from my mind because they require real answers.

"Oh sweetheart, you are so kind to think of that," she coos immediately. "I will buy you a ring to put on my finger if you want to marry me," she continues.

I look straight ahead and think of grabbing the barf bag from the pocket in front of me for security. There is a feeling that is starting deep in my stomach that may cause a wretch. I can feel that her eyes have not left me for an instant. They are burning right through me so much that I'm afraid she can read my thoughts.

She gently taps me on the hand so I look, "Will you marry me? And can we perform the ceremony ourselves?" She asks very slowly and softly. Her eyes that were scorching the side of my face are now blazing right through my own.

"Yes," I say softly, with a reservation that must be imperceptible.

She smiles and winks as she mouths, "I love you," then turns her head to look out the window. I place my head back against the seat and my mind begins to race. My thoughts arrive in no set intervals and with no discernible pattern. I think I need to have vows. What will I do for a ring? Where will we get married? When are we going to land? Should I invent an illness to force her to send me back to New Jersey? Will I have to wear a ring? What will I tell my parents? Does this count as our real wedding or will we get married in a church someday too?

I close my eyes to feign sleep until the flight attendant hands me a warm towel. Carla is already awake and smiles at me when she says, "Good morning. Did you get any sleep?" I nod and immediately think that we're already married and this is the first morning that I'm waking up to her. My quivering stomach intensifies.

Once off the plane everyone leaves with their counterpart students except me. I'm left with Jean-Michel, Carla and the principal of the school, Agnès. After our luggage is loaded Agnès drives too fast, through narrow alleys with unfamiliar street signs. The adults converse the entire ride and although I can pick up some words I am, in all ways, lost. We arrive at the apartment complex and walk up to the seventh floor, stopping on the fifth to put the suitcases down and rest. I notice a television playing loudly to remind me how far from home I am.

Agnès is clearly a good friend of Luce because she walks to the refrigerator, takes out a carton of juice and drinks a healthy gulp without using a glass before leading us to our room. As I walk down the hallway I run my fingertips along the dark textured wallpaper, peeking into a uniquely decorated parlor, a tiny bathroom with a bidet and what I assume is Luce's bedroom. Our room is small, painted dark blue with two twin beds that barely allow the door to clear when opened. Baby blue sheets and a darker blue blanket on each match the decor. The room is illuminated in broad daylight by two huge windows without screens that swing open wide into the room. Agnès opens one and wind rushes in. I smell things that I have never before. I don't know if it's pollen from European trees or foods with which I am unfamiliar but my senses go wild. Nothing about my surroundings is recognizable which causes overstimulation that leaves me feeling infantile.

The bright sunshine of noon hurts my eyes and I begin to feel the effects of having been awake for almost thirty hours. I hear the front door close and Carla's footsteps walking back down the hallway. She walks over and stands in front of me, wrapping her arms around my waist, "Well, what do you think? Do you love France as much as you thought you would?"

"I do. It's great," I say because so far it is nothing short of amazing. It bares similarities to home but is a fully functioning life for people who know nothing and care nothing for what takes place in my world. There is a comfort in knowing that everything around me is so far removed from my sphere of existence, the burdens that make me miserable are inconceivable here.

I hold my own in a one-sided conversation for a while until she thankfully asks, "Do you want to take a nap?"

I lie down and close my eyes simultaneously. She returns from the bathroom, closes the door behind her and lies beside me. I feel the warmth of her bare skin as she drapes her leg across the center of my body.

She whispers, "Don't worry, Luce won't be home until after work. Agnès said around four thirty." She undresses me as I lie still and wraps her warm mouth around me. With my eyes still closed I feel as though I might fall asleep until she increases her pace. Right as she knows I am about to come she stops, slithers up next to me again, pulls me on top of her and I realize that she already has a condom in her hand. After she opens it she hands it to me serving as foreplay so I put it on and myself inside her. Even though she assures me that no one is home she is more subdued than usual, finishing quickly before I tumble to the side against the wall and fall asleep. I feel the gentle tug of her pulling the very tip of the rubber and a few drops escape as I am completely uncovered.

The last thing I mumble before passing out is, "Don't let me sleep too long. I love you."

I am asleep immediately.

Chapter 22

I awake from my nap confused. I have no idea where I am, the window wide open and I am naked. The breeze was nice before I fell asleep but now is overbearing. As I pull the sheet over me and stretch a bit I hear something indescribable from the other room. It is eerie and otherworldly. Only after listening intently am I able to discern words but can't tell where one ends and the next begins.

Is it French? It doesn't even sound European. I have nothing on which to base any assumption. Only because it constantly loops back on itself can I make out, "Nam Myoho Renge Kyo" from multiple voices and multiple volumes yet always with the same cadence. I'm paralyzed. If I leave the bed what will I find? If I stay what will find me? Where is Carla? Where is Luce? Who is Luce? What is, "Nam Myoho Renge Kyo?"

I lie motionless and hope this will stop. I grab my watch from the floor and check the time to have a beginning point for how long this continues. I hear it dissipate but then the volume increases with intensity. "Nam Myoho Renge Kyo," I begin to pick out individual voices. I know there are at least two women but the group is predominantly male. As I focus on deciphering I become lost in the sound, feeling entranced until I snap myself awake. My survival may depend on remaining alert.

I move slowly, pausing every time the bed creaks, trying to pick up a change in the chant. Thankfully, nothing breaks, "Nam Myoho Renge Kyo." As soon as I'm out of the bed, I take ten minutes to dress thanks to intermittent pauses so I remain silent. I creep to the door and am about to turn the handle when the apartment suddenly becomes hushed.

I freeze again, this time better prepared for whatever may come through the door because at least I'm dressed. It falls completely silent distressing me anew. I crack the door slowly, just enough to see down the hallway.

Before I can make out who is coming the door opens and hits me in the head. I put my hand where it hurts trying to see around my wrist. I immediately feel another hand on my own and hear a familiar voice, "Oh my gosh, what happened? Why were you standing there?"

"Ouch, what the fuck is going on?" I say too loudly.

"Shhhh, Don't curse." Carla says.

I snap back, "We're in France. Nobody knows what I said. What the fuck was that noise?"

"I guess you heard them?" she asks with what I think is a chuckle.

"Of course I heard them, what the hell is that?" I say. I'm tired, scared, cranky and now my head hurts.

"Relax," she says as she kisses my forehead an inch lower than the pain.

"Come meet Luce," she says taking my hand and leading me into the hall.

"No, no, wait, I'm not leaving this room until you tell me what that was. I'm freaking out," I protest driven by confusion. I'm not sure I've ever raised my voice to her but I'm not ok with any of this. She grabs me by both shoulders and tells me again to relax which is having the opposite effect.

"Luce is a Buddhist, actually a priestess. She has an altar in her parlor and people come to pray. You heard her friends praying. I let them in but couldn't tell you because you were asleep. I'm sorry, that must've been weird. Do you feel better after your nap?" Her voice calms me and I feel bad for snapping but she can't override my foul mood.

"I guess I feel better," not willing to concede much forgiveness.

"Come meet Luce please?" She says with a smile and a kiss on my right cheek.

I don't want to meet Luce. Jet lag is making this difficult situation worse. There's a variety of thoughts competing for prime space in my mind.

"Wait, is there a bunch of people out there?" I ask her with a nasty tone, able to put the first obstacle into focus.

"No, everyone is gone, it's just Luce," she says sweetly.

As I walk down the hall I notice different pictures on the walls than my first time past. When I turn the corner into the kitchen I see Luce sitting at the table, with what looks like a bowl of coffee cupped in both hands.

She stands up with a huge smile and says, "Eh, bonjour. Et vous, vous êtes Jacques, n'est-ce pas? Le neveu bien evidemment. Alors, enchantée de faire votre connaisance." I don't understand anything past, "Bonjour," but her gestures are warm and welcoming as she leans in and gives me a kiss on each cheek. She turns to Carla and they begin conversing, clearly about me. Luce is almost sixty years old but looks younger. She's top heavy, with a giant chest that I first feel when she kissed me enjoying each large breast as it brushed up against me. Her flowing blond hair smells pleasant, yet earthy. Every moment brings something newly overwhelming.

Chapter 23

Over the next few days we visit some of the most beautiful places that I will ever see in my life. We agree to come back to Notre Dame de Paris and conduct our wedding ceremony sitting on the banks of the Seine with the cathedral in front of us. I raise the ring issue again because it bothers me, after crossing that off my mental checklist I move to the unshakeable anxiety that I only have three days to come up with vows. I'm tired of feeling inadequate and as though I'm constantly trying to catch up with my girlfriend. I feel the power imbalance and although I'm sure she has to feel the same, she never acknowledges any such feeling. She writes her own vows so even though she allows me to use traditional ones I know the bar she will set. Just a few days after arriving, I consider calling my parents to ask if I can come home. So much about my own life is foreign. I'm constantly fatigued from working just to be me.

We alternate our nights between going out and staying home in some unplanned enactment of tertian fever. Our trips are to either Paris or the quainter Fontainebleau. When we stay home we have dinner with Luce, sitting at the table for hours but since Luce does not speak English, she and Carla converse exclusively in French. Occasionally Carla will interpret for me during a lull but when I become bored I excuse myself. Television is pointless so I lie in bed and read the few magazines I brought for the plane.

I try to slip away inconspicuously and fall asleep alone, not often successfully.

Our third night at home instead of staying up with Luce, Carla follows me immediately into the bedroom, closes the door behind her and attacks me without a word. Her motions and gestures always have a sense of urgency but this particular night borders on ravenous. Her hands and mouth are ubiquitous making it impossible to focus on any singular sensation. Small moans escape her lips as she runs her tongue down every line of me.

After completely undressing me she pushes me back on the bed and strips herself also. She flips me over to my stomach and violently pulls my hips up so that my back is arched. She begins to kiss everything between my hips and thighs while her hands reach between my legs. She gropes my left nipple, pinching hard.

Pain momentarily overrides confusion. I involuntarily push back into her, wanting to apologize but she is undaunted. She slows to tease. Still on my elbows and knees, she mounts me.

The first thing I feel is her hair brush my shoulders and her crotch press against my sit bones. Her entire head of long wavy hair envelops me and I feel her tongue gently touch the crease formed by my compressed shoulder blades. She runs her tongue down the middle of my back and her hair follows after. Somewhere in the middle of my body I wonder how she's going to conclude.

She anticipates my reaction by placing her hands on my hips preventing my lower body from collapsing when her mouth touches my asshole. I jump. The only place that I can go is forward, soliciting a sigh that signifies her tremendous satisfaction. Her mouth follows, allowing me no time to react before she is at the same feverish pace. She grabs me with her left hand aiming to gain control by stroking me. I wonder where her right hand is an instant before I feel it at the middle of my back beginning its decent down the same crease her tongue first outlined.

I giggle almost uncontrollably every time her tongue flicks my taint. She laughs in between moans of approval. "I guess that tickles," she says with disappointment in my juvenile reactions. I'm laying fully prostate now and she has used her knees to force mine apart. Parts of me that have never been exposed are now no longer my own. Her palm is lying flat on the bed with me on top of it and she knows that despite my laughing, some part of me is enjoying this.

She probes and caresses with her mouth while her free hand keeps me down. The massaging is working in circles that gradually move downward. When she reaches the very small of my back and I feel her dangling bracelet touch me, I panic. With her writer's palm she moves down all the way into someplace that makes my heart pound. I feel the sweat bead on my forehead and my pulse in my ears.

Before any other physical reactions can take shape I feel her middle finger move in tiny small circles lubricated by saliva. My natural reaction is to bite the pillow underneath as she enters. I bite so hard my front teeth hurt. I clench every muscle below my waist just to find an instant of relief from the painful pleasure I cannot define. The pain feels steely to me. I want to describe it as the sound that a sword makes as it is unsheathed. She tries to use her other hand but my stomach blocks her, I drive my hips into the bed.

I wonder how far inside me she will travel. With each thrust she delves minutely deeper at barely perceptible intervals. Each plunge fills me with a renewed disgust. I lose track of how long this lasts, consumed with finding the apex of my pain. I think I might shit and try with all of my might not to let that happen because although I have never felt embarrassment like this I am certain that type of release will be superlative.

With no warning she grabs my hips and pushes me to my side. She takes my leg and throws it over her head laying me flat on my back. I assume she's going to climb on but instead, moves her body toward my head and lies on top of me in the sixty-nine position. I do what I imagine she wants and the second my tongue touches her she begins to move her hips in rhythm. She moves her hips faster and her whole body quivers which despite the repulsion still causes me to ejaculate in her mouth.

When I can think again, I am preemptively appalled at the thought of her telling me, "That was beautiful." She lays her head on my thigh and I feel her mouth those exact words, my stomach reacts as always. It feels like a cramp and a spasm over top of nausea like something rotten and unwholesome was just force fed to me.

Chapter 24

We always take the same train into Paris. Although I know the landscape and the stops by now, this particular journey is unsettling. I didn't pack especially nice clothes except for Easter but I certainly don't have anything appropriate for a wedding — my wedding. I'm scared. Carla talks all the way from Fontainebleau to Paris. The ride seems rougher than past trips. It might be my fragility that causes every turn of the car to rattle my bones. I'm sure many reasons have caused people to vomit on their wedding day but I'm fairly certain that this set of obscene circumstances is unique. I take no comfort in my individuality.

Her rambling allows me to revel in the white noise. When I do pay attention she tells me how wonderful it is that we're going to a place as sacred as Notre-Dame de Paris. I find it sanctimonious. She rattles off a list of famous people from some era, unknown to me, who have gotten married there but I'm sure that she means inside the building. The illicit, deceitful ceremonies must be reserved for outside.

We stay on the train to the Métro stop St Mîchel-Notre Dame which puts us on the Left Bank. It is not a far walk to the first set of stairs that leads us down to the river. This section of the city is busy and I can barely hear her over the life that surrounds us. I have no idea where I am nor our destination but I follow and still she talks. I feign interest but am playing back the conversation I had with my mother before we left Fontainebleau this afternoon.

I didn't have anything significant to say to my mom but it had been a few days since we last spoke. I was terribly nervous about the threshold I am to cross, the burden of managing it alone overwhelming. Pay phones in France don't accept coins, rather a Carte Téléphonique must be purchased at a news stand. The card is inserted into the phone and the denomination purchased determines how much time there is to talk. Before I made the phone call I bought three cards. Even though I had thirty minutes on an old card, I hoped my mom would hear something in my voice and ask, "What's wrong?" I didn't know if she could stop the momentum of events but I feel like if anyone could, surely it's my mom.

I called while she was making breakfast and the first thing she said was, "Oh your Dad just left for work. You missed him."

"That's fine," I really wanted to talk to her anyway. We made the usual small talk and like every other conversation I can tell she was interested because I'm her son, not for any reasons of her own. She is a good listener anyway.

There were a few uncomfortable silences, me out of things to say and her, depleted of polite questions. Seemingly, neither of us wanted to end the conversation. When I saw the number five blinking on the LCD screen, I knew one card was almost done. I doubted she was going to ask.

"Listen, Mom, there are only a few minutes left and I don't want to be disconnected," even though I had three more cards in my pocket.

I surrendered, "I should get going."

Saying, "Goodbye," wasn't just until the next time we spoke and it wasn't until I see her again in New Jersey. I said it with more finality because I knew that once this happens tonight I will be different because Carla says I will.

Carla and I make our final decent down old stone stairs to the quay. We are greeted by a loud, bright tour boat, immediately reminded of their inescapable laps. We find the bench closest to the cathedral and sit. Some people walk by and the honking of car horns is intermittent but nothing stops her from staring through me and somehow ignoring what she does not want to see. Things like my reticence, fear and discomfort fade away at will.

She can overlook my immaturity and fumbling for words at the stress as though they are inconsequential nuances. Even the imbalanced stages of our individual lives are conveniently leveled to diminish the dysfunction. All cast out and replaced with her conviction that we are meant to be divinely united.

She explains, "I can see it in your eyes when you look at me and feel it when you hold my hand and of course, most of all, when we make beautiful love it pervades all of my senses down to my soul."

She stops speaking only when the boats pass. Although the light blinds my eyes, I feel like everyone inside is staring, just like at school. Hiding this indiscretion in plain sight takes on a brand new meaning in the context of conducting an illegitimate wedding ceremony mere feet from the literal center of Paris.

By the time the second boat passes she already has the ring in her hand and has pulled out what looks like a crib sheet. I can't imagine what she wrote until she begins. Her voice, deeper than normal conveys the depth of her emotions. She speaks slower than she has all night making me drowsy.

I can sense her words being etched into my memory, knowing I'll never forget the monologue. I'll be able to recite this for the rest of my life but never allow the words to leave the safe confines of my secrecy. The entire soliloquy is laced with admissions of love and praises my exceptionality. For the moment I feel like the once in a lifetime catch of which she speaks but I'm swept up in fantasized romance.

As it seems that she is concluding she moves her hand toward mine. I can't see what she is about to put on my left hand but also don't want to look. She moves the ring down the last finger of my left hand and all I can think of is how much the sensation resembles what it first felt like to put on a condom. When she removes her hand I see a crucifix ring on my pinky.

She describes, "If the body of Christ is facing out," as she has situated mine, "The marital status of its wearer is indicated as 'taken.'" It looks like her eyes are welling up with tears but it could be the reflecting lights across the river. The religious symbolism is too ironic for me to integrate into my thoughts.

When she suggested Notre Dame de Paris as our ritual site I chuckled but Jesus truly puts the exclamation point on this evening. Years before the initials appear on a rubber bracelet I ask myself as I look at my hand, "What would Jesus do?" Did Carla ask the same thing to solicit his heavenly response? "Carla, you must marry this boy to make your indiscretions tolerable."

I'm about to remind her that I couldn't buy a ring when she pulls a small bag from her purse and says, "I know you couldn't do this on your own, so I picked it up for you," handing me the bag. I'm tempted to look inside but also afraid. Instead, I recite my vows which are really just one. It doesn't include for richer or for poorer, nor the sickness and health. I can't vow them to her because I don't know the meaning of those concepts.

"Carla, I've never been in love before. I know I care about you and I love you. I want to spend the rest of my life with you and live happily ever after. I think this is a special place and a great place to get married. I hope to always make you happy. I love you."

When I look at her recurrently she is starting to cry. Her lower lip quivers and she bites it to stop. As I finish speaking I reach into the bag and find a box. Inside the box, a plain band of gold I place on the ring finger of her left hand.

I'm being slowly drained as I say those words because they are void of validity. The truest thing I said is that I have never been in love before. I thought of what a wedding vow should sound like and tried to write my weak reflections. I imagined what she would want to hear because I try to please her. After the ring is on I look at her, she looks back at me and there is no mistaking her tears.

She leans and kisses me after she says, "You may now kiss the bride." I taste the salt of a tear that has run into the corner of her mouth. I'm unable to take my right hand off the crucifix. I fondle it to convince myself of the tangibility of right now because it borders on fantastic. The ring convinces me that I am actually living this life. I feel compelled to believe that we are married because she is so convinced of this reality but somehow I cannot. This whole trip is surreal, I want to believe that I'm here in Paris but there are unwholesome truths that cause me to question that anything I think is genuine.

Chapter 25

The train ride back to Luce's is quiet. I feel like I've done something wrong because she is no longer talking. When I overcome my fear of her possible answer I ask, "Is something bothering you?"

She smiles a melancholy smile and tells me, "There are so many wonderful things on my mind. I can't stop thinking what a dream come true this is." Her response seems insane, unanswerable but I press no further. She moves against the window, lays down putting her head on my lap and places my hand under her arm where it's warm. The closeness makes me feel momentarily safe. I think of the parallel of how she took me under her wing in many respects and analyze the normal connotation of that expression.

During the ten minute walk to Luce's she starts talking again and although I cannot concentrate on what she is saying I like it better than her silence. I drag my feet from both physical and mental exhaustion at two in the morning. She replays the ceremony in Paris and anticipates the consummation of our wedding night, "I cannot wait to make love to you as your wife." I'm unable to contribute. I know what an annulment is and my mind wanders to wonder if this has grounds to be annulled, if anyone even believes me.

The apartment is dark and silent but Luce has left cookies on the kitchen table where we sit and debrief. Our late night conversation is no different than any other where she does most of the talking and I do all of the agreeing, except when she asks me direct questions like, "Where do you want to go to college? What would like to study?"

She even asks me for the first time, "What do you want to be when you grow up?" The cookies are good and since I don't drink milk I have a glass of water which from a French tap, is lukewarm to match my affect. Apparently she notices my boredom and allows the dialogue to taper.

Before any detectable discomfort she pulls me to my feet, "Shall we go make love as husband and wife?"

I feel ill.

I'm surprised when sex is no different from any other time. Missionary until we both orgasm and then when she is ready, she rolls me onto my back and begins to rub me until I am too. I'm still jetlagged and my body has not yet adjusted to the change in diet. I have been waking up in the middle of the night with terrible leg cramps, the painful, whole leg spasms that sneak up without warning. My body is rejecting all of the deprivations of this experience.

Regardless of the reason, it's five-thirty in the morning and I cannot get an erection. I feel the frustration in her grip. She seems to think that tighter and faster will expedite my arousal. It does not, it only hurts. When I stop her she uses her mouth and as soon as she deems me ready she rises to complete our ritual.

For the first time she puts the condom on me herself, climbs on and moves aggressively. As she starts to writhe, the typical indicator that she is about to finish I feel something different, my pleasure doubles. I come instantly.

She slows and says through her groaning, "That was beautiful as always but this time as your wife," and lays her head on my shoulder. Something is different and something is wrong. I pull the short chain to the light that rests above the bed and when I look down I see the condom has broken.

It takes all of my faculties at this time of the morning after this type of night to keep my composure. I'm convinced there is torn flesh hanging from my penis. My initial reaction is panic, but I'm proficient at keeping my emotions in check at all times. The condom is sheared all the way down to the tightly wrapped elastic ring at the bottom. She catches me staring and sees the look on my face so she looks too.

Before I can say anything I hear, "Oh, no."

She speaks not a word but rises, puts on a T-shirt of mine that barely covers her ass and walks out of the room leaving the door open. I'm still lying naked on the bed looking as though I have torn through the last barrier of my innocence. I quickly pull the blanket up when I hear voices from the bathroom. I lay silently wondering if she is mad at me.

Fifteen minutes on my watch till she returns, yet seems like an eternity.

I can smell soap from a fresh bath as she sits beside me, "Do you know what went wrong?" I keep quiet about the strange sensation before I popped because she's already upset.

Instead, I tell her solemnly, "I don't know," and quickly ask who she was talking to in the bathroom.

She tells with a distant tone, "Luce had just gotten up for work." Carla was so upset that she stripped right in front of her and stepped in the bath even though Luce was still talking.

Sitting cross-legged, still in my T-shirt but now wearing underwear, she looks nervous. Her eyes shift between me and the window. She occasionally glances at my crotch as if placing blame, unsure what about my covered penis attracts her attention.

She says, "I think I'll be ok because the spermicide, Nonoxyl-9 is nothing more than soap. So I took a bath and scrubbed down there." Her face does not reflect the consolation she speaks.

She ask again, this time with more incredulity, "What happened Jim?" and picks up the blanket to reveal the defective condom. It looks worse now because I am fully flaccid, like a sick flower with the shards resembling limp petals. She stares and I stare to avoid eye contact.

"Maybe I nicked it with my nail as I was putting it on you," she offers.

"Maybe," trying to not incite her to say anything worse. I feel my eyes grow heavy equally from exhaustion as escape. I'm asleep before she turns the light out and leaves the room. I don't know what she does or where she goes but I discern nothing until after noon.

When I awake the room is empty. I walk through the rest of the apartment, finding it also empty. It scares me and I immediately blame myself for having slept. I feel abandoned, unsure of anything after this morning. I take a bath and dress just to do something that nears progress. I leave the bathroom to find Carla straightening our room.

"Oh hi," she kisses me, "I went to the patisserie and got us some pastries. Do you feel better after having slept?" I don't but I tell her I do.

"Did you sleep at all?" I ask.

"No, I laid out on the couch for a while but couldn't relax so I went for a walk. I feel fine now." She is remarkably calm compared with the last time I saw her, almost bubbly. Since she drops this incident I'm happy to forget it too. Instead, I ponder what the other students on this trip may be doing today with their families.

Chapter 26

Two days after our unholy union we walk up all six flights of stairs continuing the same casual conversation we began on the bus home. When we arrive at the front door it's ajar which seems bizarre but the day we arrived Agnès walked right in. Carla notices the door but doesn't seem to think much of it. After walking down the hallway and into the bathroom she sees the door to our bedroom also left open, speaking as she moves out of hearing range.

As I'm looking through the fridge I hear something strange down the hall. It sounds like hyperventilating. Carla's breath is quick and shallow, the more she wheezes the more nervous I become.

My own voice cracks as I ask, "What's wrong?" but she is already on the phone, speaking in French. I hear her say Luce's name and talk about the next day's excursion into Paris but can't be sure.

She puts her hand over the receiver and whispers what I think is, "Luce knows you're not my nephew." I think Carla is crying but can't tell what she is really saying. As I'm about to ask for clarification, she blurts French words into the receiver again.

After another few minutes on the phone she runs into the bedroom and yells, "Come in here now." I walk in, she points at the sheets and hisses, "Look at the stains on those sheets. They know you're not my nephew."

I have no idea the connection but I suppose there shouldn't be semen stains when a boy is sleeping in the twin bed next to his aunt. What I'm really trying to wrap my mind around is my first acquaintance with what semen stains look like. Carla's bedroom is always dark and no one has sex on my bed at home. The dumbfounded look I must be wearing only makes her angrier.

She steps close to my face and says, "Don't you get it? Luce probably walked in, saw the stains and called someone." She spits on my face when she says, "Probably." I can't tell how the phone call concludes but she hangs up in the same state as she began and is becoming increasingly hysterical.

"How do you know she saw them? How do you know she called anyone? How would she know that they are from us?" I ask, all innocently and for my own curiosity but also hoping to calm her down. She pulls the sheet off of the bed and begins to wash it in the bath tub while mumbling something like, "How could I be so stupid to leave the door open? How did I forget to make the bed so someone could see?"

Maybe because I'm a kid, but I just don't see the connection. I walk back into the bedroom to see if I can gather any further information. The windows are wide open, I stand idiotically still, and my mind wanders to determine my next move. I feel the volatility of the situation and do not want to make anything worse. I walk into the bathroom where she is vigorously scrubbing, more like trying to cleanse something from the fabric than just dried semen.

After painful deliberation I say, "Maybe the window blew the door open. Maybe it wasn't Luce who walked in. I don't think she saw anything," in an attempt to help.

She only scrubs harder and the staccato rhythm of her speech matches the beat of her hands, "No, Jim, I'm sure she was the one who opened the window in the first place because I didn't leave it open. She went in to open the window, saw the stains, put two and two together and God only knows who she called, I'm sure she called Jean-Michel at the agency. And maybe she heard the bed squeaking at night which only verified her suspicion." The anger in her voice somehow implies that any of this is my fault. With the guilt stalking me again, I wish I could lie down and fall asleep but could never get away with that.

I walk back into the bedroom and sit on the other bed and although I feel like crying I don't. I would go for a walk except I'm afraid to be out by myself. I can't talk to Carla and I can't even call home because it's eleven o'clock at night in New Jersey.

When my emotions can no longer remain harnessed, I surrender and weep. I stay as quiet as possible to not make Carla angrier so I pull my shirt over my face and silently sob until I hear the front door to the apartment open followed by Luce's, "Bon soir."

Carla cuts in front of me as I walk down the hall and begins conversing immediately. I have no idea the content but the few words I can pick out seem to indicate that Luce has no inkling of the dirty truth. I actually watch Carla's entire body relax as she speaks. When she pulls out her earrings I know, for certain that we're safe to unwind. I'm lost and outnumbered all over again so I walk back down the hall to the bedroom where Carla joins me just a few minutes later.

She closes the door behind her, sits down next to me and puts her arm around me like she were my big sister, "I'm sorry I bit your head off. I thought that we were going to get caught."

A voice I've never heard before from somewhere inside screams, "WE?" but what comes out are a series of questions I decide need to be asked.

I list, "What did you say to Luce? What did you say on the phone? How are you going to explain why the bed sheet is soaking in the bathtub?" Much like every other time that she needs to rise to the occasion everything adds up after her spin is crafted. We always arrive at some gross misunderstanding that can be laughed off and forgotten, most often at my expense.

Chapter 27

By the time we're preparing to return home I don't speak. My mind is simply full. I can take no more on my shoulders and still function. I speak neither to Carla, nor my classmates, nor the friends they made in France. Even my last phone call to my parents is unusually short. I barely say goodbye to Luce and when I walk away I'm certain Carla is making some excuse for my hostility. Our return flight is much like our first, adjacent seats, sequestered conversation.

This debacle of a trip, which will live vividly in my memory forever isn't punctuated until we arrive back at my high school. The bus parks in front of the school and since it's a Saturday afternoon nobody else is there but our parents. I lock eyes immediately with my mother who hugs me with an uncharacteristic sense of urgency followed by my father. They ask rapid fire questions about the flight, meals, on-board movies and the ride to school. They want to know where my luggage is and who I sat next to on the plane and I tell them all of it, with as few words as possible. After I retrieve my luggage from the bus and begin to walk to my parent's car I hear Carla greet them, gushing about what a great time we all had. As I listen to her and my parents begin their conversation panic brings me to edge of hyperventilating. I have no idea what she is going to say and I cannot imagine how this will unfold.

My vision blurs from the tears that fill my eyes as I hear Carla detail the wonderful aspects of our trip. It's a masterful display as she weaves in and out of stories that are quasi-true, omitting it was just us two, fabricating things that she knows I did with my host family. Her intimate knowledge of what happened when not in her presence clearly puts my parents at ease.

With no chance to regain my already slack composure, I cry. She just recreated my study abroad experience in the most wholesome and natural way imaginable, and now I envy even lies. I want my parent's newly programmed memory to be mine too. I want to feel like I got the most out of their money like they do. The other students had what she just described and the gaping hole left by it's absence is agonizing. I still want to be an exchange student, willing to exchange my life with anybody.

My mother whispers some things that resemble, "We didn't know if Jimi would be too homesick." The irony of my mother confiding in Carla is heartbreaking, I sit on the curb and wait for the end.

Carla approaches for the grand finale, "Ok, Au Revoir, Jacques, tu me manques." I know she will tell all of the other students that she will miss them too but it seems a ridiculous thing to say. Her pure and bland tone is the final erasure of the hell that was my life for the last eleven days.

I sob audibly.

Carla's bewildered look shocks all of us. My mother speaks of me as though I'm a child, and it makes me happy, "Oh he's just tired, he gets like this when he's cranky."

I'm thrilled to hear her say such a thing, reclaiming ownership over my youth. The youth that Carla feels entitled to twist into whatever she wants. I enjoy a small sense of relief that her last image of me is recorded with tears streaming down my face.

I don't fool myself that she will care but I allow it to mean something to the kid I was before this trip.

I feel minute. My life is in tatters and whether I'm half a world away or living in my house, nobody knows. Carla's reach is international and omnipotent. Once back in my house, I finish speaking with my parents and walk upstairs to my room. After I strip to my boxers, unplug my phone and lie down I remain in bed until school Monday morning.

Chapter 28

My life coasts right back into the same routine as before we left for France. The Foreign Language Forensics competition, still a month away, gives Carla the perfect alibi four days a week. School becomes a blur. I go through the motions because none of it matters anymore. I rarely see the need to brush my teeth. I shower only when my parents force me, just to masturbate anyway, I no longer wash my hair or body. Homework and classwork are done on autopilot from years of obligation indoctrinated by nuns. Each day I find a slightly renewed hatred for my life and each time I have an orgasm in the back of her room I hate her exponentially more.

This is me for an entire year. She invents creative ways to fuck me with the ignorant blessing of my parents. Phantom exchange students come to New Jersey that need accompanying, traveling troupes of actors perform at my school, her parents have her best students for dinner, celebratory parties exist for Forensics competitions. All false, all to conceal me and all for the simple purpose of securing me into her bed.

I feel apathy like none I have ever known, my emotions so blunted that I am simply unable to care any less. My parents scold me for typical adolescent offenses, dirty clothes on the floor, leaving my cereal bowl in the sink, overgrown grass. And with each admonition I shrug, I chuckle to myself. Am I really supposed to care about those oversights with the images that perpetually clog my mind? Pictures of a grown woman obsessed with my penis.

Carla's actions cease to surprise. Her cunning becomes commonplace and I never fight. She continues to confuse my lack of rejection for acceptance because she still fails to realize that I cannot stop her. No other boy in my position would deny my opportunity and she knows that too.

This is my junior year of high school except now she is my teacher again. I co-exist with her for forty-two minutes a day and act like she is just as wonderful as everyone else thinks. I feign fantasized arousal when other boys recount their plans if they could get her alone. There are days when I cannot fathom leaving my bed, I consider staying in homeroom all day, going to a toilet stall in the bathroom simply to avoid hearing about, thinking about, or being bathed in her ubiquity.

My existence continues in the same controlled and monitored manner for perpetuity with seemingly no end. I've cultivated a state of mind as a means of protection that disconnects me from my surroundings with a bizarre objectivity. Slight glimpses of hope appear only to be quashed by Carla's ingenious deceit. She confides in me not only the dilemmas she faces when colleagues confront her but also the solutions she crafts to circumvent prying eyes.

The superintendent and principal call her into a meeting where she is told, "Be careful, Carla. You don't want to risk ruining your reputation because of a star crossed crush by a student." They neither know me nor ask who I am. They hear the same rumors as everyone else and dismiss the possibility just as quickly counting on the same infallibility that Carla manipulates. She assuages their suspicions and alters our routine to conceal her actions in minute ways.

She picks me up in an adjacent development and makes me duck down in her car. We sit in the library during study hall to show her fearlessness of being in public together. And most laughably I only go to her room after I've eaten lunch in the cafeteria, my body her dessert. Small fixes that only veil the pollution.

My senior year begins and despite my alternate existence I am still swept up in the wave of being at the top of the social ladder. I'm excited to be graduating but for reasons unique to me. Perhaps it's subconscious, or preconscious, or simply a product of forward looking but as a new year turns familiar, I pull away from her. Once I make the seemingly impossible decision to wean myself it feels instinctive, like survival.

Separating myself is easy when only part of my mind is with her, only part of the time. I ignore her calls more regularly and Kevin's always. She finds one reason or another to call on my parent's line and I encourage her, hoping to arouse suspicion. I turn into someone nasty and cold. When I feel crowded and alienated from everyone in my life because she has sequestered me I ignore her too. She softens her approach but it means nothing because I'm beyond the ability to care, beyond distant.

My passive approach replaces what I am petrified to do. I have recurring dreams of walking into her classroom and telling her, "You're sick and I hope you rot in hell." Sometimes her room is empty, sometimes full of past and current students to witness my catharsis. It's the same choreography each time and they are all there to see me make recompense for my objectification. In my waking hours I push back against her just hard enough to make her feel resistance. She cries or begs or sometimes even yells, but whatever her reaction, I relent. In each instance, I surrender.

I know other students and faculty see me treat her rudely but I don't care. Sometimes, she comes to my other classes and asks my teacher see me for a moment. She knows I can't tell my English teacher, "No, I won't speak to Miss Danza."

As I walk to the door, I feel everyone's eyes follow, I hear what they whisper. Before I can prepare myself, I'm standing in front of her and she is asking me questions for which I have no answers. I can't respond because I don't know how to articulate these things. I don't know because I can't understand anything anymore.

My decision is going to hurt, reminiscent of ripping off a bandage. The pain is inevitable but air has to reach my wounds in order to heal. That's what I need more than ever before, air. I've been suffocating for years. This is what people like me do. We put bandages on our problems, healing not always an immediate option.

Life rolls on at a deafening pace, my mind never able to catch up. Sometimes when the bandage is placed over the wound too tightly or pulled off too quickly, a piece of the scab rips off too. With the flow of blood, old wounds open. Ones that may have been forgotten or worse yet, injuries that were unknown. But I feel them now.

Lying is inescapable, but not until I start lying to Carla do I realize that I am by default, a liar. I lie to everyone. Sometimes for no reason, just to be in control of my own reality. She was a hovel from that unsavory characteristic until my survival depends on lying to her too. Now I have alienated everyone and I'm left with nothing when without her.

Because this relationship lacks any predictability I cannot apply normal logic. This isn't like breaking up with a girlfriend. I don't know how to navigate these feelings. The first question I ask myself is, "Did I ever really want this?" I believed so but were they my reasons or hers? Overcome with disarray I choose subconsciously to act the only way for which I'm trained. Being dishonest, no matter the reason, is for the purpose of self-gain and in some cases, self-preservation.

After months of half-hearted attempts I know she will never leave me alone unless I make it happen. I create issues that anger me even if there is no basis. Fear of the real crisis paralyzes me from telling her how I truly feel. I try to make her feel guilty for normal things to illuminate the real dysfunction. For as long as we have been together, she goes back to her parent's house, forty-five minutes from school, on the weekends.

"I don't like when you're at your parent's because it cuts into our time on the phone," I manufacture. I'm not old enough to have mastered forethought, only lashing out with what sounds good at the moment.

To my amazement, the following weekend, she stays at her apartment and tells me, "I stayed here for you, Jimi." I don't really want to talk to her any more than already forced but I play rejection tag to ensure she feels the dismissal that she projects on me.

I ask her not to talk about her nephews because I don't like hearing about someone my age who spends time with her when I cannot. The things for which I choose to needle her only send a mixed message but that's because they come from my own distorted place. I don't want to talk to her anymore, I don't want to be tethered to her for one more second but my lashings only convey the opposite. The appeals I make only exist to wrestle control. It's the only way to be relevant in my own life. I hear nothing more regarding the close relationship she has with her only sister's sons.

When I tell her, "It bothers me when you stop to talk to another teacher while we are walking together," she raises her voice the next time, "Sorry. In a hurry. I'll catch up with you later."

This even extends to the principal one day as we are walking through the cafeteria. Now I wonder how far she will travel to ensure my contentment. My own sway frightens me. I have no such power over myself. How do I have it over another person? The power imbalance shifts daily without warning.

I feel in control but not how I want. I don't want to regulate her, but me. Instead, I create a two way street of a strengthened bond where she expects correspondence. I have no valid reason why I don't reciprocally ignore other students who talk to me. Why I don't spend more time on the phone with her on the weekends in lieu of time with my parents. I don't have the maturity, emotional or otherwise to outline the sacrifices a healthy relationship needs. I oblige her and kick myself for digging a deeper pit. Slowly I realize her power over me is imaginary.

I learn the power I have beyond the scope of what she gives me in the closet. I understand just how badly she needs sex with me. My only solution to feeling powerless is to battle back. I become sullen prompting her to ask me what is troubling me.

I say, "Nothing," with a dishonest pout.

"I'm worried because you aren't acting yourself," she attempts to pull me out of my funk. Her attempts to console me are more heartfelt on the days we have a scheduled tryst. She is willing to bend and flex around whatever my complaint du jour is when the threat of cancelled sex is on the line, entertaining my gripes as if they are legitimate.

I push the limit each time toward the inevitable, increasingly nervous to test her boundaries. One argument, I hold my line all the way through the car ride, the ten minute conversation outside her apartment and even after she asks, "Please come inside where we can talk."

I refuse her apology for whatever the contrived offense and see her agitation grow as banishment from my penis looms.

While sitting on the loveseat in her apartment she finally asks, "Do you just want me to take you home?" I sit silently, searching for what seems like an eternity although I'm not debating a response. I'm focused myopically on one issue. What will her reaction be? I've always surrendered to her litany of explanations but this time I want to test her. I have a knot in my stomach, worried about what hinges on my answer.

"Yes, take me home." I say coldly.

Without a word she stands and stares. I'm frozen, she takes me seriously. She walks toward her purse so I stand up and head to the door but she cuts in front. She grabs the knob, swings it wildly open and it slams against the nearby hutch. The noise forces me back in fear. The door bounces off the hutch and closes, prompting her to open it again just as forcefully. This time she catches it as it bounces and slams it against the curio once, twice, three times and then slams it shut. She bounds at me.

I'm afraid she is attacking but instead wraps her arms around me, buries her face in the crook between my neck and shoulder and sobs uncontrollably. I immediately snap out of my attempted torture. All I can think about is that I have hurt her such that she is irrational. I've never seen her raise her voice in class, never heard her say anything hateful. Never has she slammed a door, or shown any temper. This outburst is a direct result of what has happened between us, concocted by me.

She shakes as she cries and all she says is, "I'm sorry. I'm so so sorry."

I don't know why she is sorry but I rub her head, "Shhh. Don't cry."

As she nuzzles her face into my shoulder it turns into kissing my neck, which leads to my cheek and naturally my lips. The kiss is reminiscent of our first, soft and unassuming. It grows with steady intensity to be erotic just before she pulls me to the ground in front of the recently abused door. Quite voraciously she places one hand on each of my shoulders and pushes me down.

She orgasms and her entire body collapses after its rigid stance for, what had to be an uncomfortable amount of time. Carla pulls me up, grabs me and shoves me inside her bareback, all in one motion. The shock of everything that has just happened has its culmination with her warmth now enveloping me. I feel like I can come immediately but restrain myself because I know she has plans for something greater. My emotions and my knees are raw with rub burn for how long we spend in the spot where we fell. After we're done she rises, puts her clothes back on and continues unfazed by her own volatility.

Chapter 29

I am consumed by boundless longing. I want my life back but am powerless to retrieve anything that would seem normal. I would like there to be a moment of epiphany where the course and justification are blared as if from a trumpet. Instead, it happens as ambivalently as the rest of my actions. I decide that I will no longer subject myself or anyone else to the torture that has been my life.

On the phone I tell her, "Carla, I'm done. I don't want to be with you anymore."

She begs and pleads through sobs, "What is it supposed to mean that we got married in Paris?"

I don't answer because I know she remembers that decision differently than me. I'm certain that it is committed in her memory as a joint conclusion between two people madly in love but I have that event framed otherwise.

Just yesterday, she brought me backstage in the auditorium and for the first time, we have sex in school. At her prodding, she pulled her oversized black sweater up, followed by her purple mini skirt and put me inside of her, moaning too loudly for my comfort.

"So what was yesterday then? Were you just throwing me a bone?" She says through her tears. I don't think she means the pun. She insists upon making me feel as though I guide the course of action in this abortion of a relationship.

"No Carla, that was your choice," I reply shocked at my conviction. After hours on the phone, I think I agree to give us another chance.

One week later I wake up with the same suffocation and tell her again, "I cannot do this anymore." The response is the same wailing and gnashing of teeth.

She points out, "Jimi, we belong. More than any other man and woman have ever belonged together. Don't you see all that we have overcome to get this far?"

She quotes lyrics from various mix tapes, "Jimi, like Peter Gabriel says, 'I see the resolution of a thousand fruitless searches.'" I feel embarrassed for her desperation but can't bring myself to correct the misquote. By the end of the several debates over the coming weeks, I leave them all believing she is my destiny. She wears me down and eventually I cease broaching the subject. What she keeps well hidden is that I wear her down too.

One morning, mid-November the year that I am seventeen years old, I dutifully walk into her room carrying the normal amount of tension from the previous night's argument. Neither of us ever remembers the minutia that causes our squabbles from one day to the next. I know that I'm mad and that I should be mad but the source of my anger is beyond my intellect.

She grabs her keys and says, "Come with me, please."

She's cold and although I feel like I tug her control away at times, the power she exerts at this moment is palpable. We walk abreast without a word spoken. She leads us into the dark auditorium, illuminated by two amber glowing spot lights on the left side of the stage. Her heels are loud on the wooden steps that lead us in front of our phantom audience, announcing our entrance into this large space.

As I hit the top step, the phrase, "Throw her a bone," echoes in my head. She stops at the risers and sits. She doesn't invite me and doesn't wait for me to join her before speaking. I've become adept at ignoring the inane babble of her love declarations so as usual, I check out.

I'm awoken, however to hearing, "So is this what you really want?" Her voice somehow different, missing desperation, detached from the typical brooding.

"Is what what I want?" I ask, bewildered.

"Do you really want to be done with me?"

The magnitude of that question and this moment are placed squarely on my shoulders and I feel as though a strap is being tightened around my chest. I know what I want to say but simply cannot articulate the thought. My pause lasts long enough that I begin concentrating on the length of my silence instead of an answer.

I heave the word, "Yeah," quickly and quietly so she'll ask me to repeat it. Based on her speculative reaction I may renegotiate a new answer.

She responds unimaginably, "Well then, you have your walking papers."

In spinning our severance as abandoning me, she steals the last shred of my self-respect. Her release ignores my unsuccessful attempts, insures that the drama of our final act is written as a termination from my job as her boyfriend. The last clear reminder that this always was a power imbalance.

No feeling before and none after can prepare me for the swirling chaos that stems from her dissolution. I want to speak but can't, want to run but want to hug her for giving me the gift of my life back. I think I can gauge the look on my face but also think I have no idea what I portray. She doesn't look at me, only stares at a piece of paper in her hand appearing as though she wants me to reject her offer. However, her body slightly turned away creates the characteristic enigma.

I can't walk past her down the stairs because this moment is surreal; I still may be imagining it. Is this a delusion of reprieve? I can't walk to other steps, they're too far. I might not make it before I'm pulled back. I walk to the edge of the stage and leap down to the orchestra pit stopping one more time to look back. A condemned man, immediately before his execution, gets the illusion that he might be pardoned at the very last minute. I'll see her in two periods, in her classroom but that's different. This is the last time I will see her as a daunting figure in my present. The next time I see her she will only be my French teacher not my captor.

She must know I'm staring at her but refuses to look. Does she feel the part of me left there on the stage, a part I never really new? I walk up the aisle to the exit and open one of the double doors. I stand immobile while my eyes adjust to the fluorescent light of the hallway. It hurts because the auditorium behind me was so dark. I also use the moment to adjust to the novelty of what just occurred. The temptation to walk back and apologize grips like the belt again. I feel the need to return out of obligation.

She is and always will be a part of me to which I will remain loyal. We are inseparable on more levels than I'm even aware exist. Some of them wonderful qualities that will make me a man people gravitate toward.

Not until someone walks past the open door and snaps me out of the daze am I able to think. "Is everything ok?" an underclassman from my study hall asks in a soft, sweet voice. Everything is not ok, but things could be if I walk forward, out of the darkness.

"Yeah, I'm fine, thanks for asking."

I leave the auditorium thinking the worst is over.

Entr'acte

Imagine opening a bottle of seltzer. The hiss, the impending overflow. Quickly, tighten the cap. Wait a few seconds, try again and hope the pressure equalizes. Sometimes the cap can be cracked a half turn at a time to slowly release all of the pent up force. It takes time, it takes patience but it can be safely opened.

Imagine now, no equalization. Imagine the frustration when every time, no matter how long the wait, the tiniest twist of the cap causes continued effervescence. The anger of the futility is only outweighed by the realization that it's forever impossible. Next fear takes hold; maybe the bottle will never be opened, followed by confusion. Finally, choices must be made that are unwanted, unwarranted and based on no set of previous experiences.

Whether opening quickly or slowly a mess is inevitable.

This chaos is what becomes of my day to day existence because I never had the time, knowledge or ability to equalize the forced pressure in me. I was shook like the bland bottle of seltzer, in all directions, in multiple, unforeseeable ways and then left with everything contained in an undersized and ill-equipped package. Shaken over the course of years and for the next fifteen, I tried opening up a little at a time.

Life was thrust upon me. Other girlfriends my own age, college, marriage, a child, another child, a house and a third child. Each one brought hope that they might bring relief. But after each, the horrible hiss and the burden.

I can feel the bottle, painfully tight against my hand able to burst anytime. And when everything finally erupts there is no doubt that everyone around me that I love, now or in the future, will be covered in a wet sticky mess. I'm unable to protect the people so dear to me as much as they were unable to prevent this for my life.

The remainder of my time in high school is spent pining to leave out as though imprisoned. I graduate college after declaring my major in the only thing I could, French. Still absent the ability to think for myself I make a sickening variety of decisions based continuously on what I think Carla would want. I try to please her and preempt her fickle fancies now without daily contact. She evolves into a different type of ghost. I compile the endless possibilities of what she would want but am able to vary the degree of depravity I attach to her indirect decisions.

After graduating with a degree in French Translation my twenties go by in a fog. Because of this haze, a decade of my life where I watch my peers gain awareness passes in a flash. This is different from the typical way that people reflect on the passage of time. For me it seems vaporized into a vacuum where everything is a void. This vapid feeling allows most things that would be considered watershed to become bland.

Occasions that transpire are in fact, life-changing but looking back, I have the feeling once again of watching from afar without control. Carry-over dissociation from not having felt anything for so long; an unshakeable residual numbness. I wish to God I felt the things I pretend I do. I wish I remembered and enjoyed these milestones accompanied by loved-ones but it's hard to feel any kind of happiness. The man who blossoms from that murky boy is malformed.

I need to be wanted, need to be perceived as desirable. It's a common modicum that people who worship money are never able to find enough. People who pursue power can never satiate that hunger. Those sorts of ideas are usually the thesis of a sermon or a motivational speech where the warning is to value the truly important things in life. I've heard those platitudes and can easily quell material temptations. However, I'm subconsciously driven by the need to be sought after by other human beings.

My obsession pervades my every action yet its persistent presence is conveniently ignored. I crave the attention of people around me, needing to know they want me. I like feeling eyes on me, suspecting that someone is thinking about me with impure thoughts. I act in subtle, sometimes unnoticeable ways to cast my spell, shades of invitation that sit on just the right side of my subconscious. The reality is that nobody misreads my signals. I'm good at sending them without full grasp of what they actually are.

Such is my game and it's a game of conflict. I work tirelessly to have a perfect body yet cover it with baggy clothes leaving only suspicion of what's underneath. I perfect the habit of self-flagellation in many ways. My legs cut up and bruised from Mountain Biking, hands calloused from any kind of work I can find. My arms are sinewy and tight from weightlifting to draw attention to them yet require a second look and maybe repulsion from their abuse. I am and have been tied to one woman and one woman at a time since I was fifteen to add to the allure of prohibition.

I like the look of being clean shaven yet only reduce stubble when a five o'clock shadow grows into unkempt. It's all a dichotomy and all defines me as what is wanted but can't be had. Feel it but don't allow it to be felt. It starts and ends with me and causes wonderment and second guessing. I bring the constant war with myself to your front door. Neither of us can easily discern our feelings and thoughts. Don't think you know me because knowing the real me is impossible.

I'm the je ne sais quoi that eludes explanation.

I make myself a sex object in every way I know. The psychological parts are much more complex and harder to detect but the physical is just under the surface for everyone to glimpse. Being a sex object creates the illusion of control. I may possess power over a conversation or even an entire friendship because I can speak a certain way or make too much or not enough eye contact. I would like to be comfortable enough with myself to not attach such value to my desirability but I'm far from there. If I can't trust that people want me and want to have sex with me, I'm not sure on what I will subsist. I only feel alive when I flirt, when I risk.

Part Two

Chapter 1

Mr. Cunneely stands in front of the class. Like every person, at every moment of their lives I am the culmination of all my experiences and decisions. The difference is my individual parts are disjointed. Sometimes I don't know from where certain aspects of my personality come and what degree of normalcy they contain.

However, like a beacon guiding my every action I'm overly aware of my sexuality at all times. I know how to stand and how to sit, distinguishing when to put my hands in my pockets. I choose carefully when to pause while speaking, not because I'm collecting my thoughts but because I feel as though it gives me the pensive air that the females will find coy, if not rakish.

I'm a paradox. Underneath the oversized clothes, lies a body that is desirable. I work hard for the wiry, ripped arms and the barreled chest hidden under a dress shirt two sizes too large. I squat over four hundred pounds to add mass to my quadriceps and do calf raises until they cramp but my dress pants are too baggy to ever allude to their texture. Maybe, sometimes on a Casual Friday, I wear something uncharacteristically form-fitting to make the other four days curiously tantalizing.

It matters neither that I am a teacher, hired to educate young adults nor that the female audience is comprised, exclusively of teenagers. My need to be admired is elemental, my exclusive identity. I don't understand the body language cues I subconsciously emit but I don't need to. I need to look good. I will never act on any advance that would come from this display anymore than any homosexual proposition would be accepted.

My need to teeter on the edge of this precipice is overwhelming daily. My sex appeal, the only value I covet. I can only ride with these emotions as they surface pursuing them in the same manner which I pursue everything, with full force.

I go to the gym five mornings a week before work because I have the feeling of being pumped for hours after. This engorgement with blood provides the appearance of even bigger muscles. I take supplements, vasodilators to unnaturally prolong the feeling. I have mastered my pose in front of the class, flexing a bicep or placing my hands behind my head. I play like I'm contemplating a deep thought but really I'm showing off the size of my shoulders and the definition in my traps. I can feel their eyes on me, not because what I'm saying is all that riveting but because my body is cultivated to be appreciated.

I operate, most comfortably, on multiple channels. One channel speaking French, discussing homework, or a verb while the other channel makes sure that what come out of my mouth is coming out sexy. Freshmen, Sophomores, Juniors, and Seniors alike all receive the same treatment. My principal, Barbara is treated likewise and I'm sure my favorable post-observation report is a result of the sexuality I exude in front of her.

I teach for eight years like this, coaching girls' soccer and becoming known as one of the more liked and respected teachers in the building. I win awards for creating engaging lessons that become best practices in my school. I'm recognized as a "Golden Apple" award recipient for being a noteworthy teacher for one quarter. My marking period award is a precursor to being selected as the "Teacher of the Year" by a panel of parents, administrators and colleagues before I am thirty years old. This culminations of events, decisions and work cannot overcome the eclectic collection of fears and anxieties that ultimately topple my whole life.

Chapter 2

I don't remember the first time I call her name. Undoubtedly, the first day of school in 2006, third period, French I. It must be somewhere at the beginning of the attendance list because her last name is near the beginning of the alphabet. I neither remember our first conversation nor the first question she answers. I cannot put an event to when she stands out as different from the rest. What I will remember without details, is how quickly and efficiently she endears herself to me. What stands out most is how vehemently I feel beholden to watch over her.

I don't know how I become a haven for her either. It's more muddled in my memory than any other event in my life that I beg for a beginning. Despite my search for the genesis it lives very inauspiciously. Early one March morning, after the sound of the first bell, Natalia storms into my room. She enters and walks in the direction of her seat, throws her books on the floor and with the rush of scattered papers comes the purge of tears and poisonous emotions.

Without thinking of perceived impropriety which admittedly, should be closer to the forefront of my mind, I close the door so she can retain some dignity. I don't speak because no words can help undo this. I put my hand on her shoulder and let it rest, motionless letting her know that although tears are a very lonely place, she is not spatially alone. I do not ask and she does not offer the reason for her dirge.

The bell rings again, letting us both know that students will be coming into my room and she has two minutes before first period begins. "Would you like me to write you a pass to guidance so you can collect yourself?" is all I can say.

"I don't want to go to guidance. They don't do anything," she sobs.

"Well, Natalia, I don't think you want to be in here when my class comes in and you don't want to go to your first period class like this, do you?" I reason.

"I'll be fine," she says as she gathers her things and walks out.

I only make mental note that when she returns she will be upset perhaps, but I don't think that this is anything serious. She is, in fact, silent in class, but comes to my room after school much more upbeat and wanting to discuss mundane things about her day.

"So I assume you are feeling better than this morning?" I ask

"I'm fine. My father is an asshole." I look at her with disapproval but she just grins.

"But he is," she begs.

"Well, you're entitled to your opinion and I don't know the specifics but he's your dad. And please don't talk like that ok?" I say, my best attempt to be non-judgmental.

"Can I tell you what happened?" she asks.

I'm sitting at my desk grading tests before I have to teach my college class. With three hours before I have to leave, I initially regret not closing my door. As the words, "Too late now," run through my head, she tells me a story that sounds like others I have heard about broken families. There is fear in her voice as she talks about her father, including fear for her mother's safety.

Nothing she says is secretive and doesn't request my discretion but when she walks into my room the next morning she seems to have a swagger absent the day before. She wears a smirk, suggesting something of a bond created by my listening and asking questions about her family.

After this dilemma, Natalia comes to my room more frequently outside of her class period. She comes in before basketball practice and in the few minutes she has once softball starts. She is a good student with an above average work ethic who still talks about her dad but also her other classes and occasionally asks me questions about my life.

The liberties she takes I neither correct nor draw the distinct line as when other students press. She sits behind my desk and uses my computer. When she goes into my drawer for a pen or a paper clip, instead of seeing a student violating my privacy I see a girl looking for acceptance. I rationalize my silent permission as allowing her the trust to be herself but overlook the reality of not delineating what behavior I accept.

Weeks later, our conversation meanders toward food. She asks, "What is your favorite cereal?"

"Cookie Crisp," I share.

We talk about ice cream, pizza, desserts, my mom's apple pie and the brownies that bake in the microwave. The next morning she walks into my room with a disposable soup bowl from the cafeteria and a carton of milk. She pulls out a Ziploc baggie with Cookie Crisp, places the bag in the bowl, hands me the milk, a metal spoon and says, "Enjoy."

I feel inexplicably touched, unable to decide if it's because she listened or thought about me outside of school. I sit at my desk, eyes fixed on her, speechless. I know it's erroneous to feel this, but I'm helpless to prevent it. I know she has a crush but

I detach myself and focus on the thought behind the gesture. Unfortunately, I do not know how deceiving my emotions can be and choose to trust them.

The evening of the cereal gift, while my wife, Dana is at work and I'm folding laundry I hear my phone beep in the other room. I don't like my cell phone the same way I've never liked any phones. I don't check it often so I forget about the message until after dinner. Once my three children are in bed I see a text from a number neither in my contact list nor that I recognize.

The message reads, "I better get my spoon back before my mom notices it's missing."

The feeling in my stomach is a rush of panic that prompts me to hide my phone. I slam it shut and grasp it with both hands as if I am encapsulating something dangerous. I immediately fear anyone else seeing this message because I know it's Natalia. I've never gotten a text from a student but I know it's wrong. I should report this to the administration immediately. At worst I should delete the text and tell her that it's inappropriate.

Instead, I take none of these actions, I feel a distinct satisfaction. It feels sordidly good so I reply. I make a joke about holding her spoon hostage until she brings more Cookie Crisp. The exchange feels safe and natural, far from dirty. It is the first step in a pattern of crossing lines that should never be crossed. Boundaries are broken slowly but then so rapidly it's like falling down a hill where grabbing for purchase is pointless and painful.

As spring arrives Natalia has more time to spend after school and our conversations continue to revolve around the benign. There are times we teeter on a more profound discussion but I divert her for all the same reasons I allow no one close to me. The day before my birthday she asks me for the key to my classroom explaining, "I have a surprise that I can only give you the morning of your birthday."

As a rational man, turning thirty years old, who has taught for eight years, I would never give my only key to a student. Not only does it scream of impropriety but breeches the appearance of security for my professional and personal belongings.

This choice would certainly be frowned upon, if not censured by school administrators. Absent those conscious thoughts I hand her the key with my only warning, "I don't have another key so you cannot lose this."

Somehow, unbelievably that seems to be the only caution that fits the moment. I would scoff at the idea of another student having my key but I see something in her that I have not sought to find in anyone else.

I see a lost child. Someone suffering from a past injury at the hands of an adult, possibly a parent. It's not anything drastic that would make someone feel sorry for her yet subtle and barely detectable. I sense this subconsciously and feel for her.

When I walk into my room the next morning the lights are off. I flip the switch and before the fluorescence fully illuminates the room, I am doused in Silly String. The stream lasts forever as I stand in the doorway, eyes closed covered by what feels like wet spaghetti listening to multiple unknown voices giggle. Natalia and two friends ornately decorated my room with streamers and homemade signs. They adorned plain white T-shirts each to comprise a different part of the phrase, "The Big 3-0."

The thought and effort that she put into this acknowledgment are, once again touching. With each step, with each time we speak about topics more personal it seems a stronger bond is forming. I hope that she doesn't feel the same because I know it's growing in indecency and I'm unsure how to slow down.

Chapter 3

In one conversation after school, we chat about music. I ask, "You know the band Nine Inch Nails, right?"

She does not. I ask about other bands at the core of my musical library. She has no knowledge of Radiohead, Nirvana, or Depeche Mode. When she tells me that she has never heard of The Cure I demand her iPod to create a playlist. The title jokingly reads, "Songs you need to know if you are going to be my friend." Although I think the name is used in jest, I affirm that she is more than just my student. Without verifying that I reciprocate her feelings I admit that her knowledge of these songs makes us friends.

Subliminally I convey that this friendship can blossom into something greater. I have difficulty navigating my feelings toward Natalia as our contact increases. I'm constantly torn between the guilt of this unique interaction and the pleasure I derive from our conversations. The thought of losing her in my life seems tantamount to losing me.

The final draft has forty-five songs after paring down from twice that. Mixed with alternative and post-punk classics I hide a couple of songs whose lyrics could be interpreted as an indication of my growing feelings. Head Over Feet — Alanis Morrisette, With or Without You — U2, Heaven Beside You — Alice in Chains and Something I Can Never Have — Nine Inch

Nails. None are out of place but contain just enough suggestion to stimulate curiosity.

I hand her the iPod at the end of the school day and say, as an afterthought, "Oh, by the way, I forgot to give this to you before. Enjoy."

I'm shocked when Natalia finds me the next day to tell me which songs she liked and which she's heard before. "There is no way that you listened to that whole thing and remembered all the songs unless you stayed up all night?" I say as soon as she is done rattling off titles.

"I basically did. I really wanted to hear it. Plus it was the least that I could do since you put all that time into making it," she says, embarrassed for her excitement.

The frequency with which we text increases in tiny, almost imperceptible increments. She asks random questions about movies or music or homework and they all lead to lengthy conversations. It's not until the message appears on my phone notifying me that my inbox is full twice one Saturday that I realize how out of hand this is. As I go through and individually delete each message I calculate that I have spent more time in contact with her than anyone else throughout my day.

Finding the opportunity to text however, is a challenge. I fabricate nonexistent excuses to go to the shed in my backyard. I take multiple trips to the bathroom, when I read a book I place my phone inside its open pages. I hide it behind the open newspaper or in my lap. Only seldom, does my wife ask me who I'm texting, forcing me to make up a random person as well as a topic needing to be discussed. Although she knows something is amiss she is unable to ascertain just what.

Before I realize how exponentially the texting increases I step back and admit to myself that it seems to never stop. She texts me first thing in the morning and she is the last person I text before I go to sleep. Right as the school year ends she takes a trip cross country to visit relatives, despite the impetus being her family, we communicate just as frequently.

She begins asking serious questions about my past and the present status of my marriage. She asks about my sex life, past sexual experiences, and my personal sexual preferences and still none of it seems out of place, nothing too personal. My judgment is clouded by the fact that I feel important and she is taking an interest in me. She cares about things that most other people do not or have not for a long time and I am swept completely away from conscious and moral thought.

I answer her dishonestly whenever I fear that the real response will accentuate the chasm that factually exists between us, telling her only what sounds good. I answer her with the intent of sounding attractive outweighing the truth. Reality is what I'm afraid will scare her. In different places of my mind I've yet to explore and with which I doubt I could even connect, she holds a special place. The inquisitive text messages have the undertone of flirtation, yet never address the tension we successfully evade.

Chapter 4

We converse so much that when I don't hear from Talia for an extended period of time I wonder why. Two weeks prior to the end of school she tells me about a Portuguese festival in Newark she desperately wants to attend. Her father being half Portuguese intrigues her, "I'm dying to learn more about their culture."

Her dilemma is that her mother will not take her, leaving no way to go. She alludes to wanting me to take her but I cannot entertain that possibility. Shortly after leaving school I receive a text bubbling with excitement that her friend Corinna's family is going to take her.

My response is simple, "Have fun. Be careful. Newark is not the safest place." And with that I enjoy an evening with Dana and my children.

At ten o'clock the message on my phone reads, "Im atthe bar. Danbing and so drunk."

Her inebriation shocks me – Where are the adults?

"Are you ok?" I send back.

For the rest of my evening none of my questions are answered. All of my text messages receive responses but not in the context of anything I ask. "I luv dancing", "Sangia is so gooood", "You ttally shold have comeeee."

I cease to respond only because I don't want anything misconstrued when she reads my texts tomorrow morning. She tries to tell me what she eats and the names of bars that she bounces in and out of but her drunken Portuguese is unintelligible. The last text I read before I turn my phone off for the night reads, "I'm so tried from dancig. cant wait t show u whjat I learnd."

I don't take notice until sometime around noon the next day that my phone is silent. I assume she is recovering and let her alone. After we eat dinner I wonder if maybe she lost her phone or more likely, if her mother grounded her. I don't send any texts in the event that someone else has her phone, a veiled attempt to avoid suspicion.

Saturday night comes and goes but before I go to bed I play back my day, realizing that I checked my phone semi-hourly, noticeably missing our contact. I wonder now not only if she is safe but also selfishly, if our communication has been cut off because her mother suspects something. It scares me to think about the unknown quality that my life has taken, having put such small dilemmas in the hands of a fifteen year old girl and perhaps the irrational reactions of her mother.

As I'm returning home after a trip to the supermarket late Sunday afternoon, sunburnt, and smelling of gasoline from a day of yard work, my phone sounds. Natalia is the only person who texts me so as soon as I hear the beep I put the bag of groceries down and rip the phone from my pocket. Warm relief washes over me. I have two options with this and all texts, "View Now," or, "View Later." Something unexpected lights my screen, "Can you talk?"

My immediate reaction is fear. Talia has never requested an actual conversation. I snap the phone shut in a panic. I imagine any topics that she could want to discuss to prepare responses. I know that I haven't done any more than carry on a multitude of conversations on topics that would be, at worst, considered immorally candid. But everything being over-analyzed, I'm afraid how they may be interpreted.

After I bring in the groceries and put them away I tell Dana that I'm stepping out to return a call to my mom. That story should buy me twenty minutes before raising suspicion. I walk back outside and call Natalia. As soon as she greets me with, "Hello," I ask, "What's wrong? You sound like you've been crying."

Her voice is weak and tired. I hear a faint whimper on the other end of the phone then audible sobs.

"Hey, Talia, what's wrong? Why are you crying?" softening my tone. She sniffles hard, pulling everything into the back of her throat before exhaling deeply.

She speaks uninterrupted as I listen intently, "When we were at the bar, Corinna's step-father, Jared got up to dance with me. Because of the loud music he put his face right to my ear. So we were talking for a few minutes about nothing really and when he was done he leaned in and kissed me. Our lips locked for a few seconds but I pulled away and just looked at him. I was shocked. I played it off and didn't make a big deal so nobody got upset. I didn't want to ruin the rest of the night because I was having such a good time and nobody else saw." She goes on to describe hopping from bar to bar, drinking Sangria and eating ethnic food.

She continues, "Still far from home, we got a flat tire. Corinna's mother called AAA because nobody wanted to be out on the highway changing it. By the time we got home, it was three thirty in the morning. Everyone walked into the living room and passed out either on the couch or the floor." She starts to cry again. I heard her cry the morning she told me about her father but that was an explosion of emotions. This sobbing is from a wound.

I refuse to say, "It's ok," because I don't know yet how this ends.

"Talia, just relax. You're doing fine. Get it off your chest."

She sniffles hard again, clears her throat and says, "I woke up right as the sun was coming up to Jared's hand down my pants. I fucking freaked out and rolled over onto my stomach. He pressed his whole body up against mine and whispered, 'Oh, so that's how you want it?' and all I could do was cry. Thank God, someone's cell phone rang and Corinna's mother jumped up. As soon as he heard, he rolled away and pretended to be asleep. I think she just turned the ringer off though and laid back down. I didn't move until I heard him start to breathe kinda loudly. Once I knew he was asleep, I got up and ran out. Corinna lives in the same condo complex as me but on the other side and I didn't want to run all the way home. I just ran to the closest neighbor I knew and knocked on their door. They called the police, then my mom. Oh, so when I ran out, I left my cell phone and I didn't get it back until today when the police gave me all of my stuff back."

After I'm out of questions and she has told me all of the details, I remember that Dana thinks I'm still on the phone with my mother. My mind wanders briefly to what story I'll make up to explain my prolonged conversation. I'm snapped back to Natalia when she tells me that she has to hang up because the police are at her house to ask more questions. She ends with, "I'll text you later. Thanks for listening. See you tomorrow."

I find myself more affected by her story than I should be, lost in the sadness that she had to endure that fear. I'm left wanting to know more, unwilling to leave the conversation. Instead, I just say, "I hope you feel better. Goodbye," and hang up. I collect myself for a moment before I resume my own life.

Chapter 5

After our first phone conversation there are thousands upon thousands of text messages exchanged all hours of the day and night, with an endless variety of topics. Everything carries on quite seamlessly until the one irreversible conversation that unfolds shortly after school ends. Natalia innocently texts, "I wish I could stay in Alabama because I like it soooo much better." Her sadness and perceived solitude pains me despite its root in typical teenage angst.

She continues, "Nobody misses me at home anyway."

I respond, "Don't be silly, that's not true."

"Who misses me?"

I list several names of friends ending with, "And of course you know how I feel."

The combination of my ability to manipulate a conversation and her desire to play along prompt, "No, how do you feel about me?"

"Well, I love you," and hit send.

I have never said those words without feeling the full gravity they convey and as I sit at my kitchen table feeling my heartbeat in my ears, I feel the gravity this time too. I don't necessarily regret sending that, resigning to the contingency that if she has a negative reaction I will explain it as platonic, familial love.

Although the feelings are from a twisted place, they register as real as any feeling I have ever felt. The authenticity of these emotions makes them impossible to deny despite the impropriety that unmistakably swells. I want to stop, wish I could go back and undo what has been done to make her feel as though our relationship is acceptable. But the veracity that I sense every time I see her name on my phone brushes that feeling back down and allows me to continue on the same self-destructive path. The quest for her happiness lies somewhere intuitively intertwined with my own.

"Say it again," I see on my screen.

I snub the escape she provides and pause to wonder. Did she accidentally delete it? Is she saving it to show her mother or the authorities because I have crossed the line? Does she not believe me?

"I love you. Why did you ask me to resend?"

"Because I wanted to make sure that you really meant it," she fires immediately.

"Yes I mean it Natalia," I send after three attempts to spell her name correctly using her full name for final emphasis.

My mind races all night. Neither of us sends another text, perhaps both digesting the disconnected conversation. As I lay in bed I remark for the first time that I'm a French teacher who told a student I love her. The irony existing only on a plain of coincidence, not an omen.

With school done for the year we become creative in the ways we see one another. When Talia asks me if we'll be able to get together one Saturday my first reaction is, "How will you get out of the house?"

"I'll tell mom you are going to help me with the summer assignment for your class," immediately back. Talia tells her mother that I've offered to help her on weekends. Unheard of, inappropriate and so transparent it's laughable. I'm amazed how easily she can leave her house with a story so close to the truth, yet avoiding suspicion.

"I'll tell her that I'm going to watch one of your bike races," she very naturally suggests as an alibi. Natalia knows that I ride my mountain bike every weekend so she asks what kind of bike I have and where races are held. She asks to better know me but has also committed the information to memory to use as a pretense in her excuses.

Our time together is spent going for walks and talking about the same basic things that comprise our text messages. The slight edge of intimacy is missing to save us the agony of confronting the reality that clearly lies ahead. One day, driving her home from school, in the course of conversation, I put my hand out, palm up in the natural gesturing of my speech. As it is outstretched, hanging directly over the top of the stick shift she places her left hand on mine and we interlace our fingers quite ordinarily.

I only glance at her a second as she grins, shy and uncomfortable. Her eyebrows sheepishly arced to ask, "Is this ok?" Without a word, while trying to keep the car on the road I return her inquisitive glance with a look of reassurance, clear my throat and continue the pointless conversation.

She texts absent any discernible segue, "Are you a good kisser?"

In tune with the already flirtatious environment I have created my reply is, "I guess you'll have to find out for yourself."

My response solicits the exact ruse for which I was striving. It opens up a conversation about when we will kiss and how long before we can. She plays right along, "So what are you doing tonight because I'm free? LOL."

We continue with no resolution other than, "I think we'll know when the time is right," assuming some nebulous higher power will guide us. My surrender to a predestined faith makes me sound not only sage but also non-committal. Now that the wheels have been set in motion I can make it happen.

I tell Talia I have a bike race two weeks in advance so that she can clear it with her mother but I know it's going to take more juggling for me. Firstly, the race is my son's birthday and we already have a party planned. I also have to call a friend with whom I teach because he races too and I need to avoid an uncomfortable situation when we see one another. Dana ok's my absence because I'll be back in time for the party. I call a colleague, John, who also races and give him the basic run down of how Natalia has latched onto me because of her problems – someone else who buys my bullshit. Once I have all of my obstacles hurdled I tell Talia to clear her Saturday morning which thrills her.

I pick her up just after six a.m. and we drive to breakfast. Before we leave her street she asks, "Can I put on my iPod? I made a playlist to commemorate the occasion."

The first song that comes on is "First Date" by Blink-182. She looks at me and smiles, proud of her creativity. I miss some of the songs while we are talking but comment on the ones I hear. When I recognize, "Come a Little Bit Closer" by Jay Black and the Americans and "Kind and Generous" by Natalie Merchant I tell her, "Oh I love this song."

When the diner comes into sight my heart races. I think to myself, "I should not be here with her," but I push through. I put the car in neutral, apply the parking brake and ask, "Will you wait here a second so I can get something out of the back?"

I fumble around the trunk as though looking for something but I'm really trying to flush the last butterflies from my stomach.

When I'm done I close the back hatch, walk to the passenger side and open her door. She steps out and begins to walk toward the restaurant, before she reaches the end of the car I take her arm.

The look of confusion on her face makes my heart hurt. The misperception disappears almost instantly when she realizes what is happening. As a nervous smile forms on the edges of her lips, I lean in and kiss her with enough conviction so she knows I'm not afraid, yet not too forceful. It's a long kiss and once we begin I'm anxious to see her reaction. My gut tells me she'll pull away, to the contrary, she leans closer.

Her lips are soft and her tongue seems small, reminding me of her age. That thought is rushed from my mind when I recognize the mint toothpaste she used this morning. Her tongue moves slowly in the space between our mouths. This feels wrong but good simultaneously. I keep my eyes closed, afraid of watching life go by normally while I behave so egregiously.

When the kiss ends she opens her eyes and smiles a shy, adolescent smile expressing so much more than I want to see. I have no idea how I want her to react but having not thought about it prior, I'm at the mercy of inertia. I say exactly what I'm thinking, "I'm fucked if anyone finds out we just kissed."

She giggles, "Oh don't worry, and nobody's going to find out."

I successfully force my mind to disconnect while we enter the diner, are shown our seats and right up until she shows me pictures that she colored on vacation. They are Care Bears, each one complete with a theme and a meaning. The similarity to how a daughter would treat a father makes me achingly uncomfortable. My ears are hot from the embarrassment that she colored them for me and my tongue was just in her mouth. I feel dirty but switch to the detached ego state and do what comes naturally, I block out the awkwardness and continue seamlessly.

Seeing the different hues of rainbows and lollipops that brightly highlight the page I feel a bizarre sensation between my stomach and chest. It feels like nerves and feels like hunger to the point that I dismiss it as a muscle spasm. The feeling leaves as quickly but before it subsides I feel lost, like a blackout, impossible to focus.

Once the wave crests, I'm able to listen to explanations of what each picture represents. She talks about where she was when she colored them and why she wrote each caption underneath. "I love rainbows, sweet candy lollipops, what cute Care Bears." Her captions are absent innuendo and full of pure innocence. I'm relieved when she reaches the last picture, allowing me to change the subject to something less juvenile.

Part of me is dreading the race knowing I have to introduce her to people I know. I can only say, "This is Natalia and she is a student of mine." I'm hypersensitive, feeling like I must prepare for anything. I imagine how I might react to the same situation or more accurately how I should react. I find no peace but more interestingly, no cause to reevaluate my motives.

Reactions are mixed making me too scared to truly interpret them. Some of my friends greet her warmly and without adverse feedback while others stop in mid, "Nice to meet y—." Natalia is composed and to each person simply says, "Hi, how are you?"

I don't do well in the race, too concerned with looking good in my spandex. This obsession comforts me in a unique way, consuming my thoughts during each lap. When I come past the start/finish line each time instead of using the flat open space to sprint, I search for her in the crowd. I think about our kiss wondering if she is too. At times, I'm regretful but also remember how it felt good to have my body pressed up against her feeling her lips on mine.

The kiss awakens the latent physicality underlying all of our contact. We spend several afternoons together in the beginning of summer but do not work on her assignment. We spend the time in the back seat of my car. I can sense her exploration, curiosity driving her hands. I feel her linger at places not because they are erogenous zones but because she has never felt hair on a man's chest. The first time I take off my shirt she sits back and stares for longer than is comfortable. Long enough that I wonder if something has frightened her.

I ask, "Are you okay?"

All she seems able to do is nod hesitantly, making me terribly sad. I feel the reality that I am doing something wrong without the ability to process it. I never take this feeling to the next logical level which would be the impetus to stop and undo the already wreaked havoc. The path toward any sort of introspection is a dead end because somewhere underneath that depth of thought lies answers I do not want to distinguish. My despondency convincing enough that the destination is not somewhere I want to explore. I dangerously disengage to the point that I doubt my own presence in the moment arriving at a dreamlike state where we are both left staring at one another, both of us in awe of me.

It's difficult to offer an explanation as to what it's like to be entrenched in these decisions, feeling as if I was illustrated into this landscape, the events leading me here only half-decided. I have merely a cameo in every decision, not a supporting role. I have the opportunity to say no, to change my mind at any time but at the moment the threshold is crossed I feel chauffeured down this road and am now lost. So many decisions seem to neglect my influence on the outcome of events, feeling disempowered to exert my opinion by my own ambivalence.

When Natalia is done silently dealing with unknown inhibitions she presses her lips to mine again. I let her take all of the steps that stretch beyond the limits of our current scope. Much like everything else up to this point, I lead her to the edge of the final step and allow her to push through the barrier. It's essentially her decision to progress.

Chapter 6

In the midst of a typical phone conversation, Natalia tells me, "I saw my therapist this afternoon." She explains how I came up in session as someone trustworthy with whom she has a positive relationship. I know nothing about the therapeutic process. I understand neither how nor why someone goes to a stranger about their problems. As she speaks, my mind wanders to what it would be like for me to sit on a therapist's couch, unable to fathom telling anyone my secrets. Talia concludes, "Chris thought it would be a good idea for you to come in for session with the three of us."

I immediately see the opening for me to ingratiate myself further and potentially win over her mother as well as Chris, but Natalia tells me that she is nervous, not wanting to risk suspicion. I agree but explain, "It could be useful to have an ally in case we ever need their support."

"What if they're able to sense there's something going on?" she asks.

"Hey, don't worry. I'll answer their questions and I promise I can convince them that there's nothing bad about this." Part of the reason why I alleviate her fears so nonchalantly is because the meeting seems far-fetched.

One week after I forget about the conversation, I receive a voicemail from Chris asking me to join them exactly as Talia said. What is most unnerving is that I know her ulterior motive, certain I'm being sized up. Kathy, Natalia's mother, Chris and maybe even Natalia are going to be feeling me out to ascertain my intentions. I suspect Kathy will sift through some underlying reservations about why I'm a mentor in her daughter's life and Chris will be verifying that all this is psychologically just. I fully understand the search for the supporting ethos, as well as what I must do to receive their stamp of approval, and sadly, am exhilarated by the challenge.

I arrive first and sit nervously in the waiting room. Kathy and Natalia arrive after only a few minutes. The awkward greeting hangs over us only momentarily before being rescued by Chris. In that tongue-tied moment I'm overcome with a strange feeling that Kathy might not mind if I fulfilled all the roles that come with standing in for a father-figure. Chris emerges from her office with a wide smile and extends her hand as I turn to say, "Hello." I have a discomfited feeling, knowing I'm here to lie in a place where honesty is necessary to facilitate healing.

Everyone except Chris fidgets in their seat as we begin, throwing illegible sideways glances. Chris brings me up to speed with what has gone on in their sessions regarding the events in Talia's life and their effects. She speaks of abandonment, confusion and feelings of loss and regret, beginning with the depths of sadness over the loss of her father's mental capacity in a car accident.

When Talia was nine her father was seriously impaired in a head-on collision. She had told me the story before but I listen intently anyway. He absorbed the majority of the impact on the back of his head, causing major brain damage. Natalia has discussed with Chris how the accident has left him almost impossible to have a relationship with because of his limited capacity. Chris continues by telling me how Talia thought she found the acceptance of an adult male in Jared, Corinna's step-father, only to be betrayed. I listen and nod despite my already intimate knowledge.

After the recap she looks at Natalia very intently before turning her eyes towards me, "Natalia has spoken very highly of you. She feels comfortable speaking to you and trusts you."

Chris knows I have offered a shoulder to cry on and the in-depth discussions Natalia and I have had on a variety of emotional levels. All of this makes Natalia, Kathy and Chris happy but they must make absolutely certain I'm not going to be the continuation of a disturbing pattern. Nobody in this room can infer from what has been conveyed today that it's already too late.

"Jim, before we go any further, we must all make absolute certain that you're not going to be another man in Natalia's life that disappoints her," Chris says to me with a snarl that I feel projects some of her own past onto me.

I ask for no elaboration, I simply reassure by leaning a few degrees forward before I say, "I will not let Natalia down." I may have emoted too much but the silence in the room coupled with the look that Kathy and Chris exchange reassures me they are sold.

The plan is to form a therapy team where Kathy serves as the eyes and ears of Natalia's life at home and I serve as the same in school. Chris details everything systematically before asking, "Do you understand what we are striving for here?" I nod in agreement so she continues, "What types of positive peer groups can you put Natalia in touch with?" My safest route is the alibi I've already used, mountain biking.

I know that this is the perfect cover for Talia to be out of the house and take up the majority of a day. Chris turns to Talia and asks, "How does that sound? Do you think you'd like to learn to Mountain Bike?"

Natalia's response is an unconvincing nod that falls far short of the effort I have just put into our story. I wish that she would act slightly more enthused at the solidarity I have created. In any case, the topic is concluded with her underwhelming agreement and Chris punctuates it with a definitive, "Ok, good then."

Chris then asks Natalia to leave the office so that the adults can talk, of all the people in the room, I relate best to the teenager. I feel the urge to leave too knowing the adults are going to ask the tough questions now. But this is my time to shine. This is the area in which I have honed my true expertise and I feel a flash of excitement at the test that lies before me.

Chris begins by sitting up straight and telling me directly, "If you weighed three hundred pounds and were bald and ugly, I wouldn't have to say what I am about to. But since you are such an attractive young man it must be made very certain that we take all necessary precautions to make sure that Natalia does not grow to have a crush on you. Talia tells me that you are the topic of conversation amongst many girls at your school, and I can see why."

I feel like I'm blushing, having no idea how to respond to her shrouded and potentially ensnaring compliments.

"More importantly," she quickly reiterates, "It must be clear that you cannot be another male in her life who lets her down. If you do, it will be a devastation that she may never recover from."

I don't know why she does not strike a chord that I have already violated this request. Somehow, instead of seeing a thwarting of my responsibility, I vow to not disappoint her. I convince myself that if I remain in her life in this exact capacity I will be realizing that promise.

Chris suggests we set ground rules that protect against any situation that could possibly compromise Natalia's fragile emotions. The primary provision is that I am never alone with Talia. This includes in her house and in my car. Chris tells me that she has, "Omitted any school related restrictions because there is already a policy in place for how a teacher should act with a student, I'm sure." She assumes that my familiarity with those policies covers me in such situations.

I've already violated this stipulation with her mother's consent so the silence surprises me. Chris turns to Kathy and asks her if there is anything that she would like to add. Kathy squirms uncomfortably in her seat and shifts her gaze between the floor, me and something on the desk over my left shoulder. She launches into how great of a guy I am before, "Deep down I know that you have been a great influence on Talia. Her grades have improved and she is just happier around the house." Her preamble seems slightly overdone but calculated to be so. As she continues, she cannot sit still in her chair and I know that something unpalatable is about to be said. And here it is, "It's just that every time you come to pick her up, I feel like I'm letting my daughter go on a date. It makes me uncomfortable sometimes."

Is she just saying this to sound good in front of the therapist or does she really mean it? She comes across so sincerely yet is a contradiction from what I'm greeted with in her foyer. Before the sentence ends and before anyone else can respond, she tries to clarify, "Jim, I know full well that there is absolutely nothing going on between you two. I also know that you truly look out for her best interest but it's hard sometimes to tell myself that everything is ok." I can't help but feel deceived and pointlessly irritated at her uneducated choice of words.

I prepare to reply and falsely put her mind at ease but Chris interjects, "So Jim has already been alone with Natalia? Where has he driven her?" She asks the question looking at me but thankfully shifts her gaze toward Kathy once finished speaking.

I feel a wave of panic climb up my body but before Chris can see me fidget in my loud leather chair Kathy squirms again, "Well yes, he has taken her to a bike race and once brought her home from school because I asked him."

Without replying to Kathy, Chris looks at me, "Do you know what the board of education policy is where you work?" Her tone direct, almost angry. I tell her the truth, only because it benefits me. The policy is that a student can be driven by a teacher if the parent has given permission. I looked no further into the policy as to whether it must be written or can be verbal or how far in advance is necessary.

Chris looks flustered for the first time and asks Kathy, "Why didn't you offer this information earlier in light of the rules we were putting in place?"

Confusion grips Kathy's face when she explains, "I didn't think it was a big deal but I agree now that it might not be a good idea." I feel bad as I watch her vacillate on this critical point knowing that she feels embarrassed for her cavalier attitude after being scolded. Her stern façade is transparent but I refrain from saying anything.

I can feel the shift of the entire atmosphere in the office after Chris finds out she was so far out of the loop. The session was well choreographed until Chris and Kathy divide on this point. They were representing a united front to prevent Natalia from being exploited that has crumbled.

"Is there anything else that I should know before we conclude?" Chris asks with a pitch to her voice that clearly sounds perturbed. She seems to feel not only like an outsider but as though she realizes her stance was the anomaly. After we agree on the reiterated terms of our direction Chris asks me to leave the room so she can just have a few final words with Kathy. I am confident and relieved to be finished.

When I walk into the waiting room Natalia is staring intently at her phone. She looks up at me and what I read on her face is a sense of accomplishment. It makes me feel ill to have this harmful bond but at the same time it provides a sense of relief. Perhaps this will alleviate some of our necessary concealment. I wish that my distorted differentiation between privacy and se-crecy was not such a prevalent aspect of my personality. This is the place where duplicity should be seen as not only harmful to me but also to Natalia.

Right now she theoretically has a perfectly suitable associ-ation with secrecy. All of her confidences are age appropriate. Maybe she smoked a cigarette or took a drink from the liquor cabinet but those are the types of things that a girl her age should be managing. Kissing your French teacher is too surreptitious. I see her being a kid on her phone and I want something different for her than forced silence. I want it but am powerless to pre-clude her from it.

I have just enough time to make small talk about what she is doing the rest of the weekend when Kathy and Chris exit the office. "It was nice to meet you and thank you for including me in this," I say to Chris before I file out behind Kathy and her daughter.

Once outside, "That was tough Jim. Come on I'll buy you a cup of coffee," Kathy says as she nods her head toward a coffee shop next door. We exchange a few more pleasantries as we walk inside. Standing in line waiting for my coffee, Kathy turns to say,

"You know, that thing about not driving her places, I'm not worried about that. I just said it to agree."

As she speaks she places her hand on my shoulder in a gesture that seems to create another unsolicited bond. Her touch says she knows we're breaking the rules but doing it together makes it permissible. As I am processing I realize that her hand lingers just a bit longer on my shoulder than is comfortable. Perhaps the meaning of this meeting is altogether different from what I originally thought.

I'm snapped out of my daze by, "Sir, your coffee. Large, regular." I open the tab and take a sip burning my tongue slightly, a welcome sensation after choosing to be numb through the last hour.

After we see the therapist the advice and parameters set down are completely disregarded, providing a heightened sense of protection. A feeling that Kathy is even more lackadaisical than we previously thought permeates our resulting plans. Natalia and I spend several hours on the phone debriefing what took place in the office. I tell her what happened when she left the room and she tells me what her mother said on the way home. I don't find it odd that she tells me her mother wouldn't stop talking about how attractive I am and what she would do with me if I weren't married because it's clear that she is just another female who my sexuality has infected.

Chapter 7

One day, midmorning, at my summer job, running a boy's day camp, a text reads, "I think we should smoke pot together." Much like all other suggestions that push the limits I feel the same exhilaration. The potential to keep another secret from the world that only the two of us know attracts me magnetically.

I respond easily, half the plan already formulated before I hit send. I have smoked pot only a few times since I returned from France after having lived there in college, taking a few weekend trips to Amsterdam. The fear of being caught has prevented me from experimenting more but here is an opportunity I wish not to forsake. I revel in her faith and love the control I'll have when this comes to fruition.

None of the necessary lies seem a deterrent as I strategize. I fish for answers to find her comfort level and what I should expect from this day. She doesn't hesitate when I offer, "How about we go back to my house," as an option for where we can smoke, knowing I will call out of work.

Dana works at the same camp and our kids go there with us so I have several bases covered all with one excuse. She is shocked when I wake up the chosen morning and tell her, "I think I'm going to call Sr. Karen and stay home today," because I never skip work during the summer.

With unforeseen difficulty, I shake off the guilt at having all four members of my family kiss me goodbye and say, "I love you Dad, hope you feel better."

As soon as they leave I clean the house, trying to hide the abundant evidence of three young children. I set out the clothes I'm going to wear when Talia arrives, a gray sleeveless T-Shirt with baggy blue jeans exactly as she has said she loves. As I prepare to pick her up I account for many different pitfalls but the unforeseeable ones scare me most. I try hard to gauge Dana's demeanor in the hour before she leaves for work and nothing indicates that she is suspicious. I make my final commitment to act.

Since Talia lives close to camp I ensure that there are no surprise visits. With a stop in the camp parking lot, I loosen one of the terminals on Dana's car battery so that when she tries to start it she will have to call me. I'll know if she intends on leaving earlier than when I'm expecting her and better yet, may have to come rescue her. Either way I have guaranteed a warning call. The mindless and depraved decisions I make are difficult for me to comprehend in reference to the person I have been my whole life. But for now, with my goal clearly poised, I am focused intently.

I pick up Natalia and we go straight home. My house is situated three quarters of a mile down a dead end road in a small lake community. Dana is friendly with most of the women on my block, the fear that one of them may ask her who I was driving with is almost enough to make me cancel the entire tryst. I contemplate asking Natalia to duck down in the car or dropping her off on an adjacent road but cannot degrade her that way. I drive down the road as quickly as possible without seeming erratic and luckily no one sees us.

Part Two

As soon as we're safely in my house I tell her, "I have to shower because I'm all sweaty from work this morning." I'm back out in three minutes after dressing to her specifications. When she sees me walk around the corner she swoons as though out of breath. She walks to me, throws her arms around my shoulders and steps into a hug with her whole body. We stand, locked in a long embrace eventually leading to an even longer kiss.

As it tapers I ask, "What do you want to do now?" needing her to verify my control.

"What are the choices?" she asks.

I pause, trying to focus on too many factors, "Well, we can go play miniature golf, watch a movie, take a walk, we can smoke of course and....Well that's about it, I guess."

"Let's smoke," she says without hesitation.

After we walk out to my small, enclosed sun-porch I show her how to use the bowl by taking an imaginary hit. She watches with a grin but tells me that she still doesn't understand and needs my help. I chose the porch so that the smell of pot won't be overpowering when my family arrives home. We sit so closely on the small bench right outside the front door that our arms touch.

I pack the piece all the while explaining the important of separating stems from leaves. Her silence tells me she doesn't care what I'm saying but I talk to alleviate our nervous energy. I take the first hit and immediately feel the rush of euphoria, enjoying it for just a moment before paranoia overcomes me. She is on my right and I have my arm around her with the cigarette lighter ready to ignite.

I ask in a calm voice, "Are you ready?"
She replies nervously, "Uh –huh."
As I flick the lighter I tell her to inhale. She takes a hit, holds it and coughs. It takes her longer than I would like to calm down,

she hacks long enough for me to panic when it seems she may not stop. I wonder anxiously what I would do if I had to take her to the hospital or call 911. This only accelerates my heart rate and consequently my panic. Finally, she collects herself and sits back to relax.

Two more hits each, then we banter aimlessly, attempting to kill another uncomfortable silence. It could be the crest of the paranoia but I think I'm coherent enough to realize I've made a bad decision. I just backed myself into a corner from which I have no escape. She breaks the silence and my concentration when she whips her head around and sticks her tongue in my mouth. I hear little moans escape her not from anything that I'm doing but just from the sheer desire that she is exuding as we play out this unspoken part of our plan.

Because the porch is mostly glass and it's the middle of summer it's uncomfortably hot, we move inside. I think walking to the bedroom is too presumptuous and what remains of my conscience reminds me that it is the bed my wife and I share so I sit down in the middle of the couch. She straddles immediately. I allow her to dictate the pace. I gently place my hands on her hips and kiss her only as hungrily as she kisses me. She moves her hips in a rhythm as she kisses harder while I move my hands to massage her back because that's what feels safe. Everything is calculated to make sure that there is no misinterpretation that I'm pushing.

We kiss for hours. I make sure that when my hands move to her side she doesn't flinch. Her head moves to my ear and she nibbles it a notch harder than I would like. I grab her and she grinds harder. Her short shorts ride up even higher on her thigh allowing me to feel her tense muscles. She stops for just a second and I wonder if it's me or because she has lost her capacity to concentrate. The ensuing audible sigh lets me know it's the latter. I move my hands up the back of her thighs to the center of her body and feel stubble. It excites me but I am also aware of her reaction. She is unwavering.

As time passes, I become weary, more scared, she asks hurriedly, "Are you ok?"

When I answer, "Yes," she throws all of her energy back into her hips. I judge our time together by how badly my jaw hurts from my mouth being opened. My legs have fallen asleep from being in the same position and my wrist also is sore although she is showing no signs of tiring. Her arousal only increases.

Without warning and suddenly enough to startle me, she pulls back, takes a deep breath that borders on a sigh and says, "Let's go play miniature golf."

It's somewhat forced and isn't exactly what she wants as much as contrived. Despite her abrupt interjection, I honor her request without inquiry. I corral her toward the door and walk to the car, my head on a swivel. Thankfully, no neighbors.

After I close the passenger door and walk around to my side, I say through the open window, "Oops, I forgot something inside. I'll be right back."

I walk back inside to put all the toys and kid's books back on the floor. In the event that we don't return I need to leave the house as Dana last saw to avoid suspicion. I return to the car, hop in and start it. She says nothing, just sits next to me with a grin that looks as if she's in a stupor. I wonder if I look as incoherent. I'm awake enough to drive but still pensive.

It's unlike Dana to not have called by now. She has always been clingy and a bit claustrophobic but that is largely my fault. I only know how to keep secrets and am adept at existing behind a constant shroud of concealment. I play everything close to my chest and without ever trying, have become an unknowable person to everyone around me, especially my wife.

One night, two years ago I was awoken at two a. m. by the overhead light being turned on and Dana screaming, "How could you do this to me? How could you embarrass me like this?"

"What are you talking about?" is all I could mumble.

"I went into your email and read about your little dalliances with Jackie, and Lourdes and Stephanie, and Brittney. You make me sick Jim, you really do."

I could not fathom what she was talking about, I had no dalliances. I recognized the names as former students with whom I occasionally corresponded but not as a source of necessary suspicion. Some of them inquired about getting together when home for semester break and although taken with a grain of salt I did not tell them, "No," and that is what upset her. Dana was angry because I had led them to think that time alone with me was acceptable while putting her in the position to look foolish.

I saw nothing wrong with these correspondences, enough in control that if an e-mail was misconstrued I would be able to quell the desire. This is the naïveté with which I live my life and I cannot avoid feeling the pain that it causes Dana. Sadly, I find neither the empowerment nor the ability to change my behavior.

As Natalia and I are driving to play miniature golf, Dana calls. I turn down the radio and shush Natalia, hoping her presence is hidden.

"How are you feeling hon? Headache any better?" Dana asks with genuine sympathy. Her kindness and concern hurt me for her.

"Eh, so so. Ya know," I reply, trying to say as little as possible for my benefit as well as Natalia's.

"What have you been doing? I hope you are resting," she says softly.

"I am," choosing only to answer the latter question because the former is an impossibility.

"I feel ok, I guess. A little bit better," I think of Ferris Bueller's Day Off as I speak these words, amazingly finding another channel of functionality.

"Do you want me to bring anything home with me?" I feel my pulse increase but before I can react she continues, "Do you need me to come home now to take care of you? I can tell Sr. Karen that I need to go."

I delay my answer to not seem panicked, "No, I'll be ok, I'm just resting so there is nothing that you could do anyway. But thanks for offering."

"Ok, well I hope you feel better and I'll keep my phone near me just in case, I'll call you on my way home. I love you Jim. Bye," she ends.

I want to say something to alleviate the tension in the car but don't know what. "So obviously my reason for playing hooky today was that I was sick," I say with a chuckle that sounds more embarrassed than apologetic.

"Yeah, I figured that," she says apathetically as she looks out her window. Since the look on her face already displays that the moment in unpalatable I decide to broach a conversation I've been delaying.

Dana is the only other person with whom I've ever discussed Carla. When our relationship began to blossom I told her out of the same guilt I feel now and her reaction shocked me. She felt that it wasn't a shared responsibility, rather, "How fucked up it was that someone could do that to a teenager." At the moment that Dana began to ask questions I became defensive, distraught over the conflict I felt to justify that chapter of my life. I opened up to let her into my world, yet felt angry that she was attacking Carla. I felt it was my responsibility to the person that Carla was in my life to explain why her behavior was acceptable. I didn't fight to make anything tolerable, just tried to make Dana understand that it wasn't all bad. Carla had her reasons, which I neither understood nor agreed with, but they existed, nonetheless and were therefore valid.

I was so upset with Dana and her vicarious defense of my childhood that I had to stop the conversation. I withheld the rest of my details and hurried to the end searching for a futile segue. I ended by asking, "Do you think less of me for what I just told you?" petrified of the answer but amazed to hear an assault on Carla for which I was unprepared.

"Are you crazy Jim? How could I think less of you? I feel so sorry for you. How could an adult in a position of authority allow that to happen?" she followed with renewed venom. I had never felt sorry for myself and didn't think anyone else would either. This conversation uncomfortably changed that perception.

Her incredulous questions kept coming, "You don't really believe that she was a virgin do you?" and "You realize that you never truly married her right?"

I took immediate offense and defended the details upon which Carla insisted. With each answer I detached further, my only validation being, "That's what Carla told me," therefore it had to be true. The possibility that Carla was not a virgin steals the breath immediately from my lungs but I do not let Dana see. My only coping skill is to chase the reality immediately from my mind and agree. I walk away, into the same bathroom where I masturbated endlessly in the shower and sit on the edge of the tub, rubbing my temples, repeating, "Carla did not lie to me. She loved me. I was her first."

"So there is something that I have to tell you," I begin to Natalia, "When I was in high school I had a long term, sexual relationship with my French teacher."

I thought about how I was going to broach this for weeks. I came up with nothing that seemed to make sense so I speak extemporaneously. I didn't intend to convey a unique coincidence but as I speak the words they ring like I'm informing her of one more thing we have in common, instead of a straight line connection between two sets of offenses. With my tone of voice and fancy wording I manipulate the conversation, omitting the grievance.

I don't even have the consciousness to fear Natalia jumping to that conclusion herself. "Do you still see her? Was she pretty? Did you end it with her or did she end it with you?" are her only questions. They are teenage concerns that appeal only to her immediate perception. I respond and wait for how she processes my responses.

Her next words are, "I'm hungry. Can we stop for something to eat?"

I'm relieved, happy as always to disassociate from the reality right in front of me.

Miniature golf is a farce because I'm still stoned. Every time Talia brushes up against me I feel arousal, immediately followed by a dirty sensation. Luckily for my conscience the hierarchy of immorality operates on a sliding scale. As if being in public makes my choices any worse than sitting on my couch.

The later it becomes the more paranoia grips my every thought. I fear Talia's mother finding out where her daughter is or Dana taking it upon herself to come home out of concern. If she does, my plan is useless because she would avoid bothering me. She may simply call her dad to fix the battery, or a friend.

I begin to feel an unnamed dread that occupies my entire mind until Natalia asks with a sad face, "Why are you so quiet?"

"Oh, it's nothing. I'm just starting to come down," which is the truth but I need to show her more attention so she doesn't feel slighted. I regret this whole day now, realizing how close I am to being caught compounded by lamenting my choices because Dana is a good person who cares about me. Her offer to come home makes me feel loved, a feeling I have so desperately wanted from her for so long. Despite Dana's ignorance of my need to be desired, I fear we have drifted irreparably apart. All these thoughts interrupt any attempt to exist in the ugly reality I've created.

Natalia and I arrive back at my house and sit on the couch simultaneously. Immediately she kisses me hard as though the three hours spent without our mouths locked have exponentially built her arousal. My mind races. I think about taking her home and being back before Dana arrives. What if Natalia's mother is looking for her? Do I have any incriminating receipts in my pockets? I need to spray the porch again to make sure the smell is gone.

After kissing for much less time than earlier, I say, "We should really be going."

"Oh, do we have to?" she whines and puts her head on my shoulder, nibbling my ear at the same time.

"Yeah, we really should," nervous she may put up a fight. After a few more exchanges varying in playfulness, we reach the car. In my haste, I'm much less cautious, having almost forgotten the potential for neighbors to see us. As she slowly walks to the passenger's side, horrid premonitions of Dana's minivan pulling down the street flash in my mind. I have literally and figuratively trapped myself in this decision.

Conversation is pleasant during the ride to her house. "I had a great day with you," she tells me with a cute smile, accentuating her dimples.

"When can we do it again?"

Feeling the full weight of accumulated stress, "Real soon, I hope," I fake through my best smile.

Five minutes before we reach Natalia's house Dana calls. With exasperation she explains, "My car won't start, Jim. I think it's the battery. What can I do?"

Panic and pot wiped that part of my plan from memory. More specifically, I detached myself from that step once checked off of my list this morning. As I'm about to speak I hear her ask someone for help. I don't know and don't ask who but after more background noise the car starts.

She barks out of frustration, "Ok. I'll be home soon," and hangs up.

I drop Natalia off with neither discussion nor ceremony. As far as her mother knows Natalia was home all day so she cannot arouse any suspicion otherwise. We kiss goodbye at the red light before her development which serves as our farewell.

When I pull in front of her house she simply says, "Ok, I love you. Bye," and hops out of the car. Her calm demeanor is exactly the opposite of the fright that envelops me. Before she even turns her back to walk away I begin the mad dash driven by speculative horror if I arrive home after Dana. I look at the clock and do quick math to figure out two different scenarios, one with the traffic lights on my side and one against.

My breath is shallow and accelerated until I pull on my block and see an empty driveway. I bound up the steps, three at a time taking another sweep everywhere to make sure that there are no traces of my day. I left the sun porch windows open and sprayed half of a bottle of Febreeze to kill the lingering smell of depravity.

Dana and my children arrive five minutes afterward and the second I see them I feel the tight, nauseas knot in my stomach. I don't know what causes it but it's a vaguely familiar feeling that hurts increasingly worse as I resume normal life. This sensation washes over me the way I imagine anesthesia grips a person. Except instead of numbing, this is acclimation to feeling again. It's an allover pain that makes focusing difficult.

All day I have detached from the truth, yet at the sight of my family, I return. My stomach aches of regret. Sadly, my remorse is fleeting because I will text Talia tonight. I will entertain future plans. I will discuss what a great day we had, joking and laughing about mini-golf and getting stoned. I will trivialize so much of my distorted realism unable to foresee worse deeds than today.

As I tuck my kids into bed I feel like I'm reuniting with them after a long absence. I'm extra sensitive, kissing them twice as much as I normally would and spending extra time with their bedtime stories. I reunite with them as much as myself, the part of me that's a father was gone all day. This represents the longest I have ever been away from me. My two worlds came crashing in on one another, and the little boy with the big secret met the father who would do anything for his children.

The abandoned ego was unstoppable in the quest to satisfy adolescent desires. I fall asleep unable to peacefully decide if I feel proud that I put so many pieces of the puzzle together successfully or if I should explore the terrible shame of myriad betrayals.

Chapter 8

Frank has been my best friend since ninth grade. He was much better adjusted to the social aspects of high school and was more like minded than anyone else I had met freshman year. We shared much of the grief when Kevin's mother passed away and despite our inability to process, that experience created an unspoken bond. I would always admire his confidence to approach anyone, especially in college and introduce himself, astonished by his warm manner, devoid any egotism.

The testament to our friendship was the phone call I received a year after I was married. The phone startled me awake at six a.m. but the voice on the other end was more disturbing. It was Frank, in tears. He had recently moved back to New Jersey after graduation, but was offered a job in Washington D.C.

He cried because his father advised him against moving away which we both knew was because of how much Frank Sr. was going to miss him. I felt the same selfish urges, knowing if he moved he was never coming back. As I wiped away the sleep, "It is a great opportunity that you should seize. You know your parents will always welcome you back." He left that morning to flourish personally and professionally.

Dana and I visited often as our two families grew together, the distance never impeding our friendship. Unfortunately, neither Frank nor his family could escape being tainted by my self-interest. Late in the summer Natalia spends a week in Maryland with family, coinciding with a long weekend we are spending with Frank.

I send Talia the typically coy text, "Ya know, I'm gonna be in Virginia while you're in Maryland….rendez-vous? Haha."

Simple bait that she takes, "YES!! Where?"

Frank's computer is kept on his kitchen counter which means I spend the first two days of our visit trying to view MapQuest without being seen. My sole purpose is to search the distance from South Riding, Virginia to Rock Hall, Maryland. I am discouraged when I scan to the bottom of the screen and read, two hours and thirty-two minutes.

This plot was a foregone conclusion before I even proposed the idea so the distance only serves to quantify my infatuation, fueled by the six weeks since I've last seen her. All that remains is the familiar task of concocting my story to feed everyone around me. I need to make it acceptable to be gone at least five hours for the travel time alone, overnight is the only option.

Dana has already posited that something is very wrong with me and consequently, our marriage. She has sat me down several times, "Jim I don't like the way things are between us. You never talk to me and are constantly on your phone."

She has never been one to sugar coat her feelings, much to my chagrin, "Are you fucking someone else?" Her language often abhorrent in front of our kids or anyone else unlucky enough to catch the shrapnel of her outbursts.

"No," I promise refusing to elaborate any further. No conversation is resolved and the further I withdraw the stronger she persists.

She shoves a book in my face one evening, "Male Depression: How to Recognize It and How to Treat It", begging me to read it as she has. When that diagnosis yields no results she theorizes drug abuse followed by homosexuality. She has already spoken to my parents to see if they have noticed a change in my behavior and if so what suggestions they might have. Unfortunately, none of what she describes to them is that outlandish from the son they have always known. Characterizations of a withdrawn, sullen, and suspicious husband don't sound too far from their own experiences.

One day I come home to find our wedding album left open on my pillow, a card on top. The card speaks of a deep and never-ending love, as well as a devotion to making me happy and making our life together work. Sadly, it falls on deaf ears because I'm already too far down the path of self-destruction. Dana tries desperately to rekindle our relationship, attempting first to find out why I am behaving erratically and what she can do to help bring me back to center. I try tirelessly to convince everyone that I'm the unlovable person who exists in my own self-perception.

"I'm going for a ride to clear my head," I tell her after dinner.

Although she suspects something is wrong she has not yet definitely leapt to infidelity. My request for some time to myself is met with no resistance certainly because the distance we are from home acts as an indisputable alibi.

I put the kids to bed and spend a few minutes with Frank, explaining to him the same lie, "I feel like I need time to work through things in my head."

He asks me what is on my mind and I give him the best generic explanation. He knows everything in my past and although, no one truly understands an experience like mine, I let him think his empathy is sufficient. I walk away wondering if he is skeptical but chase that worry from my head and proceed.

I put the address that Natalia texted me into MapQuest and have one final moment of vacillation. Like many other seminal decisions, I find myself with no control over the forces that drive me. Somewhere in my preconscious I know it's wrong but that poses no threat to prevent me. As I jot down the basic directions I run through the checklist of lies before leaving. I decide all bases are covered as I close MapQuest and make sure I delete it from the browsing history. I kiss Dana and the kids unsure of where I'm going, knowing even less, why.

As I start the car my stomach begins. The feeling, so old but now stronger in its renewal, reminds me of nerves but that would mean I'm nervous all of the time. Nervous of being caught, nervous to see Natalia, and nervous about where my life is headed. I overcome the panic, successfully disassociating from reality.

I drive for an hour, still texting, feeding off of our collective energy. She asks for half an hour's notice so she can be ready to leave. My emotions are driving me to the point of turning back but with each song from my iPod, it becomes harder and harder to think about actually abandoning this plan. Natalia sends me an occasional text to check my status and with each I am further entrenched to complete the journey.

I pass Annapolis and see the lights of other small unknown cities. My exit from the highway dumps me on a road with corn fields on either side for forty-five minutes. I am lost in someone else's thoughts for longer than I can remember. I think I hear the echo of my music off of the hollow farmland because I still have it at highway volume with both windows down.

I have no concept of the time. The further I drive from my family the more my stomach hurts. I look back at the time stamp from her last text message to calculate how long I've been in this daze. I worry that I'm lost, having seen nothing resembling a town for longer than makes me comfortable.

I'm strangely relieved to see my phone light up from a call. It's Talia. I know she'll have no idea where I am and no idea how to direct me because she didn't come this way, moreover, she doesn't drive. I tell her my predicament and much as I foresaw she is of no help, "I know there is a lot of farmland around here."

I tell her excitedly, "If the MapQuest directions are to be trusted I should be to you within ten minutes but I've never been there before so I'm not sure."

All she offers is, "Ok, well, there's a gas station with a convenience store on the corner. Pull in there and call me. I'll walk up the block to meet you." There's a slight shortness in her breath which I interpret as anxiety.

I hang up the phone and sink further into the reality that I am completely lost in the middle of the night. I know for certain that I'm in Maryland, but what if there are two streets that share the same name and I've plugged the wrong one into MapQuest?

I park at the convenience store she described and call, "I'm here, I think. If you're able to come out, now would be a good time."

She whispers, "Ok," and hangs up. She sounds even more nervous than before but that could be transference of my own paranoia. I look at the clock to gauge how long I should wait before calling to tell her I'm not at the right place. As I'm ready to make that terrible call I see her familiar gait walking toward me. I'm enveloped with an immediate sense of regret.

This tiny town sits across a small inlet from what looks like a dirty industrial area. It's dark, so my initial opinion may not be accurate but the scent filling my nose matches that first impression. The unforgiving daylight could only make it more obvious that the houses are run down with broken fences and in desperate need of improvement. This could also be a simple projection of the landscape of my morality. I have taken my mind to a dirty place where all of the outer edges of reality have a tainted hue.

As the person walking down the road draws closer I'm certain it's Natalia and my heart pounds in my ears which are ten degrees warmer than the rest of my body, already sticky from the salty Chesapeake air. She speeds up her pace as she draws nearer and, without looking at me, opens, sits down and slams the car door in one motion. Although we text daily, it still feels odd to be back in her presence. Her breathing is much too accelerated from having just walked down the road but I'm afraid to ask her why she pants.

"Hi," she gasps with the smile of a girl meeting her crush for the first time. "Am I dreaming or are you really here?" she says just above a whisper.

"Um, I'm really here, I think," I say trying to be cute. As I lean in to kiss her she moves her face quickly towards mine and puts her tongue in my mouth more forcefully than I had anticipated.

"Let's drive somewhere," she says as if nervous even though she assures me there is no reason to worry.

When I ask where she reminds me, "I've only ever walked to the shitty little beach and the convenience store."

Of course she hasn't ventured anywhere that would be suitable to park. My regret accelerates. I jumped in the car to drive here but never thought about what we could do inconspicuously at two in the morning. I drive to the small inlet and we walk from a swimming beach onto a rock jetty that grinds on my feet with each step. I keep all my pain silent.

I smell low tide and pollution which fits my stomach. I cannot tell her about my doubts. All I hear echoing loudly in my head is, "Why am I on this beach in a town I've never heard of?" I carve it off and cram my regret someplace quiet where it can't disrupt this plan. I cannot guess the magnitude of the message she perceives at my presence, here on a whim and with so little thought about so many risks. My real life, unknown to her, has greater importance than this impetuous decision.

We walk back toward the car where there are four picnic tables and a run-down gazebo in which someone has placed a fifth. The table clearly does not belong, occupying all the available space. I sit first on the table top and she beside me leaning her whole body against mine. When I put my arm around her she leans back in harder. It's awkward and I don't know where to put my hands or where to look. I place my hand on her thigh and realize for the first time that she is wearing sweatpants, absurd given how humid the air is. The heat hangs in front of my face making it impossible to breathe.

I ask, "Aren't you hot in these?" then fear that my question may have come across as innuendo.

"Yeah, but I had to make it look like I was going to bed," she responds. It bothers me without taking complete form that she is learning to cover her bases so secrets remain concealed. The thought of pajamas and bedtimes and lies makes me feel dirty like colored Carebears. Everything feels sullied as though a parasite is relentlessly clinging to me.

She intertwines her hand with mine as it rests on her thigh and I squeeze. After an unbearable silence she leans her head back and puts her lips to mine. While we kiss she manipulates my hand to rub her thigh from knee to hip in a strangely forced rhythm. Every so often she allows her hand and consequently, mine to fall off the ridge of her leg and graze her inner thigh. Her hips rise and she moans coincidently in rhythm with the crashing of tiny inlet waves.

She stops abruptly, and takes a deep breath, "Where can we go?" I don't know exactly what she means.

"Where do you want to go?" I ask inflecting my voice higher.

"I mean let's get in your car and go somewhere where we can be alone," she says with conviction, absent uncertainty.

We walk back to the car and drive in the only direction that I know, the one from which I came. After a few minutes I see an auto body shop littered with imperfect cars both inside and out of it's fence. Once inside the yard, I find a spot between two cars that look no older or newer than mine. I ask her to wait so that I can put the kid's car seats in the very back of the SUV, clearing room for us. As I unbuckle the belts I pause, bend over and make certain I don't vomit.

It tears me up to know that I have not been able to apply the brakes to this. I want to be home with my kids but crave this attention from Talia too. I miss my life but I'm not sure exactly why. I want to stop but don't know if it's out of obligation or because the pain I am causing so many people. Worse yet, I fear the realization that I'll not be able to prevent tonight's events before they're over.

I climb into the back seat, as soon as I sit she's in my lap with her mouth pressed against mine. She tastes fruity, like whatever flavor gum she was chewing at the beach. Passing cars startle me not because I fear anyone coming into the parking lot but the road is so desolate, they pass infrequently. Our kiss lasts a long time so I open my eyes often to see her reaction. I only see the tiniest sliver of white peeking through her eyelids, she is engrossed. I'm more daring with my hands, relying on this special occasion to provide dispensation. She offers no protest when I remove her shirt and bra, only contorts her body in ways that invite me to continue. I glance at the clock on the dash board, reading 3:25 and realize I will not be home before daybreak even if I left at this moment.

She becomes more voracious, I reciprocate. She takes my hand and puts it down her sweatpants, first feeling the perspiration where waistband touches skin. I fumble slightly from nerves and a trace of conscience to find what she wants. She sighs deeply and sensuously, extremely aroused. Her hips quiver and rock upward violently as if my reluctance has only served to entice. She is beyond excited and I am distraught at earwitnessing the throes of her passion. Within moments of adjusting my hand, providing relief for my aching wrist she puts her mouth to my ear and says, "Please make love to me."

I am frozen. I knew this was coming, even speculated that she may ask tonight because she is swept up in Mr. Cunneely coming to see her.

My answer comes from someplace genuine, "No, Honey. Not here. Not in the back of a car. I will not let that be the first time that you have sex." I sicken even myself with feigned chivalry. I mean the response but that request should have never left her mouth. I should never have put her in this position, manipulated into thinking that anything about this is altruistic.

Nobody likes being rejected when requesting sex, especially for the first time. Her expression is hurt and confused.

I hug her and explain, "It'll mean so much more if it isn't in the back seat of a car at four in the morning in an auto body parking lot."

It seems to placate her slightly but I know she's upset, which I'm about to amplify, "Listen, I should be going."

She immediately pulls away, angrily puts her shirt on and says, "Fine, just leave."

"Hey, Talia, come on, I have a long ride and I've been up all night. Can you please take it easy on me?" trying to make sense of the senseless situation I've authored.

She stares before wrapping her arms around me, "I know you drove far and I don't want you to get into an accident, but I just don't want you to leave."

I seize the moment of solidarity, "I don't want to leave either but I have to."

As we are drawing to a close, I feel it, the panic that precedes the disgust in my gut. I'm beginning the transition back into a father who does not engage in late night trysts with a student. My regret is building. I'm torn between wanting to be back with my children, the part of my adult life that I love, and wanting to stay here, hiding from the frightening realities of that same life.

I drive back to the same convenience store and watch her walk into her cousin's house. I leave, nervous about reversing the directions correctly and nervous about facing Dana, almost certain she'll know what I've done. I am worried that my story won't fly because I'll need to account for my whereabouts for the entirety of the night. Most terribly, I am petrified to think of my irreversible steps.

Rush hour traffic delays my arrival to Frank's house by ninety minutes so I miss breakfast. Jenny's warm greeting when I walk through the door does not balance the anger Dana shoots at me from the other side of the kitchen. I'm left speechless with palpable guilt when greeted with my son's adorable joy, "Daddy! Good morning. Where were you?"

I kiss my three children and ignore his question. My love for them is the only thing that outweighs my own self-loathing.

I wish so badly that it could overpower the inexplicable forces driving my demise.

There are many theories that try to define cancer. How does it form? Who is predisposed and how can it be prevented? An interesting yet controversial theory has been posited by the renowned and criticized biologist, Peter Duesberg. Cancer, according to Duesberg's theory, occurs when chromosomes fail to divide properly. When cells divide, called mitosis, twenty three pairs of chromosomes line up and divide perfectly to allow for the forty six individual chromosomes to take form. One from each pair of forty six is passed on to each of two daughter cells.

If the division is erroneous the pairs split eccentrically and one cell is given too much material while the other receives an insufficient amount, called aneuploidy. It is often fatal to the cells, however in some instances the aneuploidic cells survive. The yielding cells repeat this process in an exponential yet unpredictable manner causing even more bizarre changes in subsequent chromosomes.

As each generation of new cells lacks the proper information with which to bestow to its descendant the process produces cells that are increasingly unrecognizable. The cells now lack the identity of anything that one would be able to distinguish as human. It's neither a cell from a heart, nor a fingernail, nor a brain. This cluster now grows without regard for what they should be or how they should act.

The controversy that stems from this theory is based on the fact that the most commonly accepted theories on the topic contend that aneuploidy is the result of cancer not the cause. Regardless, the cancer is abnormal and should neither be the result, nor the cause of the natural process of reproducing cells. The confusing placement of normal components of my being explains how I'm able to reach this far on a path of self-destruction, with immoral, unnatural behavior yet be able to rein it in when faced with the prospect of engaging in intercourse with Natalia.

When I was an adolescent I had no choice but to split off parts of my mind in order to cope. More specifically to make sure that no one else had the ability to see their mutant formation, their carved off aspects had to be a secret. I had no idea what the next day's choices and dilemmas were going to bring. I was forced to base today's decisions on yesterday's inconsistent outcomes and capricious emotions.

I never knew what new lies had to be told or how to act from one day to the next. A malformed product of a distorted experience. A split from a misshapen split and it wreaked havoc. Like ripping off a paper towel at the perforation but missing it ever so slightly. It will continue to grow or shrink at random intervals making the predetermined rips useless. With each decision, based on a prior, unwholesome memory my moral compass diverts from true north at barely perceptible intervals.

The carved off pieces of my psyche are sometimes identifiable. They surface at times when they are useful and help the general well-being of my mind. Had that same split with my conscience spoken up at any point prior to sitting in the car and driving to Maryland, events may have been altered for the better. But this is not the case. I am always at full blown disaster level before I see the spot to save myself. At that point, bringing measures to a grinding halt is always dangerous and potentially painful. I have come to learn the harsh reality that abandoned parts of the psyche in one's youth come back with uncontrollable force later in life.

Chapter 9

Like water will find a way to infiltrate a leaky roof, even when seemingly impossible, we find ways to circumvent all obstacles, continuously feeding the obsession. We see one another no matter what. No suggestion is ignored nor deemed too risky; no possibility unexamined.

When Natalia suggests, "Since my room is in the basement of our townhouse and Mama is two floors away, I could easily get out in the middle of the night," I play along not because I like the idea, rather I'm afraid to say, "No." I agree with concealed reluctance and step further down this unthinkable path.

"Where will we go? What if your mom comes down? Where will I park at that time of night?" She has answers that all seem simple enough to ease my mistrust.

Leaving my house poses no problem. Every night since the beginning of our marriage Dana has fallen asleep on the couch only to wake up sometime in the early morning and come to bed. I convey my objections and like so many other parts of our marriage that I find upsetting the onus is turned back on me.

She tells me with her typical couth, "I would act differently, Jim if you behaved appropriately. You expect to just come home and have me spread my legs." Dana is adept at making me regret having ever broached my feelings. When I express emotions I hope to speak about them and work toward a resolution. Instead,

I am treated to a litany of my character flaws. If I would be nicer, more domestic, more compassionate she would be a better wife. With the disclaimer that nobody is perfect I assure her that I am faithful — these conversations all take place before my infidelity- and that those are attributes I not only possess but feel and express. Thus begins our game of rejection tag.

Sex is not the issue. I genuinely want to fall asleep together. I want the security of ending the day next to my wife, the mother of my children. I beg and cajole and sometimes, at my wits end I emote, telling her with transparent cynicism, "You wake me up when you come to bed so close to my alarm and I cannot fall back to sleep." It's untrue, but I hope motivation. It does nothing and I feel equally alone.

The Friday night of our newest plan, I tell Dana that I'm going to bed at what seems a normal time. I turn on the bedroom TV and wait patiently. After an hour, I slowly open our door to see what she is doing. True to form, she has fallen asleep in front of the television, always in the same position, half lying down, one foot on the floor and the other sprawled out in front of her.

Once I'm certain she is asleep, I return to our bedroom and climb out the window. As I drop my feet out first and lower myself down I'm trembling. I walk around the side of the house and to my car. Once inside I stare at my front door waiting for Dana to come running out and demand to know where I am going. Earlier in the evening I strapped my bike on the car so that if by chance, Dana did catch me, I would tell her that I was going for a mountain bike ride.

Such a story would not have struck her as odd because it is not uncommon to go for a night ride. At the very least I am going to be chastised for not telling her, but the lie is not unbelievable.

As I sit, silently rehearsing my story, I feel a stab of sadness at how easily and precisely I can manipulate any nuance of my life into a self-serving lie. I chase away that outburst of integrity and continue to recite.

It takes me several minutes to start the car because my next fear is that the sound will wake her. My life is a series of check-lists. One item only relates to the others by nature of their inter-dependent hierarchy. Each step in my path has its ancillary safe-guards that, like rocket boosters on a space shuttle, are jettisoned after they are no longer necessary.

Every phase has a contingency and a back-up for the contingency. If she comes out now I'll tell her I couldn't sleep and am going for a cup of coffee. Yet, if I get away and she questions me when I return I'll use the biking story. Being questioned anywhere in between will depend on where I am and how quickly I can be home.

I start the car, remaining still and staring at the front door. I look at the clock on the radio and say out loud to commit to record, "Ok, if she doesn't look out by 12:22 I'm leaving." The prescribed three minutes passes without seeing Dana. When no further obstacles beside my own, almost abandoned conscience stand in my way, I leave. I text Natalia, "On my way," but cannot share in her ecstatic reply.

I pick her up and we sit in the parking lot of Pizza Hut trying to decide what we should do. Choices are limited for a teacher and his student at one a.m. After much deliberation a decision is reached by default. Her unconditional trust in me is humbling if it is, in fact even voluntary at this point.

I take her to a parking lot used to access a scarcely known trailhead. It's a quiet place on a quiet road. In my estimation, no place is completely safe but this location, of all I can imagine, affords us the most privacy. This site will become our standard hangout at any time of night or day to kill whatever time we have. It is close enough to Natalia's house as well as school so minimal time is ever wasted in transit.

Chapter 10

"Maggie tells me that she has orgys all the time," is how the text reads one evening that Dana is at work while I'm sitting on the floor playing with my kids. Maggie is Talia's best friend. Talia complains often that all of her friends are being alienating by keeping our secret.

Each time she lays that pseudo guilt trip on me I tell her, "Do what you have to do. I can't ask you to keep it a secret."

I don't reflect on it until after the words have left my mouth, but the thought of asking her to keep something so big makes me feel ugly. I obsess over the decision to take such a cavalier attitude regarding her confidentiality. Times when I'm close to revisiting the topic I feel the aching reminder that I'm controlling the extension of my psychological world where Natalia represents me and I don't like that. I neither tell, nor ask, nor manipulate her to lie to anyone. If she chooses to keep it a secret, then it is by her choice not my prompting.

"What do you mean she has them all the time?" I ask, "With who?"

"With Tommy."

Tommy is Maggie's boyfriend, also a student of mine. Her text confuses me. I don't understand why she would tell me this and what bearing it has on anything.

I ask, "Um, why are you telling me?"

"I want to have orgys too."

After a long moment of reflection it finally occurs to me that she doesn't know what an orgy is. I come to this conclusion only after ruling out other, more uncomfortable possibilities.

I ask, "What do you mean by orgies?" Hoping she will recognize the correct plural form.

"You know, like she comes a lot when her and Tommy have sex," she clarifies.

A weird feeling overcomes me for participating in this conversation. There are myriad moments like this where the gulf between her mind and mine seems larger. Some topics are logical and she takes the correction in stride, but others I can tell she feels inferior no matter how gently I handle them. Since my own children are too young, I can only imagine the correct tone with which to discuss sex.

"Oh you mean she has a lot of orgasms?" trying to ease any potential embarrassment.

"Oh, I guess. Whatever it's called," she tersely replies. "Well I want to have orgasms too," turning the discussion sharply.

"How would you like to have one?" I ask. I have already offended her so I let her guide the conversation.

She tells me, "I don't care, I just want you to make me come." I'm taken aback by how candid she is.

"Well we should have this conversation then, but not through texting," I say, hoping to table the discussion until a much later date. I know the only outcome and am exclusively to blame. I allowed thoughts to hang between us that cemented a path toward this collision. Putting an end to it now will only rightfully cause confusion.

She wastes no time, broaching it at the beginning of our next telephone conversation. The necessary discussion even more uncomfortable than I anticipated. She relies on me to make decisions and provide guidance on topics that are simply unnatural.

Before we even talk about logistics she tells me, in no uncertain terms, "Jimi, I want to lose my virginity and I want you to take it." It upsets me even more that after her initial declaration she resorts to using the sophomoric term, "V card," whenever she refers to her virginity. I try to dissuade her, knowing full well that the more I try to convince her otherwise the more tantalizing I am, looking out for her best interest. The discussion fizzles this time and no details surface, only an insight into what will come.

"I can't wait to give you my V card," is the text I receive as soon as we hang up the phone.

There is a sensation I haven't felt in years as I sit on the couch in the same room with my wife when Natalia texts me questions about sex. I feel a nagging obligation to accept a sense of betrayal but somehow nothing soaks into the correct places. Nothing digs at me enough to stop. No chinks appear in the shield I have placed around my consciousness. Questions arrive such as, "Do you have sex a lot? Do you jerk off? How big is your penis? How many people have you had sex with? What's your favorite position?"

None of my responses have their root in honesty. I answer, from my negotiable-self, what sounds best to drive the conversation that I want to have, or more specifically the one I think she wants.

At first, I deflect, "I'm not sure that's something we should be discussing." She fires back with all of the anger that she can convey over a text, "Well you've already kissed me and fingered me so I didn't think you minded if I asked you about sex." I stop resisting. I talk about positions, habits, past partners and everything she asks.

"Will you give me oral sex?" she asks frankly. I'm embarrassed as I read her question. She asks clumsily, as someone without experience.

"Ummmmm, idk Talia. That's a big step and although you may want it now, in the moment you may feel differently," I respond.

"NOOOO I know that I want you to do oral sex on me," she contests.

I squirm even though no one else is reading, like listening to a non-native English speaker try to speak intelligibly. It's easy to determine the gist of what is being said but the small refining points that create fluency are missing.

"Well, I'm not saying that I'm not willing but I'm not saying yes either. Next time we're in the situation I'll let you tell me for sure," I think is a good enough placation.

I'm incorrect.

"What should I say if I'm ready?" she asks. I try to balance what will sound good but harsh enough to dissuade her from repeating. I avoid being raunchy while trying to sound legitimate.

"Jim, kiss me all over," is the best I can do.

One evening while teaching my college class, not long after our first day of hooky I receive a text, "Can we have a day together again? No weed just a day." My heart jumps. I don't care about the marijuana. I just want to see her too and am happy she wants the same.

"Sounds great. When?" I reply.

"ASAP!!"

Skipping another day of camp will be tricky, I have to not only pass Sr. Karen but Dana again. The more that I think about the likelihood, I realize it's impractical.

On my way home after class I call Natalia, "Listen, I don't think that I can skip work for a whole day. I'm pretty sure that I can take off in the morning but I have to be back by lunch," I explain. Her long silence tells me she's unhappy with my compromise.

"Well, I don't care for how long, I just want to see you," she says, relieving me of the immediate burden. I suspect that since we recently discussed oral sex she is impatient to move to that level.

As soon as I arrive at work I ask Sr. Karen if I can go to school to interview a potential candidate. She knows I'm the Lead Teacher for the World Language Department and has no reason to question my honesty. I don't even tell Dana because she works in a different part of the camp and we only cross paths at lunch. I plan accordingly and leave hoping that she doesn't even notice my absence.

I leave camp and drive immediately to Talia's. She is already waiting when I pull into the cul-de-sac behind her complex. We head straight for my house knowing that we don't have much time. She chats about nothing in particular while choosing familiar songs from my iPod. When we near my house I run through the same list of fears. Luckily, my street is again empty, only momentary relief.

The mental gymnastics of my life are so very trying. Nothing provides respite, nothing is ever restful and each diversion only sheds light on the multitude of other decisions to be made. The reward for every risk is the compulsion to take more risks. The behavior resulting from this mental breakdown has the potential to cause a mental breakdown.

Seconds after I close the front door she pulls my arm and kisses me with her mouth wide open. I move toward the couch where we previously spent all of our time but when she realizes, pulls her lips from mine and says, "Can we go to your bed instead?"

Without truly contemplating the significance I say mindlessly, "Yes," and we walk into my bedroom. The house is muggy with the air conditioning off, so I turn on the ceiling fan while she sits on the foot of the bed. When I turn and face her she looks young, her hair still wet from the shower, her legs swinging a few inches short of the floor. My initial reaction to seeing her on my bed is that her entire comportment is juvenile but I block reality. I walk to the bed and stand in front of her, she takes both of my hands and pulls me on top as she lays back.

This is the first time that we have been on a bed together. It's the first time we have been anywhere beside the back seat of my car or couch. I have only my right leg between hers but she presses against me in a way that asks me to let her spread her legs. Despite my clear hesitation she pushes harder so I shift my weight and her near leg moves underneath.

Her legs are now spread and my pelvis rests on hers. She sighs and arches her hips up into mine. The pressure feels good, overriding my conscience. She stops kissing and cranes her neck as if looking straight over her head. I take the opportunity to kiss where my lips rest. Neck leads to clavicle which leads to another startling, physical reaction. She thrusts her hips upward once again and moans an audibly nasal and disturbing sound.

We play this game for over an hour where I kiss a spot that sends waves of pleasure through her body and she replies. We discover certain things about her erogenous zones simultaneously. I reach as far south as her navel, stopping to play with the dangling butterfly on her belly button ring. I wander back up her body before reengaging her lips again as if my time elsewhere created hunger.

She only allows the kiss to last briefly before she stops, takes a deep breath and whispers, "Jimi, kiss me all over," in an aspirated, nervous voice.

The words she uses are exactly as I instructed, yet somehow she still shocks me. The state of dissociative denial in which I exist leaves me incredulous that she has chosen to take this step. I try not to seem anxious, meandering back down her body, stopping at all the junctures where I made mental notes. When I reach her jean shorts I move right over them to her thighs. As I work my way around warm, tan legs I begin undoing the button and zipper. First over one hip, then the second. I trace the line of her thong, kissing newly exposed skin, making a concerted effort to push through my crippling arousal. The reality of this moment is taking hold and my tattered sanity is crumbling.

On my way to work this morning I had a feeling I would find myself in this situation and my primary concern was how I was going to react to being this intimate with someone so young. Apparently, all conscious thoughts regarding my conscience conveniently take place out of the moment. In the instant where decisions can affect outcomes, I am absent.

Withdrawal is the crutch I wield to bridge all uncomfortable gaps. Right now I'm so far out of the realm to act with any adult responsibility that the echo of, "Holy shit, this is so fucking hot," is uncontested in the forefront of my mind.

I work my way to the tiny swath of material meant to cover her virginity. As I work my way in shrinking concentric circles I feel her hips spasm with intensity. I kiss gently, through the fabric. I pause less than an instant as I wonder if she showered this morning or if I simply notice the scent of adolescence, a sensation I was never exposed to in my own. There is nothing unpleasant, only registering in my mind.

Her hands are folded intently on her stomach, knuckles pale white from how tightly she squeezes. She startles me when she tears them apart and grabs each of the thin strings that join the front of her panties to the smaller piece in the back.

She removes her last article of clothing as she moans deeply, "Take these off me, now."

I grab the last vestige keeping her shielded from my manipulation, pull it down her body around and over her feet. Natalia is naked and I am frozen. She lays still, eyes closed except for the heaving of her chest. When curiosity overcomes her and she wonders why nothing is happening she opens them. She looks appalled as if the gravity of the moment has hit her and immediately hides again. I cannot think about why she has closed her eyes so awkwardly so I pick up where I left off.

I engage in the same game I played with her entire body earlier but this time on a smaller scale. I explore what makes her feel best and concentrate my effort there. Everything has an equal reaction. She builds to a crescendo, but from nothing I can determine, until she finally collapses in a limp surrender to exhaustion and climax.

I kiss my way back up the center of her body and lay down watching for feedback. She remains motionless trying to catch her breath, keeping her hands in the same position, interlaced over her navel. With neither warning nor reservation she jumps on top of me. She straddles my knees and undoes the fabric belt on my shorts, fumbling either from nerves or inexperience.

With my pants just below my crotch she pulls them off almost angrily. She tries to do too much and has her hands and mouth too busy to be able to feel any of what she is trying to accomplish.

Part Two

I'm exactly the opposite of her in this supine position, unable to close my eyes. I recognize this for exactly the horror show it is, there is a teenage girl performing oral sex on me. What do I do now? I fear that stopping her will be a terrible blow to her ego. There is no completion to this aside from the one I'm sure she is expecting but even that, if it were possible is out of the question.

When I take her shoulders and gently pull up, she darts her eyes at me. The look on her face drives me to the brink of a wretch. She looks in pain, panting and squinting from the stress.

"What?" she says impatiently through gasps.

"Come here hon," I feel deplorable.

"What's wrong?" she resists.

"Nothing," I assure as I position her next to me, cradling my arm underneath. When she's close enough, I kiss her to divert attention from what just occurred at the lower half of my body.

She falls right into place in the new act I have unwittingly authored so much so that after just a few minutes she pulls me on top. She walks her kisses along my cheek, to my jaw, my ear, then whispers, "Jimi, make love to me."

I am speechless. Prepared otherwise, yet speechless.

When I can finally speak, I say, "Uh, Talia, are you sure? I mean we haven't really talked about this much and I'm not sure either of us is ready."

"I'm ready," she snaps back and grabs me with her right hand to draw me close. My immediate reaction is to pull away until I realize that by letting her scuffle and grope her way through her own attempts she will hopefully frustrate herself. When she stops out of frustration I'm exonerated as the sole obstacle.

"The stupid ceiling fan must have dried me out," she says disenchanted. I say nothing in relieved agreement. I hope that she is sated enough to avoid another attempt.

269

"I really want to have sex Jim," she says breaking a few moments of awkward silence. Still no reply. Before I can provide a fictitious answer my cell phone rings from the living room.

I ignore the sound but know Natalia hears it too, she asks, "You going to get that?"

"If it's important they'll call back," I dismiss.

I take a breath to answer her with something I have not taken time to formulate when the phone rings again. Without a word I walk into the other room, tracing the ominous vibration. Before I even pick up I see, "Call from: Dana" and am stricken with panic. I didn't think that she would even know I was missing but now is looking for me. Is everything ok? Is one of my kids hurt? Did Sr. Karen come looking for me and ask Dana where I was? I pick up the phone already out of breath, fearful.

"Jim?" She asks with concern or maybe annoyance.

"Ya," is the only word I can enunciate.

"Where the fuck are you?" she asks with typical decorum.

I hadn't created a story to tell her because I thought that leaving work for just the morning would avoid having to lie. What I had not anticipated were the counselors that work under me asking her this same question.

"I'm at school, Dana. I'm interviewing someone for the vacant Spanish position," I tell her in case she has spoken with Sister.

"I called you ten minutes ago. Where were you when I called?" She fires questions and I know that if my answers are not satisfactory there will be ensuing interrogation.

I stand in astonishment of how quickly I come up with an answer once I take the first step into my own fantasy world. "Listen, the interview is over, so I had to get into the storage closet to look for books and I guess there is no service in there," I tell her while a vision of the truth flashes through my mind.

I'm awoken from that daydream, "Bullshit Jim, where the fuck are you? Everyone is looking for you." I know the second part is her typical exaggeration and now know that she hasn't spoken to Sr. Karen.

"Dana I'm at school. I spoke to Sister this morning and she said it was fine if I came to sit in on the interview," building confidence in solidarity with my lie.

"Well, all of the counselors I've seen today were asking because they haven't seen you since morning prayer," she finally clarifies the exact reason for her call.

"Well, I don't work for them so I don't have to tell them do I? Look, the longer we bicker the longer I'm going to be here. Let me go so I can get back," finding my perfect excuse to end the call.

"Fine," precedes her hanging up.

I know there will be more questions when I see her but I can now prepare myself. The nauseous feeling begins when I first hear Dana's voice, but subsides as I talk my way through. Residual anxiety lingers and waxes back to full force as I put the phone down and prepare to tell Natalia, "Listen, I'm sorry but I have to get back."

I walk into the bedroom to find her with the blanket up to her waist, seemingly very comfortable being bare breasted in broad daylight in front of me. She alleviates me having to broach the unsavory topic, "Sounds like we have to go huh?"

I give a half-frown, "Ya, unfortunately I have to go back to work."

"Did she buy your story at least?" she asks absent any sarcasm but with genuine concern for my lies.

"I think so. I guess I'll find out later," more thinking out loud than trying to console our worries.

Natalia puts her index finger to her lower lip in a very pensive pose and says, "Well I guess it's a good thing we didn't have sex because we would have been interrupted." I shudder inside at the level of thought that she puts into our daily existence. Worse than simple acceptance though is the false normalcy.

The conversation about when we will complete the act is inevitable, now arising several times a week. I sidestep as long as possible before arousing suspicion. Natalia finally puts the question to me in a cold, almost threatening tone, "Are we ever going to have sex or what?"

When I can no longer evade, I engage in the conversation. My ironic responses when finally facing reality are like advice a friend would give. I sound like the true selfless mentor I should have stayed. Even though I should be telling her to get away from me, she doesn't see through me when I say, "The first time you have sex should be with a person who you share an emotional bond with. More importantly, a man who cares for you deeply."

Mindfucking her to see only my version of the portrait, highlighting me as the only man that could possibly fit the mold.

She tells me with frightening conviction, "I'm certain that I want it to be you, Jimi."

I'm so deeply entrenched in the idea that one's virginity is linked indisputably and unfalteringly with love that I see it as the irreplaceable culmination of this union.

The conversation lingers around minutiae until we are able to decide a time and a place. She expresses her impatience despite impressing upon her the need to have all of the particulars in order. My procrastination has pushed us into preseason for fall sports season and she is disappointed, but the advent of a new school year brings added securities.

We pick a time when she doesn't have field hockey practice that we'll go to her house. Although I've been there several times and her mother will be at work, I am very nervous. I take solace only in the knowledge that her room is in the basement, providing a convenient escape route if necessary.

Chapter 11

A text message wakes me thirty minutes before my alarm, "I cannot wait for this afternoon."

I cannot agree.

I wish I hadn't made these promises, but I did and can't back out now. I lie still in my bed, recalling so many times in my life when I looked at my surroundings and asked, "What am I doing here?" I remember an overwhelming amount of instances when I should have stopped myself but fear or lack of common sense seemed an impediment to self-preservation.

I seek explanations for mistakes in college, overly influenced by girls, simply complying to garner their affection. I regret not stopping advances from men when I lived in France, knowing now I should have realized something was amiss long before it was obvious. I wish so many transgressions to be undone caused only by inane loyalty to previous poor choices. The inability to trust my own emotions is a torment all its own I have never tried to decipher. I feel such a familiar shame as I reflect on the culmination of actions that lead to now.

As I imagine myself in her house today and speculate my reactions, I feel ill. I don't belong there but I also feel vapid, as though I don't belong anywhere, ever. I should neither be making this plan nor carrying it out but something inexplicable drives me, something I do not want to fight. I'm going to satisfy an obligation coming from somewhere unknown.

There is always the same sickness every time I leave my wife and kids to see Natalia. It bears resemblance to an illness but borders on an anxious excitement that further clouds my ability to act appropriately. It's a familiar sensation, having only recently resurfaced, but as it comes more frequently I remember it vividly.

This feeling was my body's exact reaction as I would walk in the back door to my parent's house as a teenager. This was the precise knot in my stomach that would twist painful as I entered school every morning for years. I can only assume that this awareness in my body is a coping mechanism. Since my adolescent mind could not process all the mental energy I was demanding, the manifestation of the stress was a physical feeling to cope with the overflow. I had no idea the pain was abnormal, it was just part of my life.

I have already told John, my other coach, the lie that will necessitate my early departure. Dana knows I'll be staying late so I'm covered on both fronts. I leave the soccer field at eleven-thirty, perpetually on the brink of fainting. I drive to the cul-de-sac behind her complex and sit for several moments, taunted by my last chance to stop.

My phone rings uncontrollably but I'm petrified to look. It could be Dana telling me one of the kids is sick or it could be John having found out my lie. Instead it is the worst of all possibilities, Natalia wondering where I am, anxious and impatient.

I walk into her back patio door and she jumps into my arms, kissing me loudly on the cheek then my mouth while giggling. Her lips feel good on mine and she tastes like cold and strawberry. I pull away for a second, smile at her and ask, "What did you eat? You taste sweet."

"An ice pop," as she pulls me over to her bed.

We've done everything else that would normally lead to this moment, if this were normal. Still the air in the room is heavy with impending realizations of countless conversations. I'm hypersensitive to everything around me, the hum of a lawnmower in the distance and a dog barking. I hear every bird chirp and noises in the units on either side of hers' further heighten my fear. I repeat the same things to make clear that I care for her well-being, disgusting myself with each sanctimonious repetition.

What is lost in the excitement is that I have no business being in her bedroom at noon on a Tuesday in August. She should be with her friends waiting for field hockey practice and I should be standing on the soccer field waiting to be home with my family, but neither of us is doing what we should. I know all the reasons I shouldn't be here but none of those reasons matter. I have manipulated her into thinking that I care about what is best for her and that I'm the man with whom she should be losing her virginity. This wave of uncontrollable nausea is my body telling me something which my mind is incapable. I push through, already here and knowing I've done worse to reach this place.

She says with a cute and elongated tone, "Soooo, what now?"

I am frozen beyond action. I cannot speak and for the most part cannot even think, except for the two questions that echo louder in my head with each reverberation, "What the fuck am I doing here?" and when that thought dead ends, "What do I do now?"

"What do you want to do?" I ask softly, barely above a whisper.

"I want to make love to you, Jim," she says kissing me softly, but with a certain passion of long-harnessed desire. Her body shouldn't belong to a fifteen year old as I see her half-naked in the daylight. Even though she is developed more than what my instincts tell me she should be, the ghastly feeling flows over me, hindering my concentration.

My mind is elsewhere, all I think about is my need to finish what has begun. I cannot leave without fulfilling my promise. Lawnmowers and running faucets remind me the world outside is unaware of the unfolding fantasy I'm crafting.

After foreplay that delves into no uncharted territory, she takes off her thong and says, "Jimi, please make love to me."

I move slowly, apprehensive about what to expect. The expression on her face clearly conveys pain, I ask often, "Do you want me to stop?"

Each time I hope she says, "Yes," because perhaps this will never happen. Instead, she breathes deeply, pushing through and says, "No, I'm fine, just be gentle."

The bile rises to the back of my throat. The weight of this snapshot is too much to bear and I feel again, like I might faint. A student of mine just asked me to fuck her gently because I'm causing her pain. I have no doubt about the pain, but she has no idea that it's time released. The true ache doesn't come for a long time, soreness will be born out of years of confusion, not a broken hymen.

She relaxes and falls into rhythm. I would not characterize the look on her face as pleasurable but she no longer looks in agony. Every noise, whether a car or voices on the street, makes me jump. It's not as though it matters anymore, I am inside of her.

Despite the reality that the point of no return evaporated long ago, I still imagine as though I can save myself. My sexuality is all I've ever used to hunt self-esteem, the best and only tool I've ever wielded to make women love me. And now, again, I regret my misguided emotions.

I stop because her demeanor has, once again changed. She looks at me and starts to cry. The abhorrence disappears and all of the logical feelings I should have felt up to this point come flooding into consciousness in one devastating gush. I am nagged by the reality that I have betrayed and violated her trust. I ask, "Why are you crying?" as I hug her, holding her head in my hands.

She says the one and only thing that could possibly make me want to wretch even more. I can neither foresee this nor cut her off but when I hear the words I need absolutely all of my strength to not vomit in her bed.

"That was beautiful. That's why I'm crying."

I have a total body-adverse reaction. My head pounds. My stomach aches. Both of my calf muscles cramp and my arms quiver from holding up the weight of my entire life. She notices the shaking in my arms and asks with concern, "What's the matter. Are you cold?"

I instantly think of the movie, "Say Anything". Right after Lloyd and Diane have sex in the back of his car, she asks if he's cold because he's also trembling. Lloyd looks at her and says, "No, I'm just happy. I'm trembling because I'm happy." Of all the extravagant words I've used to manipulate us into this situation, all I can do now is quote a movie, the only thing I can think to respond. I wish this moment was as fictitious as a movie. I repeat the line, the fact that there is no truth in the statement irrelevant, but it mirrors how she feels and buys me time.

I lay next to her for what I hope is an acceptable amount of time to prevent the perception of escape. The sensation in my midsection can only be caused by being ensnared somewhere between my two ego states, the adolescent and the adult. The pain unbearable. Instead of feeling the knot for just the transition, I'm stuck indeterminately. It's uncomfortable enough when rumbling through my body during the switch, but to exist while the sensation underpins every thought is excruciating. I think she can hear the trembling in my voice but she does not ask. Despite her witnessing, what has become fierce shaking I'm certain she cannot know the origin. I'm working through this right in front of her but luckily, she is blissfully oblivious.

After much protest, I leave, get close enough to my car to be hidden and vomit. The violence behind the purge represents years of sickness. As if I reached the tipping point. The denial of my roots, my dishonesty with everyone around me and finally this betrayal has become too much to swallow for one ill-prepared person. This is a catharsis like I've never felt before but it's only momentary. Like le petit mort, it's gone and I'm back to reality, faced with what I've done.

Just as every other time I've pushed the boundaries she debriefs through voracious texting. I play along, using the same tone of wondrous excitement. But now I'm trapped as I've been in every other relationship in my life. I find myself rapt from a sense of obligation to prior transgressions, only perpetuating the cycle. Perceived obligation will mark so many relationships and the superficial niceties that seem innocent at the onset become layered under debts I can never repay.

Chapter 12

Sometime, early in the summer it occurred to me the potential difficulty of teaching Natalia's class but understanding the breadth was impossible. When she was a freshman, no lines had been crossed. There were hints of flirtation but nothing existed to cause discomfort. Now, I'm unable to speak when in front of her class. How do I portray this façade of a well-defined role model when she knows these flaws of my personality? She intimately knows my dirty little secret.

In another attempt to cloak my malice I explain to her, "I just want you to know that this isn't who I really am."

"What do you mean?" she asks confused by my ambiguity.

"Well, you're watching me lie and cheat and I don't want you to think that you've gotten involved with someone who is a liar and a cheater." I outwait her silence having nothing to add to the manipulative disclaimer.

After she works through whatever she is trying to formulate she pacifies us both, "Oh Jimi, I know the only reason you're lying is so we can be together. Once we can tell everybody we're in love you'll have no reason to lie."

There is no appropriate reply to such a bizarre confession but she clarifies that she is in love with the idealized version of Mr. Cunneely, exactly as I have spun him. She can overlook all of the blatant faults I have put so proudly on display, infidelity, dishonesty, conniving, and manipulation in the name of love. She has found the peace of knowing that an established, sane male finds her worthy of his time and emotion and I have led her there simply with attention.

She may never use her sway over me and may not even discover its existence but she has simply to lean toward a classmate and reveal her secret, our secret and I'm finished. My initial taste of the reality I've created comes the first day of school while explaining such inconsequential topics as homework policy and novels. I'm outlining classroom rules while there is a continuous bead of sweat running down the center of my back. It's so obvious to me that I'm afraid to write on the board, certain the back of my dress shirt is soaking wet. I can barely contain myself from panting. I look at Natalia as I naturally scan the room, but then wonder if I'm looking too much or if it's obvious I'm trying to not look?

"And we'll look at the contrasts between Le Passé Composé and L'imparfait."

Does anyone see my deliberation about looking at her? Do I smell of sweat?

"I would like you to hand in your summer assignment and pick the topic for your research paper."

Can anyone know that Natalia and I have had sex? What if someone looks at her and sees how she is looking at me, will that be obvious?

"Class participation will be the same as last year. A point for each time you speak French, accumulated until the end of the marking period."

What is she whispering to the girl next to her? Ten minutes till the bell and I hope to God Talia doesn't ask a question. Why is she smirking every time I look at her? I feel the sweat dripping down my forehead now. Thank God for the bell.

"Au revoir, à demain."

Routines are silently established by the end of the first week. She knows I'm free third period so she leaves her class, asking to use the restroom. She comes to sit in my room for just five minutes saying nothing of consequence, and leaves just as innocently saying, "Ok, so I'll see you later."

She still comes to my room in the morning and just for a minute after school. She keeps her belongings in my bottom desk drawer and her jacket in my closet so that she doesn't have to go to her locker. Everything is made to feel so normal and no one questions her ubiquitous presence neither in my room nor my career. Navigating my own life is impossible. I'm not sure anything can make me stop. This is the route I've chosen and from somewhere that I cannot access, have decided to see the completion. All I can do now is observe and regret.

Twice we run into one another during the day. She looks at me and says, "Hello Mr. Cunneely," and each time I hear her giggle causing mild panic. I seethe when she greets male classmates with a hug. I try, unsuccessfully to quash my jealousy. I remind myself that I'm a grown man who need not feel inadequate compared with a sophomore, but it doesn't work. I am possessive and covetous. Unable to function as an adult when I see her act as a teenager.

Instead of school quelling our trysts, it adds exhilaration. We both become better acquainted with the back seat of my car. Any time we can create, we seize. We share the obsession from different points of view. No reason is acceptable for me to decline an invitation and I become afraid to reject her.

She has no idea of my real life responsibilities and I've never told her, "No." She only knows my willingness to drop everything for her. She neither knows nor cares about the roots of my placation and rightfully shouldn't.

Weekends become challenging because as the weather turns cold our one solid excuse becomes impossible. I can tell Dana that I'm going to a mountain bike race and Talia tells her mother she is going to watch. The problem being there is only so much we can do to remain inconspicuous. As a result we find more secluded places to park.

The obvious appearance of impropriety is always a danger near school, so driving someplace safer, a necessity. I become creative, finding many inventive spots. I ascertain when my parents are out so we go to their house, she does the same with her mother and we seek refuge in hers. I use my parents to babysit so we go back to my own house when Dana is at work. Fighting the elements and discovery of our secret is second only to combatting my own self-loathing over unconscionable decisions. My lies pile upon one another without absorbing how many people I exploit, yet I always remember to prevent overlap. I cannot stop to calculate the tally of damage I wreak on all my life for fear of a full blown emotional breakdown. I've grown accustomed to living with a constant, soul-destroying, mental conflict coupled with unending clashes of will power.

When she complains that the constant hiding is a nuisance I present an idea I fear she will find repulsive. I hope all she does is reject the suggestion without being offended.

"Did you think of someplace that we could go this weekend?" she texts me in the middle of the week. We have already planned to sneak away on Saturday but have solidified nothing more.

Part Two

"Well, I have an idea but I'm not sure you'll like it," I hang, open-ended.

"I'm game for anything as long as I can see you," she plays along.

"I know it might seem shady but I thought we could get a hotel room. I know one that isn't far and is clean. At least we could have some privacy," I offer.

I read my text in the two seconds it remains on the screen after I hit send, immediately wishing I could take it back. It tastes seedy as I list every movie I've ever seen where ugly things take place in hotel rooms. I wait for her response, unnecessarily nervous.

"FUCK YEAH!!" She texts. I'm momentarily relieved, but that feeling fades quickly into grief when I focus on the planning for which I have just assumed responsibility.

The major obstacle is cost, ninety dollars for the night, in our case, the day. That type of money missing from our account will surely prompt an interrogation from Dana. My wantonness has no limit, as I list ways to secretly produce ninety dollars. I can dip into the kids' savings accounts or look in my parents' jelly cabinet to see if they have a stash. I'm running a fundraiser at school to support the National Honor Society that I could skim, but I finally decide to ask my brother to borrow the money and pay him back over time. He innocently agrees and the last piece is in place.

I prepare her for the experience as the day draws near by asking what she wants to do, offering suggestions such as going to a movie, playing board games, or cards. I tell her, "There are always movies in the room we can order," when my previous ideas are not well received. All of my suggestions sound lame, trying to cover up the obvious reason we're spending the day there.

285

Natalia brings us right back to the ugly truth, "I just want to go the hotel room and fuck you all day long." I say nothing because there really isn't anything meaningful to be said.

I pick her up at home and have the usual small talk with her mom. I give a new name for an imaginary race and we talk about the weather, school, her job, my kids, her kids or the myriad other topics to keep me standing in the foyer. I feel her become nervous around me, sometimes she lets her eyes linger a bit longer after I'm done talking. It may be my imagination or hypersensitivity but I'm fairly certain she flirts with me.

Natalia and I drive forty minutes to the hotel with a familiar nervous energy. I give the clerk a credit card for deposit and verify with him four times that nothing will be charged to it so I can pay cash afterward. He directs me to the room and I leave the lobby with my head down weary of security cameras.

I pull around back and find a spot between two larger vehicles that hide my car. My thought process is weak and flawed. Although I achieve the false sense of being carefully duplicitous I just gave my real name and credit card to the man in the lobby illuminating how subconsciously bad I am at covering my tracks.

We walk inside to the smell of chlorine from the pool mixed with the caustic aroma of industrial strength cleaners. Our room is upstairs and halfway down the hall. I don't feel my hand shaking until I attempt to put the keycard in the slot. The lock blinks red the first two times I try because I pull the card out too fast, paranoid. I wonder if she notices me shaking but when I see her out of my peripheral, she is looking around, calm as ever.

The room smells stale. The curtains halfway closed and the textured wallpaper stained from spending the majority of its life in a smoking room. The edges of this moment are surreal, like one of those experiences where I admit to myself that I should not be here and aver to never do anything like this again. Somehow, all the potential loss hanging in the balance does not outweigh the indolence to change.

We spend the day as planned, naked and engaged in some sort of sexual act. We stop only to shower and buy Chinese take-out. We check out by eight p.m. and as I close the door to the room I'm again overcome with remorse. The feeling occurs often enough now to be analyzed. I have no parallel but imagine this to be similar to a suicide attempt. Like eating a bottle of pills only to change my mind while waiting for the result. The thought of, "Why didn't I foresee this regret an hour ago?" creeps up violently and somehow, unexpectedly.

I despise the thought process and momentarily vow to incorporate it into future decisions but I can guarantee that this repentance will be no different than any other. I will again be overtaken with happiness and horniness when she asks me to spend a day with her. When she tells me, "I love making love to you," I will cave again, failing to control the forces that overpower my fickle morality.

Twice more we'll spend the day in a hotel. I blindly march through the same futile steps to hide my whereabouts, once even parking my car down a country road to ride my bike to the room. I think nothing of holding the room with my credit card making my presence completely traceable but my obsession is blinding. Our last excursion includes a stay overnight. By this time in the relationship we are able to revisit places in our past to reminisce, having breakfast at the diner where we first kissed.

By the time I drop her off I'm unable to sit still, overwhelmed by the anxiety of having been detached from myself for so long. I'm convinced that someone, if not everyone knows what I've done. I'm terrified to look at Dana when I walk into my house because, although she bought my alibi about playing cards, spending the night with my underage girlfriend drives me to new depths of corruption with which I'm not sure I can ever be acquainted.

Chapter 13

I receive several warnings in the nascence of my missteps. The first day of school, the crisis counselor, Sharon, with whom I have always had a positive relationship casually tells me I should come to her office. Her tone does not convey crisis but I have no doubt what she wants. I go two periods later overcome with curiosity.

Sharon's office is always buzzing. There is forever a student with a perceived dilemma or a parent with a real one causing her phone to ring perpetually. When she closes the door and sits behind her desk she looks at me and chews her gum loudly before speaking. Her omnipotent smirk irritates me, tempting me to ask what's wrong, but I have to let her speak first in the hopes that she reveals something.

She is an overly proud recovering alcoholic who thinks she knows how to deal with any problem because she has overcome her own. In a thick New York accent, through a stream of cliché phrases that only add to the mystique of her thick skin she says, "Listen, the field hockey coach came knocking on my door. I was her first line of defense to tell me the rumors coming down the pipeline."

Sharon understands the pitfalls of a student who latches onto a teacher. She only refers to Natalia by last name and tempers whatever she might truly feel with, "We both know kids like to chew the fat and if she's getting positive feedback then maybe she took the ball ran with this thing a little too far, ya know?"

Since Sharon is not only giving me the problem but also the explanation I let her continue. I let her stroke her own ego with plenty of addiction jargon about kids in need. I taper the conversation by asking what I might do to help this situation and conclude perfectly when I say, "Should I speak to Natalia's coach to smooth things over?"

She tells me without any thought, "I got your back on this one."

I sit and wonder how she is going to cover me because during my time in her office I explained nothing. It wasn't really a lie if all I did was agree with the justifications thrust upon me. Disturbingly, still no incentive to actually change my behavior appears. Every opportunity to act is instead viewed as a bullet dodged.

Dana makes her own attempt to reel me also, not simply by speaking to me or searching the root of my erratic behavior but also telling me the ancillary consequences of my repeated absences. "Your daughter is having a very hard time dealing with whatever you're going through Jim," she says as I arrive home one night after a day with Natalia. I try to ignore her for all of the typical reasons that I have found to disregard her feelings in the past. I dismiss her pleas as simple embellishment to produce guilt. I tell myself that Dana is trying to tug on my heart strings by using our kids as pawns, dismissing the possibility of any truth.

I'm not surprised that Dana would use the kids to accentuate a point because she knows how much I love being a father. Dana has heard plenty of accolades from members of her family and friends regarding the rapport that I have with my kids. She not only shares the compliments with me but also the opinion.

I never knew what it meant to truly love someone until the first time I held our first born daughter. I stayed up long nights staring at her, enamored that she relied on me to meet all her needs. It was daunting and melting simultaneously. I was nervous when Dana was pregnant for a second time, unsure I could offer the same love and attention to another child, my affection absolute for my daughter. However, the capacity to love expanded effortlessly when my only son was born twenty-three months later. I felt blessed and truly happy for the first time since before high school as I took inventory of my life.

Another twenty-three months brought another daughter and yet another augmentation of the feeling that I could barely harness toward one child yet somehow multiplied by three. Dana and I spoke about three children and here they were, omnipresent in my life. Yet something was still nagging at me frequently.

"Is this all there is?" I asked myself many times. Nothing seems to ever live up to its billing. It confuses me when an event or a milestone, holiday or happening is so anticipated. I don't know if I'm afraid to have happiness taken away from me or if I'm unable to enjoy things the way other people do. Am I the tainted variable?

I will marry and think, "Is this all there is?" I witnessed the birth of my three children and thought, "Is this all it is?" Graduate high school, college, gain employment, promotions, be chosen Teacher of the Year, compete in bicycle races, triathlons and in each instance feel the normal amount of anticipation and excitement in expectancy.

But in the quiet, reflective, solitary moments afterwards I ask again, "Is this all there is? I want to feel more. I'm dying to feel something clean and natural but the more events that unfold I fear purity may never come.

I'm so far into myself and satisfying my own needs that I am oblivious and impervious to everything. Even, "Your daughter is laying on the floor crying that she misses her dad," although terribly upsetting, does not wake me. I miss her too. I miss all three of my children very much, but the person I miss most is me.

The most serious scolding comes in December. In the middle of class the phone in my room rings, I am greeted by the principal's secretary who tells me that Barbara, the principal would like to meet with me. Her call concludes ominously, "She suggests that you bring a union representative."

I know instantly that we will be discussing a serious topic and have no doubts what that is. I find and tell my delegate, giving him nothing more than the same cursory story. He puts my mind at ease offering past stories of suspected impropriety. He prepares me as much as he can for the meeting but I know what I must do and by this time, have told the lie so many times that I'm not only comfortable, but believe the validity myself. The added caveat here is that I'm sure a decision is going to be made whether or not to take this to the next level.

I'm surprised when I walk into Barbara's office to also find Rick, the head of guidance, who doubles as the Affirmative Action Officer. There is no surprise when Barbara tells me very officially, "It has been brought to my attention that there's a female student who has grown quite attached to you, Jim. There are rumors circulating that could potentially damage your reputation. I know how hard you've worked to create a pristine reputation for both you and your department," she preaches.

She passes directly over the question of whether or not there is any truth to the rumors and begins to control the damage. She does have the good sense to ask, "I realize that Natalia is in your class, but how is it that you've come to have a relationship with her outside of the classroom?"

This allows me to tell her how Talia latched onto me in her time of need. I explain, "Her mother is aware that Natalia has confided some problems in me and she is aware that I have put her in contact with guidance as well as provided my own bit of advice." Nothing seems to strike her as odd until I mention our trip to the therapist.

At my revelation of visiting Natalia's therapist she becomes agitated, fidgets in her seat and cuts me off, "Wait a minute, you mean you went to her therapist with her?"

"Yes, and her mother," I add quickly as if saving myself from admonishment.

"Oh Jim, that was not a good idea at all," Barbara says, the wind knocked out of her.

I explain that the idea wasn't something I offered, rather was asked by a direct call. That explanation makes no difference in Barbara's clear disappointment. She directs me, "You need to explain to Natalia and her mother that guidelines must be put in place that prohibit you from being alone with her at any time."

Barbara offers to be present at this conversation to make clear the decision is coming from above. I try to appear like I'm contemplating her option but politely decline, "Thank you Barbara, but I feel as though I can handle the conversation by myself," full of complete dishonesty.

As the meeting draws to a close and I'm walking to the door, Rick, who has sat and silently scribbled notes the entire meeting says, "I have just one question," his pause sycophantic, self-righteous. "I feel as affirmative action officer I would be remiss if I didn't ask you this directly," he says before looking up from his legal pad.

"Is there anything going on between you and Natalia that violates the teacher-student relationship?"

I clench my jaw to prevent any other incriminating reaction, my heart pounds.

I know that I must answer quickly and I must lie. This is the first time that anyone has come out and asked me directly. With all eyes on me, I look at him and say, "No, Rick, there is nothing going on between me and Natalia."

I make a point to look at Barbara for punctuation. I sound so convincing, I even believe myself. As I utter that sentence I detach myself from the life I live after three o'clock in the afternoon. I am not the man sleeping with a fifteen year old girl. My answer comes from somewhere that is still living up to the self-made promise to live a good life but sadly, that person is not rooted in reality. That man will evaporate into the conniving ego that controls my actions as soon as I leave this office.

During my drive home, I cannot stop dwelling on how dirty I feel. This is the first time I lament the betrayal of myself. I don't care about lying to either Barbara or Rick. They are administrators, but I've always expected more of myself. I'm so tired of lying and so tired of creating situations where the need to lie becomes self-preservation. What I feel is constantly slamming against what I think I should do. I'm exhausted and want this to end. The mental gymnastics are demanding and are losing their efficacy. I'm running out of lies as well as the energy to fabricate them.

Chapter 14

We mold our relationship around the obstacles in front of us, our routine unable to remain static. I've been driving her home for quite some time until my admonishment makes it clear that any contact draws too much attention so we meet at a park next to school. Although a nuisance, the alternative to stop driving her home is not an option.

She knows my schedule and comes to my classroom during free periods, closes the door behind her, walks behind my desk and rubs my back or asks sweetly, "Can I have a hug please?"

She also knows the places in the building where we pass in the hallway. We both speed up or slow down to put us in the optimal spot to exchange a glance. I neither discourage her behavior nor curtail my own, constantly setting examples and reveling in the reciprocation.

It's difficult to ascertain the point when it becomes an infatuation, but taking inventory now, this seems more like an obsession than any relationship I've ever had. I amaze even myself when I lie down and recount my day before I pass out from the exhaustion of a double life.

One night, late in the fall, I sit outside Talia's job, waiting to drive her home. Periodically starting the engine to take the chill from my car. Just about the time I start to worry because she is late, I receive a text, sure to read that she will be right out. What I see is simply, "I told mom."

My first reaction is that she sent the text to the wrong person, "Told mom what?"

After I send, the thought occurs that perhaps she is referring to our secret, but easily dismiss the absurdity of that notion.

"Everything."

But before I can reply another text arrives, "About us."

My panic is inexplicable, almost enough to make me faint. My first reaction is to start the car and drive away, for good. I don't know what I would do, but I imagine the worst, thinking that the cops know and I may already be hunted. I hate the feeling in my stomach but after the wave crests, I calm to the strangest sensation of relief. Lying to even one less person liberates me. My fingers can barely find the right keys to text. While still fumbling Natalia sends another text that I'm reluctant to open.

"It's okay Jim, she's fine," I read.

I cannot fathom anything as fine with the images plowing through my mind but Talia is remarkably calm. I delete the half-typed text and instead ask her if she can talk.

She calls within a minute, her serenity counters my insanity, "Are you okay?"

I stammer, "Um, I don't know, you tell me. Am I?"

I feel disempowered and wish that I had been made a part of that decision. "Should I be running now?" I ask.

She laughs, "You're so silly."

"How did this happen?" I ask, but before she can respond I say, "Wait, where are you? Can your mother hear you right now?"

"I'm sitting on the floor in Mama's bedroom," provides an uncomfortable picture of her adolescence.

"Well Mama started talking about a conversation she had with another mom. She heard how Catherine is having sex on the weekends and drinking and God only knows what. Then Mama tells me how lucky she is that I don't cause her any of those problems."

Natalia pauses, as I'm about to ask what any of that has to do with my question she continues, "So I started to cry because I hate keeping this secret from Mama and I had such a strong feeling that she wouldn't be mad. Well, I was right."

It bothers me that she refers to her as, "Mama," and not, "My mom," because it is the simplest diversion from her earth shattering news. She continues, "I started to cry. I told her that the only problem that I cause her is that I'm in love with my French teacher. She just said, 'Oh Talia, I know you love Mr. Cunneely but that's just a dream. There's nothing to cry about.' Then I said, 'Well he loves me too.' He told me he does and we talk all the time about the future of our relationship.'"

My anxiety becomes painful before she continues, "She was silent for a moment and looked at me. I thought she was like mad or something, but I think that she was just trying to see if I was telling the truth. Then she said, 'Well you guys need to be careful that you don't get caught.'"

I try to let her finish but my disbelief makes silence impossible, "So you told your mother about us and she didn't say she was calling the cops. You're sure she didn't remain calm to avoid either of us doing something drastic before they could arrest me?"

After laughing again she assures me, "Mama is downstairs eating dinner. She's fine. She has not and will not call the police."

The last thing Talia adds is, "Oh! And I asked her if she wanted to speak to you and she said it would be a good idea but in a few days after she's had some time."

I cannot even think clearly, fear and confusion grip me past the point of paralysis. A blitz of questions clouds my ability to perform any voluntary action. Breathing, barely manageable. What happens next? Who else knows by now? How do I explain any of this? How is Kathy cool with it?

I can't help but feel betrayed. However, also relieved if all was received as well as Natalia says. I want to knock on their door right now and have the conversation but know I should wait. I wish, for the first time that I had someone to talk to, each day growing exponentially more difficult to function.

There is nobody I can turn to but me. I want to run and want to stay where I am because I feel safe sitting silently in this parking lot. I sit, watching my breath condense in the cold air wondering what this next step will become as it evolves into the new normal. I'm scared, reluctant, and as usual regretful.

We hang up so she can finish eating and I try to teach my class. It seems impossible to concentrate on anything meaningful. Three hours, I trudge through, awaiting a knock at the door and flashing lights in the parking lot. I walk out of class, fully expecting to be thrown to the ground and handcuffed. Unfortunately, my corrupt behavior does not come with any foreshadowing of how my world will collapse.

Once in my car I call Talia to find out if anything new has developed. She is even calmer, almost jovial as she explains, "Mama and I have been talking all night and she has been asking all sorts of questions."

She tells me, "It feels great to be honest with her and I just knew that she would be cool and supportive."

I still cannot believe this is happening. I feel better in some respects that my future is in the hands of not just Natalia but also her mother, another decision I will come to regret. The bounce in her voice angers me as it completely disregards the caveats of this unforeseen twist.

I have only the thirty minute ride to discuss what I should say when I have this conversation with her mother. It's set for Saturday, at her house. Natalia assures me, "Just be honest. Mama just wants to know that I'm in good hands."

She explains the variety of questions her mother has asked, providing a strange mix of comfort and confusion. With each conflicting stage of the insanity I realize that Kathy is relaxed and actually entertaining the realistic possibility of her fifteen year old daughter dating a thirty year old teacher. I'm simultaneously petrified and consoled by the incompatible truths.

When this swirl of perplexity calms long enough for me to lie in bed, I feel oddly alleviated that Natalia no longer has to keep our secret from her mother. I'm not convinced this will benefit me, but am happy that Natalia doesn't have to endure so much secrecy. I see the part of Natalia that is the extension of my own psyche as fortunate and like to take credit for that. I've listened to her speak about her mother to know how close they are. She wants to make her proud and be a perfect daughter so I'm happy to alleviate some pressure. I rationalize my anxiety away thusly until I struggle to sleep.

Chapter 15

Two days after our secret is revealed I make the surreal walk to the front door of Kathy's townhouse. I call Natalia on my way to make sure that everything is still as planned, but I cannot shake the fear that the police are awaiting me. The horrible feeling in my stomach actually forces me to moan as I switch from my adult ego to the fifteen year old. The transition is especially difficult tonight because the fifteen year old drives this part of my life, but the adult has to attend the meeting. The grown man façade needs to make sure that Kathy understands I mean her daughter no harm. I turn the last corner to their townhouse slowly and reluctantly ready to slam the car into reverse and flee.

I park and take a deep breath, completely ignorant to what I am doing. As I ring the doorbell I smell chicken frying. I'm surprised by how long I stand at the door considering they know I'm coming. When it finally opens I see Natalia, a smile on her face unlike any I've ever seen. Her expression speaks of having the upper hand but not for any exploitative purpose only that I am a guest in her world for a change.

Her eyebrows raised, her smirk conveys nebulous uncertainty. "Hi, are you ready?" she asks barely aspirating her consonants.

She dressed up for this, including makeup, trying to look more mature. As I slowly make my way down the hallway I see

Kathy standing at the stove. She breaks the ice immediately, "I said to Talia, 'What if we just don't answer the door? Then we never have to do this.'"

She chuckles letting me know that she is joking, but I'm apologetic for having put all of us in this uncomfortable predicament. "I'm sorry," I say sheepishly.

"No, it's fine," she does a sub-par job of putting me at ease.

We move to the living room and although I've been here before, my presence now makes me uncomfortable. We discuss topics ranging from what I want from her daughter to evading discovery. She mentions that Talia told her we have not had sex, which is a lie, but believed because of how forthright we apparently seem. She makes no statement forbidding intercourse only marking off of a mental checklist.

At different points I sit forward with my elbows on my knees to punctuate the gravity of my words. I feel her eyes linger on me a bit longer than is normal during natural digressions. It's voyeuristic, she appears to live vicariously through Natalia as she tells me that all she wants is for someone to take care of her daughter. Kathy asks about my marriage and my career and amazingly my long term plans in teaching as if I am being interviewed for the position of illicit lover for her child.

I lie about my marriage, "Dana and I are in the process of getting a divorce," which tears my stomach apart when I mumble the words.

What else can I say? That I am living two separate lives? I have strayed from Dana for a variety of reasons, but this betrayal should feel worse than any I can imagine. Remarkably, I'm able to block the full extent of its treachery. I feel no remorse, having completely severed ties with my adulthood.

We come to all of the necessary agreements in order to receive Kathy's blessing. She makes clear that she has nothing further when she asks, "So what are you guys gonna do tonight?"

I shrug my shoulders, "I guess we're going to the mall to do some Christmas shopping," and the conversation turns to the holidays. I feel like I'm watching myself in a movie, too unbelievable to grasp that I am living this. We say goodbye in the same foyer as so many times before but this time is different. Talia and I leave as a couple, apparently no concerns on Kathy's conscience, I wear them exclusively.

We sit in the car and although in no shape to drive, I go just to avoid sitting here any longer. I stop at the first convenience store I see and without a word, walk inside and buy a pack of cigarettes. I haven't smoked in years, but the events of this evening are much too difficult to manage chemical free. I don't know what Talia's reaction will be but also don't care. I open the pack, pull one out and put it in my mouth ready to light.

Before I strike the match, I look at her and ask with the unlit cigarette pressed between my lips, "You want one?"

"Fuck yeah," she says with a grin that verifies her understanding the benefits of being with an older man.

Three quick drags and she looks at me very seriously, "We can't tell Mama that either of us smokes. She'll kill me but she'll lose respect for you. She hates smokers."

I nod. Keeping my renewed habit of smoking from Kathy seems the least of secrets that need concealing.

We sit in the car aimlessly. I don't think either of us accounted for what life would be like after this conversation simply because the content itself was unimaginable. It feels new all over again with one shroud of secrecy now absent. Something seems missing, the careful planning having lost one facet. However, it is replaced with attempts to discern the new protection now and in the long term. After my cigarette is finished and I think myself composed we leave.

Moments later we debrief the surrealistic conversation, as well as our conversion from secretive, hidden dalliance to approved relationship. I refuse to believe its existence despite the verifying memory.

Chapter 16

With full support of our liaison, Kathy recruits me into the role of co-parent. Despite the chunk of time that Talia's job cuts out of what we would normally spend having sex after school I agree to drop her off. After she explains how she wants to start saving for a car I continue the act of supportive boyfriend. She also works one day during the weekend so the times that I would normally see her are pushed back until after she is done with her shift. I secretly feel relieved that she'll have a portion of her time occupied by something beside me, providing a bit of breathing room. I think of all the things that I'll be able to do while she is at work and feel the weight being lifted from my shoulders.

One Saturday evening, after I pick her up, she texts Kathy to tell her we'll bring home a pizza. As we are waiting Kathy texts, "I already made dinner because I have company tonight." Five minutes from her driveway, after cancelling the pizza, I am awoken from my daydream, "Company?"

I pull the car over and ask, "What we are going to do? We can't go to your house," using too stern of a tone after I hear myself.

"Why can't we go to my house?" Talia asks innocently making me feel worse for snapping.

I try not to sound condescending, "Your mom told you she's having company. I can't exactly sit there making believe it's completely normal that I'm at your house."

We have normalized so many abnormal behaviors, consistently pushing the boundaries has been the only constant, but there has to be some shred of reality left to guide my survival instinct.

She looks at me seriously, conveying that she is deeply contemplating the validity of my statement. "Well, I don't know Jim, Mama didn't say you couldn't come over. She knew you were getting me from work and knew you were coming tonight so if she invited someone it must be cool."

Her response baffles me, "Natalia, that is absolutely crazy and you know it. Whoever this is, how can I just walk in your house, sit down and have dinner? Are you just going to introduce me as your French Teacher?" I sound angrier.

Her frustration bubbles, "Hang on, I'll call her and ask." She makes the phone call and I hear only her end, explaining my concerns.

She hangs up the phone and gleefully responds, "Mama said come on home. She made steak."

I open my mouth but have no words. I begin to realize the full breadth of my predicament. I have given power to two people who have little vested interest in my well-being. Of course Natalia thinks she loves me but only because I have choreographed the story as such. And Kathy, who has capriciously given Natalia over to me for the sake of what I believe, is living vicariously only loses her voyeuristic muse if I'm caught. And now after having put all this trust in them both, how do I back out and question their judgment? Without words and with an uncomfortable silent argument hanging, I drive to their house.

We walk into a full dining room table. I only see Kathy in my periphery, my eyes lock on the two strangers in the room. In an animalistic instant, I size them up to analyze if they will leave this meeting repulsed. My mind revolves, relentlessly around the idea of being caught. I try to guess who it will be, how it will happen and who will bear witness.

The woman at the table, introduced to me as Linda seems apprehensive to shake my hand. Linda and Kathy went to high school together and have always remained friends, "Best friends in the whole world" as she is explained. I cannot read if her reluctance is because Kathy has already warned her of my place in Natalia's life or her true reaction to seeing me walk in with a fifteen year old girl. Either way, the salutation is half-hearted.

Linda looks to be worn out, the somewhat ragged appearance of having been scorned by too many men, making me a prime target for suspicion. She is slender with dark hair. I think she would be pretty if she would smile or at least lose a little bit of her hatred. Her husband, Bill is personable and warm, shaking my hand readily with a firm grip. He is a typical middle aged looking man, thirty pounds overweight with a moustache that went out of style fifteen years ago.

Their four year old daughter barely looks up, yet says, "Hello," as instructed. We sit down and are served steak, mashed potatoes and corn. I cannot eat, too anxious about what is unfolding before my passive eyes. How do I behave normally, what if Bill asks me what I do for a living? What if they ask me how I met Natalia or how long we've been dating?

There are so many topics that could potentially wind this conversation toward disaster, that I say not a word. I make no eye contact in hopes that I blend into the background. They engage Natalia, asking about school, field hockey and her new job. Although I'm happy they are speaking about a topic other than me the potential still exists to drag me into the conversation at any moment. I keep my head bowed and chew as quietly as possible.

I take intermittent bites only because not eating will also draw unwanted attention. A ten second silence precedes Linda saying, "So Jim," my heart sinks immediately, gripped by that feeling in my stomach. I instantly wish for the ability to talk myself down like people who calm themselves from an asthma attack. This time extra painful.

"You're awfully quiet," she says sweetly. I choose to interpret her tone as condescending and become angry. I smile and say, "I just like to listen." Ray Liotta flashes through my mind, saying the same thing in "Goodfellas", also at a dining room table.

Kathy saves me, "Well is everyone finished? I'll take your plates," as she clears the table. I'm thankful for the diversion but regretful for her absence. Luckily, she continues to control the conversation from the kitchen.

After everything is cleared Kathy returns with a store bought chocolate cake and a stack of paper plates and napkins. "I hope you don't mind such an unfancy dessert," she says chuckling.

The din of everyone responding with some sort of placation drowns out my thoughts. When I refocus it occurs to me that with dessert being served I'll soon be free. The small talk continues surrounding foreign topics. They talk about the prom and trips to the shore, reminiscing about old boyfriends and some argument over a guy. I eat my cake in five forkfuls and when Kathy asks me if I would like another piece I place my hand over my stomach, "God, no I'm full," hoping Natalia reads my cue.

A few seconds after Talia finishes her last bite she finds a small lull in the conversation and says one click above the whole evening's volume, "Ok, we're going downstairs."

Before she can finish her sentence I have my plate in hand and stand up feeling naked except for a polite smile. I dump my empty plate in the kitchen trash can and walk quickly toward the basement door hoping to prevent any further danger.

Like nothing more than a trained animal, as soon as I smell the distinct aroma of Natalia's bedroom at the bottom of the stairs I feel the same two feelings. I have the deep, distinct nausea from an unknown part of my existence, immediately overlapped by the beginnings of arousal. The laundry room is in the far corner of the bottom floor adjacent to her room so the scent is a mixture of her natural odor, perfume, and laundry detergent. I love smelling it not only because it's pleasant but also because sex is not far behind.

I lay on her bed while she tinkers with something on her dresser. I'm inclined to tell her how difficult dinner was but refuse to acknowledge the immorality I have so cleverly disguised, so I say nothing. She joins me on the bed, "You know I kinda want to have you come in my mouth."

The rush of erotic excitement is quickly tempered by the reality of who is speaking. Not all stimulation is squashed but I am reminded that I still own something like a conscience.

"What makes you say that, hon?" I carefully choose my words to avoid her feeling as dirty as I do.

She instantly replies, "Because we have done just about everything else and I think it would be hot. I know other girls that do it and I think their boyfriends are disgusting. You're definitely not disgusting so I might like it."

I find no flaw in her logic, "Ok, I'm game."

The natural flow of this conversation illustrates that there are no vestiges of the boundaries that once guided my life.

With that, she rolls over and kisses me, moves her lips to my cheek, my ear, and then neck. As she finds my collarbone she moves her hand down to my waistline, stopping when she reaches my fully erect penis. As soon as she grabs me knowing I'm fully engorged she strokes. She presses too hard so I grab her hand and explain why that hurts.

With a seductive smile, "Well then let's take your pants off," she replies.

I'm naked from the waist down as she is kisses and caresses the lower half of my body. When I writhe she whispers, "Did you like that?"

I moan back, "Uh-huh."

As soon as she puts me in her mouth my hips surge upward. When that instantaneous rush of pleasure subsides my mind is washed over with the actuality of what is taking place. Again, as so many times before, thoughts arrive with no discernible logic. They come as couriers dropping their message with no time for interpretation before the next one overtakes occupation of my thoughts.

She's fifteen. My dick is in her mouth. Her mother is upstairs. What are my children doing right now? What would Dana think? Her mouth is warm. What would my parents, my grandparents think? Can I trust Linda and Bill? I don't think I can come. If I can't come how do I explain without hurting her feelings? Does her mother know what we're doing down here? Someone's walking upstairs. Block your mind. That feels good. I think I can come if she keeps doing that.

"Right there," I say as I put my hand on her head.

She increases her pace slightly perhaps from the excitement of controlling my pleasure. I lock my hips and drive my head back into the pillow and warn in a raspy whisper, "Talia, you're going to make me come."

With only another moment of rhythmic stroking, I pop. All of the built up arousal and excitement explodes in a release accompanied by a low moan that escapes the back of my throat.

I open my eyes to see her kneeling over me, her face blaring panic. I fight through the euphoria, trying to discern her problem. Her body heaves once as she shakes her head as if to say, "This isn't happening." I realize when she puts her hand over her mouth that she is fighting her reaction. I don't know if it's mind over matter or her gag reflex but she's in crisis. She looks at me with distress, seeking my approval to void what's in her mouth. I'm absolutely useless, riding out the orgasm. Although I have no reason for personal alarm the look on her face is compelling enough to make me share the emergency. My heart rate pinned at the same pace as when building to ejaculation.

All I can do is reach down and grab her hand to let her know that she can do whatever she needs, otherwise I'm checked out of this horrid affair. There is no bathroom down here so I look for a waste paper basket, but unfortunately, I'm still completely paralyzed. When she can hold herself no longer and the fear that has frozen her disappears, she wretches where my stomach meets my groin. She doesn't empty the contents of her whole stomach, but only the exact amount of semen she tried to swallow.

Despite my warning, not knowing what to expect, she immediately swallowed what hit the back of her throat and before she could control anything else she choked. She swallows hard a few times, a disgusted look on her face and as soon as she can gain control says, "Oh my God Jimi, I'm so sorry. I did not mean for that to happen. It wasn't you. I just wasn't ready. I'm so sorry. I'm so embarrassed."

"It's fine Talia," I say fighting through panting breaths, "I understand."

She runs to the laundry room and returns immediately with a clean towel. While still standing next to the bed she wipes from my upper thigh up to above my navel the regurgitated, chocolate colored semen. She looks as if she might cry.

I take her hand and say, "Hey, don't be upset. It's ok. We shouldn't have done that maybe, but there is nothing to be upset about. I promise I'm not upset."

She nods in agreement with the corners of her mouth turned down. This is the perfect ending to our evening where every aspect has been a glaring spotlight on how depraved this all is. But the illumination forces no end. And remarkably we have all, Kathy included been able to masterfully cram down our subconscious doubts. We have normalized the consequences of our decisions. Talia has also reached her limit and can no longer swallow the disgusting reproduction of this disease.

I leave shortly thereafter, not too quickly to make her think something is wrong. I avoid lingering which would only provide opportunity to dwell on what was just etched in our collective memory. Natalia is quiet. I want to know why but don't ask, afraid of the conversation that would surely ensue. I say goodbye and walk upstairs to find Kathy and her friends sitting on the couch. The same couch where I received Kathy's blessing.

"Ok, goodnight. It was nice to meet you," I say.

I would normally shake their hand politely but I'm too afraid. I'm certain that the events downstairs are written all over my face. I say, "Goodbye," looking toward them but walking in the other direction, out the door. I power walk to my car, start it and stall as I pull away, letting my foot off of the clutch too quickly. I start the car again and cry the entire ride home because of what I just did to that girl. I have no idea the depths of the damage, but feel distraught even attempting to understand the hurt I continuously cause.

Chapter 17

My life is reminiscent of standing on the beach. I'm lost in the peaceful illusion that I'm safe, watching the tide. Until, without feeling threatened by any of its predecessors the first wave hits. Tides move methodically, the only warning is common sense that the water level will undoubtedly rise. There is a definite wax and wane to the feeling of potential, if not imminent danger with which I live. My decisions felt precarious at the beginning because everything was unknown. The behavior that sends up red flags is anonymous, the appearance of impropriety cast well before its existence. Driving her home and listening to her problems were both aspects of what was still a genuine relationship. When those habits continued without admonition crossing over into the lascivious was simple. And of course, as the human condition dictates, each time the line is crossed, pushing further feels harmless.

As physicality progressed it felt dangerous but with each additional foray, became comfortable. Our visit to Chris seemed scary but that feeling quickly abated when Kathy clarified her disagreement with prescribed safeguards. And finally, when Kathy came on board I felt lulled into an impossibly false sense of security that I could not be enveloped by the force of the rising tide. I'm watching the waves, I know the tide must be coming, but I do nothing to save myself. There is now, very little time left before I drown under my salacious decisions.

Some time passes since the meeting with my Principal when I receive the second call to my classroom. Now it's the Superintendent who would like to meet with me. This follows the letter placed in my permanent file detailing Barbara's plan to prevent the further spread of rumors. Upon reading this letter the Superintendent summons me to his office.

George is a bombastic man who thinks he has much more power than is reality. The rural, regional school covers both ends of the economic spectrum and comprises five municipalities over one hundred square miles. George has been an employee of the district since its inception in 1975, first as a Vice-Principal, Principal and shortly after, Superintendent. By his own account, this is his small kingdom and he acts very much the king.

After I passed the initial interview with Barbara to begin my employment eight years earlier, I was called back to meet with George individually so that he could put his personal stamp of approval. I have always felt a connection to him from our first meeting because he has the ability to put a paternal spin on anything that comes across his desk.

His office, perched above the library, allows him to look down on all those meant to admire his lofty position. The stairs that lead to the administrative annex can be a lonely and stressful walk for any reason, making my march that much more dreadful.

"So, what's going on?" he leads as soon as I sit down after a sincere handshake. His tone calm and reassuring. I try to convey the same gravity that beckoned him to summon me while not seeming guilty.

"Well it seems a female student who has grown attached has raised some eyebrows. So, Barbara and I sat down and planned some damage control," I reply. I'm immediately relieved by how convincingly my first opportunity to speak unfolds.

"Jim, from the day you started here, you've been nothing but professional. I remember interviewing you, proud to have found this diamond in the rough. You started at a high level and have only continued to grow. I mean, we picked you as our Teacher of the Year and you've certainly lived up to every bit of that honor. I would hate to see your reputation tarnished by something silly. I've read the letter and just wanted to ask if you needed anything. I've heard things myself but I'm not down there in the classroom so I thought maybe it wasn't anything. But people talk and some want to put an explanation to this thing. I mean you're a good looking guy so people wonder. You're ok then?"

His overdone soliloquy only buys me time to create a response to his sanctimonious concern. "I'm fine and I have it under control. As a matter of fact, I've already spoken to Natalia and her mother and explained that things have to change. For my good but also for her daughter's," I lie.

The smile on his face hurts me. Beneath his posturing lies genuine concern, not only for Natalia and for the wellness of the school community but for me too.

I leave this meeting and feel the walls tightening. By the time I reach the bottom of the stairs I'm short of breath, loosening my necktie. The swirl of thoughts in my head range from, "Why did you ever get yourself into this?" to, "Walk back up there and tell him everything, it might be your only way out safely."

This tension in my chest is neither a new feeling nor something easily put aside. I can barely function. Suspicion has reached as high as it will go before extending outside the school. Although I realize this stark reality and can feel the rumble in my stomach it neither controls nor suppresses my obsession.

Chapter 18

Is it possible to remember the true beginning of a nightmare? I've never been able to pinpoint how I led myself into any fantastic catastrophe and this is no different. I feel as though dropped into the second act of a traditional three act tragedy. The constricting feeling in my chest peaks at Christmas. Dana takes the kids to her parents without me, our marriage so fractured that the decision is made almost automatically.

Unbelievably, even to me, I resort to where I think I will feel most comfortable and spend the day with Natalia, and Kathy, not my own children. I feel disgusting all day. Everything I see as I look around their townhouse reminds me that I am someplace I do not belong, the epitome of ectopic.

My thoughts are exclusively on my family and what they are doing. I wonder if they miss me, what they are eating and what toys I'm unable to assemble. I'm with Natalia today in body only, not in spirit and she knows it. I feel dreadful, unable to be where I want and impossibly trapped where I am wanted. I embrace my role as a lost soul and wander through two impossibly difficult days.

The culmination is February, Super Bowl weekend. It's the end of the only life I've ever known. During my free period Friday morning I'm pulled away from my desk by a knock at the door. Certain it's Natalia, I open it with a smile. Instead, I'm shocked to find the superintendent. He rarely walks the halls unless a problem needs his intervention, in which case his gait and demeanor far precede him. I step aside and he enters.

He is calm but without preamble fires, "So did you have the conversation with that girl and her mother?"

I know that there is something more to his question because he exudes gruffness with, "That girl and her mother." Despite his position he is far from refined. He makes great effort to display decorum with only middling success but like me, cannot hide his true nature.

No such effort is made here tipping me off instantly. "I did," choosing a minimalist approach to avoid entangling myself with too many words.

"So it went well, meaning you don't see her outside of class anymore?" He shoots back. It feels more like an interrogation now than concern.

"That's right," I say, "Only in class."

He only mumbles, "Ok," and sinks into thought. He is processing, clearly weighing my words against something else he thinks the truth. Some emotion I cannot discern overcomes him and it prompts him to turn and leave without a word. It may be anger or confusion or disappointment but this conversation strikes him on a visceral level.

Knowing something is wrong, I try to keep in him in my presence by making small talk as he's almost out the door, I ask about a mutual friend, "So how is Dennis doing? Have you spoken with him lately?"

Truthfully, I'm sizing him up to determine what is happening. Upon hearing my lame response to his interrogation he seems on a mission, driven by his momentary reflection. Despite my diversionary question, as he is already beyond the threshold of my door, he barks without breaking stride, "Dennis is fine last time I spoke to him." I close my door and run to the wastepaper basket behind my desk, insert my face and vomit.

The second half of my day is a blur. I change all of my lesson plans and assign individual work. I sit at my desk and stare at my computer screen wondering what will happen. My drive home is equally as mechanical until I receive a call from Tommy, Maggie's boyfriend. Tommy has been a student in my class for two years and is always friendly. He greets me with, "Hey man I just wanted to give you a heads up. Maggie's math teacher told her the Prosecutor's office is coming to talk to her Monday."

His words are confusing but I'm further dumbfounded by his nonchalance. I can only conclude that this call is a favor but anger overrides appreciation for feeling blindsided. In an overwhelming moment of epiphany I know this is how my affair will finally end. My lies are about to be completely depleted and I am helpless.

"Huh? What about? I mean why are you telling me this?" I play naive but think I'm transparent, even to a fifteen year old boy at this point.

"Well apparently it has something to do with Talia," he pauses and catches himself, fearing he may offend, "I mean I know there's nothing going on, but you know how you guys spend a lot of time together because you're helping her with her dad and stuff? Well I guess people are talking and somebody said something to the wrong person and now the cops are in on it. I mean don't worry because there's nothing going on so there's nothing to worry about."

I'm devastated by his conviction of my infallibility.

He never asks me the truth, drawing his own conclusion from the person I portray in front of his class. The man he knows as his teacher is completely incapable of something so perverse. I want to cry, seemingly the only thing left. I'm eager to know more but don't want to raise suspicion by asking for details. I thank and assure him that it's just the product of, "People who like to talk."

Unfortunately, I'm only ten minutes from home, so I have little time to debrief Natalia. I call her and relay Tommy's horrid news. She tells me emphatically, "Jimi, I have no idea what this is about."

Her silence confuses me because I don't know if she is simply afraid, behind all of this or just as thunderstruck as me. In a ploy to keep a tighter leash on my actions, Dana applied to direct the winter play at my school and was hired. Tonight is opening night so she is already gone by the time I arrive home. As I'm making dinner Talia calls back. I step away nervously, "What's up?"

"I talked to Maggie," she greets, short of breath.

"She told me about her math teacher. It was Maggie, Meagan, Katie and the teacher who had lunch this week. Meagan made some comment about a teacher she has a crush on and right after she said it, everyone looked at one another. When the teacher noticed she said, 'What? What was that for?' It was then that Meagan told her how she knew there was something going on between Natalia and Mr. Cunneely." None of what she says makes sense and seems like someone is lying.

My mind races to the worst imaginable consequences, but I quickly chase them to avoid a panic attack. I settle on the realization that if any of this is true at least I have a starting point. Whatever happened during that lunch led someone to report to George. George confronted me today before he called the police to make sure he was justified. I settle on that basic chain of events to stop my mind from wandering so I can begin to solve the next step.

Part Two

The feeling that washes over me is indescribable, waves of nerves and nausea and an instinct to flee from everything, including Natalia. It's paranoia that everyone is out to harm me and that this is Natalia's fault or Kathy's or even Maggie's. I blame Dana for not being a better wife and my parents for not being better parents.

I'm cracking, looking for someone other than me to help shoulder this colossal burden. I pace my house, watching my kids do kid things. They play with their toys and watch television and I think of all the times I could've been a better father. My heart breaks and I feel like crying but can't. I imagine this to be like having a terminal illness, waiting to die. The end is imminent but I do not and cannot know when peace will actually arrive.

After a fitful evening, I lie in bed but do not sleep. I have no idea what will happen tomorrow or the next day and yet somehow there is still absolutely no possibility of ending my dalliance. Severance never even presents itself as an option through the entirety of this turmoil. Now, even as I'm almost certainty that my employer knows and has notified the authorities, I do not distance myself from Natalia.

Quite the opposite, I call her first thing in the morning and ask, "Is there any time today that I can come over and speak to you and Mama?" I still play the subtle psychological games to make sure she is ingratiated to me. I tell Dana that I'm going to run errands which buys me a few hours. Instead, I go to Talia's house and the three of us sit in the living room as I tell Kathy and Natalia all that I know. Natalia looks how I feel, stunned to the point of numb. Paralysis coming from the fear of feeling anything, the truth unimaginable. She seems to sense the reality that everything is crashing down and no matter how I try, I cannot understand why she is taking this so hard.

Kathy is eerily calm as if she knows something she's not sharing. I wonder continuously if she is blissfully ignorant to the magnitude of all I'm describing. "Well, Natalia certainly isn't going to say anything, and if anyone asks I'll just say that I know every time you're here and I'm fully supportive of you being her mentor," she unsuccessfully tries to reassure.

Kathy oversimplifies everything to the point of sounding ludicrous. Her blasé appeasement of the concerns for my life drives me further into a panic. "Ok, good," is all I say because it's all I can. I realize that anything else would be attempting to rationalize with an irrational person.

Natalia and I go downstairs to her room before I need to leave. We lay on her bed and she puts her head on my chest. Both of us silent as we wonder. She puts her hand on my stomach, gently rubbing an innocent place and I wonder if she is trying to have sex. I don't feel attractive in this state of anonymous trepidation but I think that an escape from the enormity, if even momentary might help.

She breaks the silence, "You know if this all goes down and you get in trouble I won't be able to go back to that school."

"What do you mean?" I say in a scolding tone, "I'd be the one in trouble. I wear all of this not you. Why wouldn't you be able to go back?"

She speaks quietly but with amazing conviction, "I just know. I'd be looked down upon and seen as a slut. And my God, everyone there loves you. Out of all the girls who say how hot you are and how badly they want to sleep with you, if I were the one I'd be completely singled out."

This idea seems preposterous but I don't press, now is not the time to be divided. All I say is, "Well I wouldn't worry because

I don't think that will happen." I need someone with which to share this distress and she's all I have.

I sit up slowly and say, "Ok, I better be going. I'll see you tonight?" My parents are watching the kids so I can go to Dana's play and Natalia will be selling cupcakes as a fundraiser. Maybe if the play is over early enough I can go back to her house for a few minutes before I have to pick up my kids. I explain all of this to her as if anything matters.

"Ok," she says, as if in a trance.

I'm still baffled why she's so upset. I don't want her to take this lightly, that would be equally as frustrating but she seems more depressed than I would have imagined. She walks me to the door and gives a kiss goodbye. I put my phone on the seat next to me and ride home in silent reflection.

I don't think about anything in particular but my mind races uncontrollably. How much will my life change? Will I still be able to teach? Will I ever be able to see Natalia? Will Kathy really help me? What is jail like? Will my kids hate me? Will Dana divorce me? Could my parents disown me? I wonder what Carla is doing right now?

I have no answers only speculations that lead to more speculations. I grow optimistic at times, thinking Tommy was wrong. But then I sink into thinking the worst, I'll be put in jail and never see anyone I love again. Still other thoughts end in me being able to lie my way out of this.

If Kathy adheres to what she has agreed then our story could be bulletproof. In the back of my mind I think about asking her to say that the relationship is between me and her but I don't know how Talia would like that. I arrive home terribly needing a nap. The mental energy that I expend on a momentary basis drains me of everything, with no end in sight.

I think about skipping the play but know I will only drive myself further insane without a diversion. The play is interesting but I only use the serenity to reflect on the flurry of thoughts that arrive, happenstance in my head. More questions and new fears appear every time I open up my mind to wonder.

I sneak away during intermission to my classroom. I clean out the desk drawer I have reserved for Natalia, placing everything back in her locker. I'm grasping at straws and in my terror, brought on by Friday's news, I'm playing out my overactive imagination. I try anything to cover my tracks no matter how trivial or futile. As if the removal of books will throw anyone off of the month's long scent I have left with my outrageous behavior. It's no different than hiding my car at the hotel where Natalia and I went to have sex. It's pointless other than to make me feel as though I'm being vigilant in my clandestine security measures. I find only momentary peace from my self-created chaos.

I return to my seat just before Act II and see Natalia sitting in front of me. I know what she is doing at all times, watching her as much as the play. She looks good but for some reason, young. My mind instinctively molds her to a sympathetic form, gratifying its own intentions. When I am present in a younger ego state she is perfectly adult and functions as such, but as I switch into my own maturity I distance myself, seeing her true youth. I wish we had sex earlier but maybe it's best we didn't.

Afterward, I speak briefly with Dana and try my best to offer congratulations, but I remember nothing, my mind distant for the entirety. I offer to pick up the kids since she has things to wrap up at school. I stop by Talia's house to say hello, hoping to be quick. For as much as I feel like I'm dying a slow death, I will be losing her presence in my life also. Whether the person I'm preemptively missing or the concept of her representation I feel like I need to salvage as much time with her as possible.

I walk in her front door and find her sitting on the couch in silence, home alone. She is still sullen and when I ask her why she says, "I don't want you to get in trouble, Jimi. I love you and cannot imagine you not being in my life."

I have no response. I wish I knew what to say but I have manipulated her up to and including this point to think as though we are lovers entrenched in a forbidden romance. I have spun tales of love conquering all and riding off happily into the sunset and now my bullshit has caught up with me.

Perhaps in a world where I can bend reality, all of that is possible. But not in this world. Not in this day and age where society is hypersensitive to exactly this variety of indiscretion.

I hug her and say the only inane thing I can, "It'll be ok." She does me the courtesy of believing one more lie. I pick up my children and go home for another sleepless night.

Chapter 19

The next day is Super Bowl Sunday, February 4th. The Indianapolis Colts are playing the Chicago Bears. Much like Christmas, my erratic and unfaithful behavior has led to exclusion from my in-law's party. That works fine because I'm spared from concocting an alibi. I don't fool myself into thinking Dana believes I will be watching the game with friends. Of course, I watch the game with Natalia, Kathy and her boyfriend, my life nothing short of surreal.

The news on Friday was shocking but perhaps because the weekend was beginning, reality was still in the distance. Now, however the palpable fear looms over every thought that crosses my mind. Talia and I spend most of the afternoon downstairs in her room, talking. The conversation ranges with our emotions.

Maybe this is nothing but if it is, we're prepared because mom knows and wouldn't say anything. I might just have to go teach at another school which would be difficult but manageable. Maybe Maggie was jealous and said that to scare us. Maybe I'll be called to the principal's office again and told to stop immediately or will definitely get fired. So many delusional possibilities continue to smooth over the severity of not only the immorality, but the crime that I'm committing.

I can only play along, having planted the original seed. I groomed her to think that it's not a big deal to be texting her

French teacher, made her think it was permissible to drive her home. It's not a problem to come to my bike races and watch me parade around in Spandex, bulging through my shorts.

We can kiss, harmless because we're in love. Oral sex is an expression of that love, intercourse, the greatest expression. Now your Mom knows and she's not upset which only solidifies there is nothing shady. And now, when the truth is inevitable, there will be dire consequences that will last a lifetime, there are no more lies to tell. There are no more placations or conciliatory words that can heal these fretful feelings. All that's left are the tears to shed as we unravel the agonizing confusion.

Of course we have sex one last time before the game, wrought with overdone emotion. I look at her deeply and tell her, "I love you. I'll always love you. I will love you no matter what. We can and will make it through whatever happens."

This is what I want to believe. I need to behold this as truth because here on the doorstep of full transparency, the only way to justify the insanity is in the name of true love. A tear escapes her left eyelid as she blinks and runs down her temple. I hug her while still inside and feel it's wetness on my own face. I stop to hold her and feel her squeeze me close.

I have alienated almost everyone in my life, even if unbeknownst to them yet. The only person that I feel close to is the one I exploited to feel so. We lay motionless for a few moments just locked in an embrace until she begins to move her hips again and we finish. We silently dress and walk upstairs four minutes into the first quarter.

I'm beginning to feel the physical effects of the panic gripping me. I feel nauseas and am sweating profusely. Despite the fact that thermostat reads sixty-seven degrees I'm hot in my own personal hell. I periodically step outside with the excuse, "I need some air."

I come back in to watch the halftime show because I want to see Prince perform. The first cassette tape that I ever bought, to play on my newly received boom box was the soundtrack to "Purple Rain". I played that tape on the radio and in my Walkman on every car ride for a year. I am glued to the television screen watching him play two songs from that very album, "Let's Go Crazy", and "Baby, I'm a Star".

I'm a kid again, still my parents' son and not facing down this apocalypse. My mind shifts immediately back to reality when Prince covers "Proud Mary," and "All Along the Watchtower". One more Foo Fighters cover and then he finishes with "Purple Rain" which brings me quickly to tears.

The slow and sensuous power ballad melody brings back so many memories of being in that time with friends and people who had neither exploited nor been exploited by me. I've heard the lyrics more times than I could ever count but this is the first time I truly listen. The significance that these words have in my life right now crushes me.

Natalia comments, "Well this song is a bit overdone isn't it?"

Everyone in the room laughs.

I respond, barely audible, "I think it's beautiful."

I wish that I could convey to her as beautifully as Prince does that I never meant to hurt her. I only ever wanted to be a friend, but many things, none of which were her issues, stood in the way.

I try not to watch the clock of the second half because it only serves as a reminder that time is marching mercilessly toward judgment. I leave after a prolonged hug, steeped with emotion in front of her door. Kathy comes over before I leave and also hugs me. As I try to pull away she clings, "It'll all be ok, I know it will. We love you."

I don't know what any of that means, but I don't have any mental energy to interpret. I kiss Natalia one more time and with a look of walking bravely into the unknown, I leave.

When I arrive home, everyone is already asleep. I sit on the couch for a while and contemplate putting on the television. I pull out the newspaper and try to read, even attempting to gather enough concentration for the crossword. I give up because nothing eases the restless fidgeting, the volume of a roar inside my head. The last thing I do before I lay in bed is sit at my computer and Google, "Sentences for Statutory Rape."

Chapter 20

My attempt to salvage what's left of my sanity requires keeping the same routine. I wake up at five thirty, despite my sleepless night and go to the gym. I speak to no one. I put my headphones on and my hood up. I neither want to be seen nor acknowledged because I need to focus on what today might bring.

I cut my workout short, shower and head to school half an hour earlier than normal. Miles from school I'm smacked with the reality that my reckoning has come. As I leave the gym parking lot, the superintendent appears in my rear view mirror. In my seven years at this school I've never seen him arrive before nine o'clock. His presence this early, today indicates that he needs to be here, come what may. And it's only ominous irony that he happens to pull in the parking lot right behind me.

I put my belongings in my room and walk to the office. While collecting my mail I see George talking to the vice-principal, Ed. I walk past and try to read his face. He says, "Good morning," refusing to look at me.

He only gives a sideways glance, unable to make eye contact. In my best attempt at a red herring, driven by panic, I ask him if he attended Dana's play. "No," substantiates that there is something very wrong.

George is the type of man that would rave about the quality performance of "his" students, or give the indisputably valid reason for his absence. In between trying to read George's mannerisms and pick up on any clues, I look at Ed, also loathe to lock eyes with me.

Nobody asks but I tell them, "I could only attend Saturday night because I had the kids on Friday," to relieve my nervous energy.

Neither man says anything in response, both nodding. I walk away feeling like they were speaking to someone about to be executed, trying to normalize the absurdity. I notice my breath shallow and my hand quivering as I put the key in the lock of my classroom door.

My only goal is to survive the day, which becomes trying to endure each individual class period. Momentarily I can become lost in a conversation or a lesson but always stinging in the back of my mind is fear. Fourth period, Natalia comes into my room and closes the door behind her.

I jump from my desk, "No, don't close it. I'm sure they are watching even more closely now."

She ignores me and it probably doesn't matter anymore. She stands an uncomfortable distance away and says, "It's all true. I spoke to Maggie this morning and she told me that everything is true. The Prosecutor's office is coming to talk to her sometime after school and they're going to talk to Meagan too."

She covers her face and cries.

Because she positioned herself so far away I don't know if I should hug her or allow her space.

"I don't know what to say, Talia. We spoke yesterday about how we're going to handle this, so as long as we remain true to that plan then we have to just hope for the best," I say mostly to break the unbearable silence.

"You never told anyone anything so whatever they are going by is just hearsay right?" I ask knowing the irrelevance of my question.

She slowly shakes her head not remotely convincing me of the truth. I think she may have told more people than she'll admit, but it's immaterial now and only serves to numb my wits which I desperately need to function. She exits without another word leaving me petrified to face her class, which is next.

She walks in and puts her head down on the desk immediately making me feel further alienated. I should correct her for not sitting properly, but a scolding is likely to put her over the edge so I ignore her. She blends into the backdrop of my terror with every other student.

The last few periods carry out the same as the beginning of my day, mindlessly going through the motions. There is a strange shapeless peace I feel as my school day ends. Partly because nothing has happened yet, but also because the end must be looming. When the final bell rings I'm at a loss for actions. I can't leave for another fifteen minutes but don't know what to do until then. Will Talia dare come today?

I lock my door before anyone can bother me, sit at my desk and watch videos on YouTube to focus on something, anything other than the thrashing in my head. I sit for five minutes, watching the clock when there's a knock at my door. I freeze, too terrified to move. There are a slew of people that I do not want to see. Do I open it or walk out the back door into the adjacent classroom and hide? After a tense walk across the room, I thankfully see a student named Katie through the window.

Katie plays on my soccer team, has been in my class the last two years, attended the infamous lunch that set my demise in motion and loves French. It's not uncommon for her to often stop in just to ask a question so she causes no concern. Something appears amiss when I first see her face and she does not greet me with her typical warmth. She is out of breath as she walks past me seeming nervous, almost agitated.

"What's up Katie?" I say, happy to have a distraction.

"Hey, I missed my bus. Do you mind if I sit in here till my mom gets me?" she asks still not having caught her breath.

"No, I mean I'm not going to be here much longer but feel free to stay as long as I am."

Before she knocked on my door I was looking at videos of soccer games so I turn the monitor to show her, thinking she'll be interested. We watch for a moment interjecting our own commentary. She begins a relevant story that seems forced and as I watch her struggle it pains me. She speaks in an uncharacteristically soft, accelerated tone.

I don't press her because the longer I watch her reconcile this the more fear consumes me. Out of the corner of my eye I see her take one final deep breath and without further preamble say, "Can I ask you a question Mr. Cunneely?"

Her nerves have drained all of the color from her normally olive complexion and sadness mixes with my alarm. I have no doubt what is coming because Katie is straightforward. I prepare myself by thinking this may be the last time I will have this sham of a conversation. I sit back from the computer, "You may ask me whatever you would like."

She looks about to cry from her self-induced pressure, quivering lips and the ripple in her chin put me on the verge of tears myself. "I don't know if you have heard but people are saying so many terrible things about you today."

I'm unsure if she's waiting for a response or unable to speak as she regains her composure. "What kinds of things?" I prompt.

"They are saying that something is going on between you and Natalia, but I just know you would never do something like that. It's been so upsetting to hear and I had to ask you for myself," she says chased with a deep breath and a hard sniffle. Weight visibly lifts from her petite shoulders just from releasing the poisonous question. The fact that she has not been a part of any of the month's long gossip further speaks to Katie's maturity.

I sit back in my chair as though thinking of the best way to respond, my stock answer already locked and loaded. I take a deep breath to begin, but stop, realizing the significance of this moment. Only one other person has asked me this question directly, Rick, the Affirmative Action Officer. His question was more along the lines of an interrogation, devoid of any vested emotion. But this time is about me.

This question is brought from the place of care and concern for my well-being. She heard something that contradicted every experience she has had with me. In her eyes I am not a person that would ever do such a thing. She bestowed her trust upon me with the understanding that I will uphold the ideals she knows a teacher must. And here in a time of so much apathy and ignorance when a piece did not fit correctly into her matrix she has the courage and respect for both me and herself to put it out the open to heal her heart. How can I lie?

I swallow hard and try to pretend that the speechlessness came from someplace other than the hiccupping of my conscience. "Katie," I sigh, "I've heard the things that have been said too. And no, I did not do anything with Natalia."

I rush through the latter part of the utter bullshit because it feels grubby on my lips like a mouthful of sand. I have not hated myself as much as I do right now in longer than I can remember. Of course other people have deserved the truth in the history of this squalid chapter. Dana, Natalia, my parents, my employers and co-workers, but for some reason unknown to me, confronted with this duality of a compliment and criticism I feel more compelled than ever to shed my fraudulence.

Normally my duplicity emerges from a distortion between secrecy and privacy, but in this case being confronted with an innocence that I wish I could recapture, fear overcomes me and again, I resort to dishonesty. I have never felt filthier than at this moment wearing my chosen deceit.

Before my mind can travel too far down the path of regret she cuts my thoughts quickly and with a sigh of complete relief, "Oh thank you for talking to me, I knew it. I just knew that there was no way that you'd ever do anything like that. I stuck up for you all day. I even said something to Natalia because I think she might be contributing to the rumor."

I lose my thoughts at the end of her gush wondering what has been said and what is still left unsaid. Somewhere deep down I hope that I will be able to keep this secret from Katie. I wish to keep her protected from all of my dirty actions. I feel the same way toward her I do about my own children. I want to shelter them from all of this but surrendered that ability long ago. Sadly, this will all soon be a very public mortification.

Chapter 21

I pick my kids up from their bus stop, we do homework and watch television, trying to act normally. I assume nothing is going to transpire differently until told otherwise. I take a short nap because my body simply yields. Dana went to school to wrap up the play and is then going shopping. I make dinner, clean up and start making lunch for the next day.

What continues to stab at me as I complete so many routine tasks is that I have not heard from Natalia since she walked out of my classroom fifth period. Her silence scares me but given how depressed she was I conclude she may be sleeping or talking to her mom or any litany of things which I convince myself to remain calm.

At four o'clock, I text her something benign, "Hi, how are you?" but receive no response. At eight thirty I put the kids to bed. The girls in their room and my son on the couch because he is fighting a fever and I want to watch him. I feel in a fog. Everything I do seems like I'm drunk. I think to check my e-mail but remain standing still lost in thought as if there is now a permanent delay on every action to make sure the decision warrants the effort.

Dana calls me from the store to tell me she will be home in an hour. I put my phone down on the counter and as I'm loading the dishwasher I hear the beep of a text message. The screen reads, "Message from: Kathy."

I open it and find, "Ur so done. The police know everything."

I instantly feel as though someone is screaming in both ears while the edges of my vision become framed in a black wavy border. I recall this feeling as the precursor to the one time in my life that I passed out, but I do not faint. I put the phone back down and try as diligently as I can to think. What does this mean? Why is it coming from Kathy? Is it a joke? Is this a setup?

After a deluge of emotions I'm unable to decipher and with nothing to lose I reply, "Who is this?" I send it and think I may sound terse but accept that my veneer of etiquette is fading fast.

Every ten seconds I look at my phone waiting for a response and every time there is none chips away a substantial piece of my threadbare sanity. The next sound my phone makes is that of a ring tone, not a text message. Kathy is now calling.

"Hello?" I say in an accusatory tone.

"Hi, it's me," Natalia says, I know immediately she has been crying. "If you're going to run, now is the time," serves only to confuse me terribly.

"Huh? What are you talking about?" I snap back.

Her voice deepens as she speaks pointedly, "After school my mother picked me up and brought me to the police station," she snorts in the phone loudly. "They took me in a room and started asking me all these crazy questions about you and us. They asked me if you had any birth marks and if I had ever seen you with your shirt off and all this stuff that I just kept denying. They started making accusations that we're a couple and that we had sex and you picked me up and brought me to school in the morning and I just kept denying it over and over again, some of it lies and some of it truth. But then," she stops and begins sniffling and sobbing uncontrollably.

"They said that if I didn't tell them the truth they were going to come into school tomorrow and throw you on the floor and bring you out in handcuffs. They said that they had video of us somewhere that would prove that we were together outside of school. They said from the hotel or wherever. I just tried to protect you Jimi, I'm so sorry. I just tried to protect you. I'm sorry. I'm so so sorry." She takes a deep breath and sniffles hard in my ear.

"They wanted to know what we did in the hotel rooms and," she pauses and I hear voices in the background. "I have to go. I'll call you back," she whispers an instant before she hangs up.

I remain motionless with the phone still up to my ear as my mind wanders to innumerable places. I am numb, lost. "So this is it," is the phrase involuntarily repeating in my head. At one time or another everyone wonders how they are going to die. What is it going to feel like? How will it happen? Will it hurt? What will I see on the other side that curtain? And then when the realization takes hold that death is imminent the feeling sinks in, "Ok, so this is it."

Within seconds my mind begins its hard-wired quest for self-preservation. She said something about running. Should I? I'm sure they'll find me. I can go to my Grandmother's in New York City. I can just jump in the car and drive. Should I kill myself? Should I drive somewhere and kill myself? If I run should I take my kids? Should I tell Dana? Should I tell my parents? Why won't Talia call back? The only guiding principle that overtakes my ambivalence is confusion. The fact that I actually consider suicide in the same thought as fleeing speaks to just how disassociated I am from so much of me.

I walk into the living room, sit on the love seat and stare at my son. Knowing that his life is about to change in ways that are so unfair to him and his sisters, I mouth the words, "I'm sorry," right before my phone rings. It's Natalia again from Kathy's phone.

She omits any greeting, "Listen, you said one time that you'd just run if you ever got caught. Now is the time. If you don't run, here's what happened: I told them that we never had sex. I told them about the chocolate cake thing because I thought that would be better. They kept asking and I kept denying that we ever had sex. They told me that if your story matched mine it wouldn't be as bad for you. You might not even go to jail they said. I'm going home soon because I have to give them the clothes I was wearing yesterday and they're taking other stuff too."

She pauses but as I'm about to speak says, "Jimi, I'm so sorry, I tried to protect you but they said they were going to handcuff you and hurt you. I was so confused, they told me that they had video of us and they were getting calls from people who could agree they saw us. And Mom tried knocking on the door and they wouldn't let her in. They kept telling her I was fine, but I was hysterical. It's been absolutely horrible."

I have more questions than I can name so I instantly prioritize hoping for straight answers. "Why are you calling me from mom's phone?" I say without acknowledging her apology.

"They took mine, something about getting all of the text messages off of it or something, so mom let me call you from her phone," she detects my urgency and replies at the same quickened pace as I ask.

"Are they coming for me now?" Her answers, although spoken quickly are not coming soon enough.

"I don't know, they only asked if I thought you'd run."

"But why would they say that? How would I find out if you hadn't called me?" I'm starting to punch holes in her story not to disprove her but to gain a better understanding.

"When I had to hang up before, they walked in and saw me on the phone. They asked who I was talking to and I said no one but they took mom's phone and matched your number with my phone. When they found out we talked they wanted to know if I thought you would try to get away from them," she says before reverting back into tears.

"Ok, just relax," I say more for myself because there is no way for either of us to remain calm. "So what did your mom say through all of this? Where the fuck was she while this was going on? She didn't stop them or step in?" I let loose for a moment then realize I don't want to turn her against Kathy.

She sinks into hysterics, "No Jimi, that's just it, they wouldn't let mom in the room." She rambles slightly and my mind wanders, causing unmanageable frustration. I remember she said something about this a moment ago, but I was lost on another thought so I pay closer attention now. "Mom kept asking if I was ok. Four fucking hours I was in there. She brought me right after school and I held my own for four hours of them badgering me and screaming in my face and every time mom asked them if I was ok, they just told her, 'Oh yeah, she's fine,' or, 'Sure, we're just getting Talia a glass of water but we're just talking.'"

She knocked on the door three times. And every time they said, 'Oh, she's fine,' but I wasn't fine, I was hysterical and they wouldn't let me out. The one cop got mad and started slamming his hand on the arm of my chair and banging on the table. He was so angry that he was spitting on me as he yelled. And then when I finally broke down after they threatened us, they said, 'Ok now we need to get that on tape, so we'll ask you the questions again and answer us the same way.' They said it like none of the terrible things they did to me ever happened, like we were best friends because I told them what they wanted. Oh Jimi, it was horrible. I'm so so sorry," she speaks through tears again.

I pause to think. I know she told me all she can handle but I still need to know how to match our stories.

"So Talia, try to calm down, I'm very sorry that happened. Can you tell me what you said so I can repeat the same?" I try to sound sensitive but know time is of the essence. She takes a deep breath. I can feel how incredibly hard this was and the life it sucked from her.

She continues her effort on my behalf, "I swore to them that we have never had sex and they seemed to believe me. I told them there was one time that I blew you, but as soon as your penis went into my mouth I gagged and got sick on your stomach. I didn't tell them that you came in my mouth or anything like that. So I don't think that it will be bad because it was just once they think."

Her silence makes me think she's done, but as I begin another question she adds, "Oh, and Jimi, I told them that I forced myself on you. I told them that every time we did anything it was me who came onto you, that you always pushed me away and continued to push me away until eventually I broke you down. I tried to take as much of the blame as I could. Jimi," I feel more crying coming on, "I'm so sorry."

Each word elongated and emoted to match the despair as she mistakenly believes the betrayal is on her hands. "Listen I better go because last time they caught me on the phone they got really angry. They said that mom could be in more trouble than even you if she lets me talk to you again. I'll call you when I get home.

I love you Jim. I'm sorry," she rambles through without taking a
breath.

I hang up without saying another word. I turn the television
on and flip through the channels not knowing what I'm even seeing. I go into the DVR menu to see if there is something to watch.
I stare at my phone and sit down at the computer to play solitaire.
I have no idea how much time passes before I awake from my
disconnection.

I begin to plan. I involuntarily replay her consolation that if
my story matches hers then the scaled down version might not
be so bad. I wonder if they are going to come to my house tonight
or if there will be someone waiting for me tomorrow. In my confusion and lack of direction I think about calling the substitute
service to notify them of my absence tomorrow.

What I absorb without any true reflection is that I no longer
have control over anything. I cast my life in this direction long
ago and essentially relinquished the steering wheel, leaving me
to only wait and let my life unfold on foreign terms.

Dana comes home with her hands full of shopping bags. I
walk out with her for the rest but really want to look down the
street to see if anyone is coming. I contemplate telling her but
what do I say? How do I tell her that the police will be knocking
on our door tonight to take me away for an affair with a student?

True to my chameleonic form, as soon as the bags are inside,
I leap into her arms and bury my face in the niche between her
face and shoulder. She smells good and familiar. In this moment,
on the precipice of everyone I ever knew turning their back on
me I still have my wife. I know that in the very near future she
will know exactly why I have returned, but for now I need someone to sustain me.

"What's the matter?" she asks because all she has known is a cold, heartless husband, something must be amiss.

I stand in her arms asking myself, "Do I?" but knowing her inevitable hysterics will cloud my senses.

"Are you ok? You're shaking," she whispers.

"I'm ok, just....I don't know. Just don't feel too well right now, but I'll be fine," I lie to her yet again.

"Would you like to go lay down? I'll come with you," rubbing my back softly.

I nod. As we walk to the bedroom she asks about our son's fever. I revel in such simple and everyday topics that I wish could return to our consciousness. In the few moments of peace I think back to what were the good times. I have ousted so many good memories from my mind recently as to not interfere with my impulses. But now I've allowed them to come back, an attempt to whitewash this new reality.

I live in the past on almost a daily basis, always have. My life is and has been so difficult that nostalgia creeps in from just one day prior. I will reflect upon yesterday and remember it as so wonderful only because dealing with the pain of today is un-manageable. Yesterday was no better and tomorrow will bring nothing to wipe away today's pain, but my mind instinctively places rose colored glasses over all memories, painting them pal-atable. Anything is better than right now. All of my adult life, this was the only way that I found to press on and see another day. Nostalgia being nothing more than a refuge for those who find it too difficult to live in the present.

My wife and I lay in our bed, her supine, my head contently on her chest. Ten minutes, maybe thirty. I lose track of all time, set on one continuous loop of fear. I try to relax my heart rate but find it possible only by, once again reliving moments in my past.

Part Two

I think of lying on the beach in North Carolina with just the five of us. I think of holding my infant daughter on my chest while she napped which leads to memories of walking with my only boy endlessly as he worked out his colic. My younger daughter, only four days old before we bonded because Dana had to return to the hospital with Toxemia. I recall that frightful time as comforting, wishing I could return there.

I'm snapped out of my attempt to capture what was always the anchor of my life when I hear Dana say in a tone that conveys urgency, "Jim is that someone knocking at the door?" And I know my life is forever changed.

Chapter 22

On the way to the police station the two cops are my best friends. They encourage me to sit in the front seat. They introduce themselves and I know immediately who they are from Talia's phone call. They ask about school, how the girls' soccer team did last season, and the Super Bowl.

The tone turns serious only as we leave my development, "Jim, I think you know what we need to talk about. You have a right to an attorney. So would you like to have an attorney present while we talk about this?"

"No, I don't need an attorney. I don't have anything to hide," I say without taking my eyes from the passenger's side window. I have done many immoral things over the last six months, and for some, if not many, I could say that something came over me I was unable to control. The truth behind that statement is more closely, I didn't want to control the factors at play.

While being frisked before I stepped into their minivan something overtook me, assumed governance of my actions. It came without the usual stomach ache, apparently coming from a disowned part of my psyche. It felt executive in nature, as though driven by the ability to monitor and react with full perspective of all actions, past and present. The answer to his question channeled from the place that was going to make sure the balance of my life was carried out absent the shadows and veils of the first thirty years. Legally I may come to regret my refusal of an attorney, but psychologically this is the first crucial step to stop trying to outsmart my integrity.

My life became quite real when asked in the street, "Do you have any weapons?"

With, "I have a pocket knife on my key chain," both officers flinched and grabbed my wrists simultaneously mumbling loudly, "Ok, I'll just take that."

At that moment the severity of this is placed squarely on my shoulders with no option to shrug any longer. I ignore the remainder of the pleasantries designed to make me comfortable and instead, hear my internal monologue take over, "Just tell them the story as Talia did. Tell the story and then there is no longer a need to lie."

The temptation to avoid wrapping my whole life around some version of a fallacy for the first time in my adulthood is too great to ignore. Lies by omission are still lies so if they ask about sex I will tell the truth but I will say no more than they ask.

We arrive at the police station and they show me to a room that looks nothing like any of the ones on television. The same two cops sit down, set their legal pads and talk to me as though they are providing a tranquil outlet to clear my conscience. They are stern but cajoling. "Geez, it must have been hard, being around Natalia, knowing she has a crush on you. Seeing how pretty she is and that she would do anything for you. I mean, I would have difficulty saying, 'No,' if I were you."

I know what they want to hear. It's not about the human condition and what felt natural and wrong simultaneously. They ask the same repetitive questions like, "What happened next?" and, "When was the next time you saw her and what happened that time? I'm sure you moved on to the next level sexually with her then right?"

Part Two

I stick to the story. They know about the hotels, my car, her bedroom, her mother's bedroom, texts, cards, letters and I have to regurgitate it to them to the point that I think they are deriving a sense of gratification themselves.

Telling this story without the usual smarmy lies and half-truths is difficult. I involuntarily interject some self-righteous statement about being her mentor and providing a positive peer group but only in the context of deceit. None of it matters now, a two hour interview that could be pared to ten minutes. They want to know how far we got with one another and I'm confessing enough to convey the point, enough to essentially end my life. Does it make a difference where I have physically penetrated her and how often or in what setting? The worst part of my victimizing her is the psychological permeation that forced her to be secretive, to normalize debauched behavior.

I just want it to be over, so much that it doesn't occur to me to keep the enormous lie alive. I distemper the extent of our sexual encounters, but don't refrain from telling them neither confessions of love, nor the promises of a future. This purge is the first step toward complete honesty. I can be rid of the painful, ugly, veil I've always worn over my face, forever.

They finally leave, satisfied I assume. I sit alone , my head down on the cold steel table feeling better, cleansed before the fear of the unknown creeps in quickly. One of them reenters, "Stand up. Hands behind your back." My breath increases, tears well in my eyes. This is never where I saw my life heading and the authenticity of handcuffs is incomprehensible.

I compose myself, "So what happens now? I'll spend the night in jail?"

He stops and looks at me, confused, "Well, yes, well, I guess I didn't actually say it, but yes, you're under arrest. You'll be brought to the county jail where you'll be housed until you have a court date. We'll call the judge and he'll set bail. Once you're arraigned, if you can make bail then you'll be able to get out. That's about all I can tell you."

Ok, so I'll spend the night in jail, maybe tomorrow too. And I know I've lost my job, but so far this sounds manageable.

Chapter 23

It's three thirty in the morning when I'm given two coarse blankets, two sheets, a pair of orange shoes and an orange jump suit. I walk through a heavy door into a room with four bunk beds. It reeks of caustic cleaning products that try to unsuccessfully mask sweat and urine and shit. The only beds available are top bunks. I try to make the bed without waking whoever is in the bottom but I'm trembling.

I'm in jail and have not one item in my skill set to even begin to cope. I'm trying not to cry knowing that would be disastrous. I lie on the bunk and try to sleep or think or do anything productive. I'm on the verge of an anxiety attack focused on the reality that in a few hours everyone I work with, everyone that called me their teacher, my friends and family will all know the second biggest secret I've ever kept. I'm at the far limit, the end of myself.

In the default setting of my mind I try to plan my next move in this game I'm reluctant to quit. I've always had a feasible plan to clean any previous mess. This is difficult to formulate because I have no control over anything that could happen next. I lie awake all night.

Before I left the police station I was able to call Dana, she had apparently already done some research for herself since I left, piecing together obvious information. When I told her that I was charged with a first degree sexual assault, second degree endangering the welfare of a child, and third degree criminal sexual contact she was astonished, "First degree? Why first degree? Oh no Jim." I speak as vaguely as possible because the cop is next to me, trying to keep some vestige of dignity.

At Dana's request I put my hand over the receiver and ask, "Why am I charged with a first degree crime?"

Very officially and without thought he replies, "Any act of penetration constitutes a first degree sexual assault."

"Even though it was just for a second?" digressing into a juvenile ego state. I've penetrated her much more than once and my presence will be felt for longer than simply three seconds. My permeation encompasses not only the multiple physical occurrences, but the much more damaging psychological ones that may never heal.

"It doesn't matter for how long. Penetration is penetration," sounding like a line he often practices in front of his mirror. In any case, I plan out my immediate future, certain to make bail and be home in time to teach my college class this evening.

Trying in vain to focus on my first full day in jail, my name is called by a guard standing in the doorway. My heart rate speeds to a painful pace. I look at him in bewilderment, waiting for some indication why he has called me.

"Let's go asshole, time for court," prompts me to the door. He points to a box drawn in red tape on the floor and says, "Stand in that box and don't move."

On the counter next to him is a set of handcuffs, a chain and shackles. I am certain to vomit. The smell alone is enough to make me wretch aside from what my life has become. Everything I look at seems to have a film over it, as though looking through someone else's opaque eyeglasses. I haven't led the type of lifestyle, until recently, that ever led me to believe I was heading down this path.

"Turn around face the wall. Raise your right foot," cold shackle on my bare ankle.

"Raise your left foot," shackle on the other.

"Turn around." I shuffle my feet to put my back against the wall. The chain is short of a normal stride so I almost tip over with each step. Handcuffs are secured, linked to a chain wrapped around my waist.

I'm led into an elevator and down a long, freezing corridor. I was stripped of everything last night, wearing a short sleeve jumpsuit, no socks and no coat, fourth in a line of six other inmates going to court. We're led into a holding cell separating us from the court room by an enormous steel door, overkill considering my restraints. I'm the last to be led out, forced to hear the horrid sound of the door open and shut five times before my turn. The loud clanging sucks years off of the back end of my life every time a slam echoes in my head. A reminder of what I've done and worse yet an alarm of the uncertainty ahead.

Before court I'm brought into a tiny room with a screen in front of me as if it were a confessional. Across from me sits a man I can hardly see through the tight metal weave.

He explains briefly, "I have been retained by your father and I will be representing you in the arraignment."

He discusses my charges and gives a brief summary of what will happen once in the courtroom. Because he is speaking hurriedly I say, "Guess not," when he asks me if I have any questions.

Right before I exit he says, "Oh, just so you're prepared, there are reporters out there. And cameras."

I stop to ask for clarification, or help, but a guard pushes me into another holding area. Did he mean video cameras? Newspaper reporters? This is my first introduction into the true gravity of my situation. Prior to now I was certain this would blow over with little damage, but cameras and reporters tell a different story.

The first person I see upon entering the courtroom is Dana. She is crying, next to my father and brother. A second after I recognize them the rapid and incessant clicking of cameras begins. I refuse to look in their direction, forbidding a quality picture but the thought of what this is becoming, in the hands of strangers petrifies me. I see the same attorney standing at the defendant's table, looking different without wire mesh over his face. It's when I look at him and he nods that I'm stricken with the understanding that these people take my actions much more seriously than I ever have.

My knees buckle intermittently. People talk to me and about me, all unintelligible. The judge asks the prosecutor questions about what he wants as conditions of bail barely audible over the clicking. My attorney speaks about having certain parts of an evaluation sealed as to not prejudice a jury in the event of a trial. He pleads not guilty on my behalf which confuses me in my state of lethargy because I confessed. I want to turn around to see everyone but am far too embarrassed. I hear Dana sobbing. Her reputation for melodrama is renowned but this is one of the first instances that I believe she actually has grounds to react exactly as she is.

My plan to make bail and be home in time to teach my college class is laughable. The judge holds my bail at $75,000 despite the prosecutor's request to raise it but stipulates that I must pass a psycho-sexual evaluation. As the guard grabs the crook of my elbow to take me away the attorney leans and says, "I'll be over to you see you soon."

I'm back in the cell where I spent last night before I can process anything. I wait a few hours and call Dana, only to receive more bad news, "Your story has been all over the radio and the college called to say they've terminated you."

Long ago I could see the slight fraying at the edges of my fragile existence but only from the inside. Those were the hidden storms, left invisible to everyone else in my world. The public dismantling of my entire life is now beginning and everyone who knows me and more who don't are enjoying front row seats to watch the dog and pony show which will be the legal case that determines my punishment.

Epilogue

I'm still your son. Still your brother. I'm the neighbor who lends you his lawnmower. The one who gives you vegetables from his garden, plows your driveway, and unnecessarily keeps you up at night because I live next door. That's if you choose to see me for what I am, instead of who I am. I long to be average once again but the monthly visit from my parole officer prevents my life from returning to normal.

I want to be a good father, good son, good friend, a writer, in that order of preference. My parents are still heroes to me, embodying the unconditional love and forgiveness that I can only hope to show my own children. And my grandfather too, I admire him even more for exemplifying a trait I never knew he possessed to such a degree, always finding the good in people, no matter how poor their choices.

Six years after my arrest, still engaged in intensive therapy, I knock on Carla's front door. A trip twenty years in the making. Two years ago I wrote her a letter asking for help. I stated the impetus was conciliatory, assuring her I meant no harm. I offered my mailing address, email and phone number hoping she would contact me of her own volition. Simply hearing from her would verify that I was a person in her eyes, not just a sex toy.

Three months with no response so I called. No answer the first several times. Then, I reached an answering machine so often that I dialed mindlessly, expecting her recorded voice. One afternoon a man's voice surprised me from the other end of the phone. I stumbled through, "Hi, may I speak to Carla please?"

"Sure. Who shall I tell her is calling?" he replied with candor.

"This is Jim. I know her from high school."

After hearing the phone placed down on a solid surface, he returned, "I'm sorry, she's upstairs teaching right now. Can she call you back?"

I knew I would receive no such call but I was as close as ever to my goal. I spoke to someone who verified that Carla was alive, lived there, and was physically able to speak to me. Who is he? Her husband? Does he know who I am? Does he know who she really is?

One week to the day, I call back in the evening. On the third ring, a voice, "Hello?" soft, yet deep and rich. I picture Carla with the receiver to her face.

"Hello?"

My stomach churns, I'm fifteen years old again. I hang up, hyperventilating.

I hate myself immediately. I hate the fear and I hate my guilt. I hate the false sense of healing in which I've taken solace but mostly, I hate the wasted opportunity that just escaped. Carla just got another pass.

Through processing that collapse, in my therapist's office, I come to understand why I was afraid and more importantly, why I shouldn't have been. Over the next two years I make ready to confront my past yet again, in person. I imagine and role play and conjecture every scenario in which I may find myself to make the best use of my time in her presence.

Epilogue

With my arrangements to Florida solidified I ask two dear friends, Dan and Connie, whom I trust explicitly to accompany me, unaware of who I might find at her door, and more frighteningly, who I might find inside myself after such a confrontation.

The preparation is thorough and intense, looking at satellite maps to know her neighborhood, writing letters to leave on her doorstep in anticipated rejection, and rehearsing my opening line. Most importantly, the completion of the manuscript that became this memoir. The two hour drive to her house is excruciating. Every time I consider obeying the resistance in my head, the overwhelming reminder screams, "Don't quit now."

I bring to the forefront all of the reasons why canceling this trip is not an option, why bailing out now would be more destructive than any reception from Carla. I think of my children, how great to tell them I stared down my victimizer. I think of my parents, their incessant anger at having been duped. I can't face my therapist and tell him that all of our work over the years was in vain. I press forward for Dan, driving with me, so he can see this happen and know the fruits of his support.

Dan is also a survivor, unable to confront the deceased priest who has forever altered his life.

Strength and motivation come in strange and desperate forms when the surreal edges of one's life begin to close in around the field of vision. Fifteen minutes away, I stop at a rest area to stretch my legs and firmly focus. I switch the auto-pilot off, and make sure the executive ego is ready for what I'm about to ask of it.

I make the last turn onto her block. This is very real now. My eyes scan everywhere, not just for danger but also to etch everything into memory. The golf course and the styles of the homes not so necessary, except to create a backdrop against which today will be set, detailing the most accurate portrait.

I pass her house, once. It looks just like the picture on the internet which relieves me that I'm in the right place, theoretically. I pass again and notice that there are no cars parked anywhere on the street. The homes beautiful, hers the biggest. Her front yard landscaped more elaborately, four giant palms ominously prevent a clear view of her front door. A façade hiding a façade.

After a final pass I stop the car and let Dan drive. I grab my two letters and the manuscript copy of my memoir saying, "Ok, I'll be back." Without placing this choice into a parallel category of other anxious steps, I walk the remaining one hundred yards to her front door.

The large pickup truck sitting outside her three car garage doesn't fit what I imagine her life to be in this protected part of Florida. I head up the walkway and ring the doorbell absent any further melodramatic thoughts or self-monologue. A medium size dog barks and the sound of its nails on a tile floor pass the few excruciating seconds. My stomach aches from loneliness and residual teenage inelegance when I see shapes moving behind the opaque glass verify that somebody is coming.

The door opens a crack and out of the small opening I see Carla's face. She looks exactly as I remember. I didn't know what to expect but was ready for any physical appearance. "Hi Carla. It's Jim," short pause, "Cunneely."

"I hope you have a few minutes to talk to me." Requesting a conversation has already been done. Pleasantries became outdated two years ago so I take to direct statements.

The shock on her face is instantly recognizable. She opens the door a little more to reveal that she is still in her pajamas. A pair of sweatpants and spaghetti strap tank top. My heart still pounds and I hear the shortness of my breath as I await her response.

"Um, hi. Yeah, sure. Um, why don't you come around back and we can talk on the lanai."

"No fucking way," silently and involuntarily passes over my lips as I realize this is happening.

Instantly, as I walk from her front entrance, past the imposing pick-up truck my mind begins a primal preparation calling to the forefront all that I've prepared. I soften my initial approach knowing that I neither need to coerce nor convince her to speak. Each step is interdependent on her prior response so I need to regroup. I try to control my breathing as I find the screen door, desperately wanting to sound less nervous than I am.

Another, shorter eternity passes before she appears at the back door, now wearing a sweatshirt that says, "Université de Paris" and lipstick. She opens the door and extends her right hand. I shake it as she welcomes, "Hi, come on in."

I'm met in the doorway by her dog, a wonderful diversion from the unmanageable gravity. I bend down and pet her, "Hello, how are you? She's beautiful. What's her name?"

"Kahuna."

As I stand up and take two more steps inside I see a man slightly older than me, also in his pajamas, "This is my husband, Peter. Peter, this is Jim," my title unannounced.

She offers no explanation why I'm at his back door at 11 a.m. on a Wednesday morning to speak to his wife. And strangely, he requests none. After shaking my hand he turns to walk through the sliding glass door into what appears to be an elaborately decorated, yet typical Florida home. Kahuna follows and Carla motions to a loveseat on the other side of small patio table, "Please have a seat."

I walk around the table and position myself in the furthest corner of the cushion placing my manuscript and letters away from where I think she will sit. Everything thus far has been civil and polite, so I take a moment to admire what's in front of me. I'm sitting in a two story lanai, overlooking an enormous in-ground pool fed with a tile and marble fountain that backs up to a picturesque golf course. Characteristic southern birds bathe and play in the pond that separates her property from the fairway.

She sits on the same piece of furniture as me, an appropriate distance away, back straight, legs crossed at the ankles. She folds her hands on her lap.

"You have a beautiful home," I offer sincerely.

"Thank you. We like it."

I use some more small talk, gauging her willingness to share this moment with me and she obliges. A lull in the banter preempts anything more serious as she breaks character quickly, "I have to ask you something. Are you taping this?"

I rise, step away and pat both hands on my pockets, front and back. I shrug as I put my right hand over the breast pocket of my polo shirt, soften my voice and say, "Carla, it's just me. I mean you no harm whatsoever. You have my word."

"Ok, I just had to ask."

As I sit back down she points to the pile of papers, "So what do you have there?"

"Well," this seems a logical place to start even though I hadn't planned on furnishing any explanations, "I think you may know that my life has taken some unusual turns since high school."

Her expression turns into something difficult to discern. It looks a demure attempt to hide embarrassment as she opens her mouth but says nothing. I don't wait for a response, "Well to help me deal with those issues I've been seeing a therapist, a gentleman who has been instrumental in helping me put the pieces of my life back together. And in preparation to come here today

I accounted for a multitude of possibilities. Since you chose to return neither my phone calls nor my letters I've prepared for some time to come here. In that preparation I didn't know what I'd find so I wrote two letters. One in case you slammed the door in my face and one if you began a conversation but ended it prematurely. Each letter asks you to reconsider your refusal and tells you that I'll be back in an hour."

"Oh, I'm not the type of person that would close the door on you."

I ignore her patronization, "Also, I've written a memoir. I've used that process to figure out the confusing life I've led since I was a teenager. I brought it here today to help remind me what I've done as an adult to overcome my past."

She nods, seeming skeptical but accepting me at face value. "So Carla, I was hoping to be able to ask you a few questions with the goal of achieving some of the healing I just mentioned," I begin because no segue exists.

She nods again looking afraid.

"So I know the answer from my perspective but I came here hoping that you could tell me what happened between us all those years ago?"

She stiffens, her back straightens even more and her mouth opens, again only silence. A few bewildered sounds of ignorance escape before, "Well, I think we shared a genuine and sincere friendship."

I say nothing believing this is the beginning of her explanation, not the end. I wait patiently until a submissive gesture of her hands and a shrug of her shoulders inform me she has answered completely.

I bring my voice lower and softer, "Come on Carla. You know that was more than just a friendship. It was sexual."

The same gesture appears but more animated, "I feel like I tried to be an intimate part of all my students' lives. Maybe I'm naïve but I thought we shared something special and wonderful. I probably should have made different choices but I never meant you any harm. And you should know that I pray for you and your happiness every day."

In midstream, I lower my expectations and accept that I'm speaking with someone equally as delusional as she was twenty years ago if not more, further insulated from reality by her lack of remorse. Despite all of my planning, I'm stunned. Of all the outcomes for which I prepared, I was certain she would have known of my arrest. In knowing, she must have made the leap that she affected me adversely in adulthood.

"Ok, then let me ask you this," I instinctively slow my speech and clean my diction as though speaking to a child, "Was there ever anything that you lied to me about to fool me into our relationship?"

While she fumbles for words I silently hope for a confession. Ideally, about her virginity, tell me two laic people can't perform a wedding, she knocked a few years off of her real age, she doesn't prefer her toast burnt, I'll take anything. Instead she stammers through, "I don't remember ever being dishonest with you."

I hope now to coax her by fostering honesty, "Well you know, Carla, I did get in some trouble a few years ago. I was a high school French teacher, a successful one. I became romantically and sexually involved with a fifteen year old student. And I got caught. I spent a year in prison and although my marriage was not perfect, that situation completely dissolved what remained. I must register as a sex offender. I'm completely unable to find work befitting my level of education and things are simply fucked up on a daily basis inside my head."

As I speak she closes her eyes and sighs deeply. A single tear streams down her left cheek. I'm tempted to comfort her in this moment of sorrow, a characteristic I undoubtedly learned twenty years ago. But I do not. I sit in silence and wait.

"Oh, Jimi. It's just like Jean Valjean in *Les Misérables*. We know he isn't a criminal but he's treated like one and no one gives him a chance because he supposed to have committed a crime but in reality all he did was steal a loaf of bread to feed his family. And..."

I slowly raise my hand, "Carla, stop. It's not like Jean Valjean. He is a fictional character. This is my life and what I deal with every day. That's a story."

Her stunned silence coincides with a bit of noise inside the house that sounds like someone putting dishes away, "Hang on one second. Let me see if he needs anything," she says. It seems contrived, like an escape from the reality I've brought. When I'm out of her sight I place my face in my hands to do the same. I regroup and remark how much better than expected this is unfolding.

Carla returns after a moment with a cookie jar in her hand. I assume she's offering me something to eat so I raise my hand in refusal. "Give her a cookie and she'll be your friend forever," she says, talking about the dog beside her.

I begin to absorb the extent of her fantasy world, watching the attempt to navigate a husband and former teenage lover in the same house. Kahuna provides an outlet for this mental torment. I pet the dog after feeding her a treat to provide us both an intermission. When I stop and the dog leaves. Carla sits again so I resume.

"Listen, I told you I see a therapist regularly. I've suffered a lot of damage from my youth. You know I didn't lead a typical existence," I pause but am not waiting for a response. "When Kevin's mother died it was extremely difficult for me."

She nods emphatically in agreement, "I know you did, I remember that."

"I turned to you because I was looking for comfort and I can't help but feel like you betrayed me. I needed a selfless person to guide me through that and you turned it sexual which was very confusing at my age."

I stop speaking despite my urge to fill all uncomfortable silences.

"I remember how hard that was for you but I never knew you didn't have anyone else to talk to. Whenever I think of you in high school, I remember how good of a student you were and how well you did in the forensics competitions. As a matter of fact, Peter and I were just watching a Cyrano de Bergerac movie the other night and I remember the bar scene and how I never saw anyone recite that as well as you…" I interrupt again.

"Carla, again, no literary references. I need you to know that my life is hard, very hard and the reason I see a therapist once a week is to unravel all of the fucked up memories in my head." She interrupts me now.

"Was it hard to come here today?" she asks, a hint of remorse in her voice.

I turn my head and focus on the knee high, circular fountain babbling over into the large in-ground pool. My breath increases and my vision stings as it blurs from the tears that gather. This is the first time I allow myself to feel how scared I've always been to confront her. I regroup, keep my head still but cast my eyes in her direction, bite my lower lip and slowly nod. She looks at me with mirrored sadness.

"It was really fucking hard," I whisper.

She looks away in the other direction of the lanai where her husband is now setting up a power washer. I wipe my eyes so she can't see the tear about to drop. "As I was saying, my therapy is an ongoing process, constantly filled with adversity. Having said that I would like to continue to correspond with you, whether via email or snail mail doesn't matter but my questions are endless and I could use your help. As you now see, I mean you no harm. I just want to be okay."

"Oh Jimi, I want you to be okay and I know you don't mean me any harm. I always knew you to be a good person, a person of integrity and a good Catholic," she responds immediately.

The coincidental absurdity of her words unhinges my composure again but this time I chuckle audibly.

"Well Carla, it's ironic you should choose a word such as integrity. You see, the entire goal of my therapy, as well as my life is that exact quality. It's been impossible to integrate anything regarding you into my life. Do you know how difficult it is to normally integrate a sexual relationship with your French teacher into a teenage existence?" I ask rhetorically.

"It was impossible and has been for years. That's why I need your help and frankly, I think I deserve it. I want your email address so that we can continue this conversation indefinitely."

She tried to deflect me twice but realizes I will not rescind my request. She sits back, breaking her stiff posture for the first time and sighs. "I'm not sure about that. I believe you just want healing but I'm unsure if I'm comfortable with that. I will take you email address and give your question serious consideration. I don't do facebook or any of that but I'll think about emailing you."

My immediate reaction, although I say nothing contrary, is to wonder why she should be uncomfortable if we simply shared a genuine and sincere friendship. What would she fear me re-cording if I were just another student with whom she took an intimate role in their life?

"I will definitely think about it and try to help you, but maybe next year if you're in Florida again you're certainly welcome to come back and visit," sweetly wraps up her response.

"Well then, I thank you for your time and I hope to hear from you soon." I know I will not receive an email and I know, despite sharing the same loveseat, we live in two very different worlds. I leave her house feeling different, more adult, and less afraid. I pause a second outside her back door trying to etch the conversation into my memory. There will be much to process, much to learn from what she said and what she wouldn't say that I need to save for when my nerves calm.

Though all of my efforts are to think steadily, I feel washed over with a feeling of celebration. My life is a daily struggle to decipher the confusing, misleading emotions that arise from the strangest of origins but, I no longer share a delusion life with anyone else. It saddens me that Carla still lives in a world some-place between French literature and whatever fantasies she has created. I know that she is unable to help me even if she were so inclined because she seamlessly switches between an adult and child to suit her needs. But most importantly she can neither help nor harm me because I'm no longer the other half of her folie à deux.

Afterword

By
Michael J. Fiore Ph.D.

Jim walked into my office three weeks after his arrest defeated and confused. He explained, "I was a teacher and I had an affair with a student." Jim spoke those words with what seemed to be an appropriate amount of remorse, given the gravity of his offense. He further explained, "I had a long-term, sexual relationship with my own French teacher," he explained. Jim did not use the terms, "abuse" or "molestation". He spoke of both teacher-student relationships as though he were speaking of love.

The work that needed be done to unravel the mess that his life had become was overwhelming for him. Not only was he trying to assuage his own shame for the public embarrassment he caused, but also the loss of his marriage, fear of losing his children, alienation from the community, and the lengthy prison sentence looming over him. The treadmill of confusing and complex emotions that defined his life since childhood, that contributed to his demise only seemed to speed up at this intensely stressful time.

Jim tried to prepare himself for the isolation of prison. The anxieties that he expressed were typical of someone facing down his type of reality. I suggested that he document his experiences in a journal to provide him an opportunity to continue processing his emotions while incarcerated.

Upon his return from prison, Jim began the truly difficult work of breaking down chronologically, the events of his life. I watched him speak candidly and honestly about the multitude of confusing, contradictory lies he was fed to groom him as a man-child. I asked the questions that allowed him to search his own feelings, to find his own answers. Never did he shy from a difficult topic. He dug deeply to root out the true cause of his feelings, not always the explanations present at the onset were the most accurate.

What is considered to be the worst traumatic effect of sexual abuse is the keeping of secrets. Jim struggled most tumultuously with how to amend his relationship between secrecy and privacy. Immediately, upon admitting that he kept secrets from me too, he set out to explore the reasons why his subconscious fears compelled him to live a double life. Only through time and difficult choices did he dissect every relationship in his life to determine what transferences and projections were the impetus to resist integration. At a particularly low point in his healing the possibility of writing to facilitate his progress was mentioned. This project, this memoir that you hold in your hand, was begun as a vehicle to make sense of the roller coaster ride that he experienced. Good days were neither an indication nor an omen of a bad one to follow. Jim set out to channel the feelings of a bad day into something positive on the page. His objective was, from the beginning, to hand his story to the people most important to him so that they could understand the reason for his breakdown. He spoke about providing this for his children to read when they were old enough to do so, hoping it may help ease the pain of their father losing everything and betraying their mother.

As the writing process endured, Jim shared with me the fruits of his introspection and I recalled our correspondence while he was incarcerated. I suggested to him the possibility of seeking publication for his manuscript because I noticed real talent in his writing. His concerns were obvious and understandable given the personal and delicate nature of his story. He was most concerned about re-victimizing his victim and again, causing his family embarrassment.

The road from idea to manuscript has been arduous and I can assure you, not one taken lightly. Just as no question was avoided in Jim's initial quest for harmony, no topic was left unaddressed when considering the possible outcomes of publication. The transformation from sexual abuse victim to survivor is never easy, often the pain that results from unraveling ones past rivals that of the offense itself.

I've watched Jim process his life in conjunction with the person he wished to become instead of the one dictated to him; the one he created to cope with his terrible past. However, he never sought to blame others for his action, only to find causes and serenity within himself.

Jim's story should evoke a range of emotions across a broad spectrum. Although his experiences may seem unique, is he that much different from anyone else? Incapable of being quantified into neither black nor white, acting out the scripts written in childhood over and over again?

Feel every emotion that surfaces while you read Jim's story. What lies herein is the truth, absorbing in its honesty, absent prurient value, and void of justification. He painstakingly leaves its validity to be seen as naked and raw as he has lived it.

Upon realizing that he cannot leave his past behind, Jim choose to bring it forward, no matter how painful. I leave you with the assurance that every reason for telling and not telling this story has been carefully considered in our sessions by this accidental author.

Made in United States
Orlando, FL
14 March 2022

15772172R00205